The Church nov

Contributors

ANTONY ARCHER, OP
ANTONY BLACK
RT REV. ALAN CLARK
JACK DOMINIAN
DAVID FORRESTER
MICHAEL P. HORNSBY-SMITH
NICHOLAS KENYON
FERGUS KERR, OP
DAVID LODGE
DAVID LUNN
JAMES MACKEY
V.A. McCLELLAND
ENDA McDONAGH
LOUIS McREDMOND
TERENCE MORRIS
RASHID MUFTI
ROBERT NOWELL
IANTHE PRATT
ANTHONY ROSS, OP
TERENCE TANNER
DESMOND WILSON

THE CHURCH NOW

An inquiry into the present state of the
Catholic Church in Britain & Ireland

Edited, with an Introduction, by
JOHN CUMMING & PAUL BURNS

GILL AND MACMILLAN

First published 1980 by
GILL AND MACMILLAN LTD
15-17 Eden Quay, Dublin
with associated companies in
London, New York, Delhi, Hong Kong
Johannesburg, Lagos, Melbourne,
Singapore, Tokyo

7171 1082 6

Designed and produced by
PROCESS WORKSHOP LTD, London
Typeset by Randall Typographic, London
Reproduced from copy supplied,
printed and bound in Great Britain
by Billing and Sons Ltd,
Guildford, London, Oxford, Worcester

Contents

Acknowledgment

The passages from *How far can you go?* by David Lodge quoted in the Introduction, pp. 8-9, are reproduced by permission of Martin Secker & Warburg Ltd.

Introduction

IT IS NOW generally realized that we live in the secular city. Since the
1960s it has become a commonplace of popular religious sociology to say
that the Christian Churches have lost not only the social control they
possessed in the age when they were parts, guarantors and beneficiaries
of state power, but the very motives that enabled them, notionally at
least, to transcend an uncaring world.

The process of secularization is now affecting more or less committed
church members, not the masses. They were lost long ago. Some would
even say that the Churches never had their allegiance. One of the most
perspicacious French historians of religion has maintained that the
peasants of Europe in the Middle Ages were never in any real sense
Christian; that the vast efforts of the Protestant Reformation and the
Catholic Counter-Reformation from the sixteenth to the eighteenth centuries were devoted to the first real attempt to Christianize them; and
that in the nineteenth century the now industrialized masses, with
insignificant exceptions (including, until recently, the Catholic Church
in the British Isles), finally rejected a Christianity which had never had
anything to offer them anyway: 'If everything in the Christianity of the
Ancien Régime that was constraint, conformism and official worship,
everything that was rejection of the world despite the fact that it was the
only world men had, everything that was magic, Manichaeism and fear,
had been excised, what, for many people, would have remained? Have
we not for too long called "Christianity" what was in fact a mixture of
practices and doctrines with frequently but little connection with the
gospel message? If this is so, can we still properly talk of "de-
Christianization"?'[1]

All over the world, in the last twenty years, major Christian bodies
have tried in various ways to assess and re-assess their nature, functions
and prospects in a world where the process of rejection, indifference and
secularization has taken forms proper to local cultures. Inevitably the
dominant experience and model for investigation has been the rôle of the
Christian Churches in industrialized western society. This of course was
one of the major problems that bedevilled the attempt of the Fathers at
the second Vatican Council to offer an analysis, programme and prog-
nosis of the Church for the whole world. Those more valuable parts of
the Vatican II declarations which approach social self-analysis rather
than transcendental genealogy present (if at best through a Rahnerian
glass somewhat darkly) the Church's belated realization of the

European-American version of the experience described in the forego-
ing. The knowledge that the process has been very different in various
countries, and especially in the Third World, has led to a refinement of
this understanding in the form of liberation and local political theologies
which, in their turn, have helped to revise the self-understanding of
European Christians.

The Catholic Churches of England and Wales, Scotland and Ireland
have been special cases. Though undergoing the same relentless trends
that have changed the function of religious communities in western peasant and commercial, and then industrial, imperialist and moderate
state-interventionist societies, their common and several self-
understandings have diverged from the general as well as from the particular realities. Although much fragmentary work has been done since
the early 1960s to discover, then analyze the nature of the Catholic communities in these islands, most of it has tended to replicate the general
work of Catholic reawakening and re-assessment elsewhere in Europe
and in the United States. Hence the *succès de scandale* of *Objections to Roman
Catholicism* (ed., M. de la Bedoyère; London, 1964) was due to its raising
locally general questions of the inappropriateness to humane and gospel
values of international Roman Catholic teaching and practice (supersti-
tion and credulity, worldliness, authoritarianism, conformity and guilt,
anti-contraceptive morality, and so on). In spite of the pioneering work
of the journal *Slant*, associated books, and certain articles in *New
Blackfriars* which attempted a sociological (often quasi-Marxist) analysis
of the practice of Catholicism in the British and Irish contexts, it was not
until the late 1970s that research work began to be published, and
surveys to be conducted, which could give British and Irish Catholics an
idea of their true history and practice against which to measure their
historical and their new self-images. In works ranging from *The English
Catholic Community, 1570-1850* (John Bossy; London, 1975), through the
studies of Irish and church history published by Gill & Macmillan, and
the astonishingly belated yet courageous survey of English Catholic opinion produced by Surrey University (see pp. 55-65 below), and other
surveys conducted in Scotland and Ireland, to the forthcoming major
study of the Catholic Church and the working class, *The Two Churches: A
study in oppression* (Antony Archer, OP; scheduled for publication, London, 1981), Catholics in these islands have been and will be offered
evidence of a truth that diverges sharply from the long-established
legend of a triumphalist Church, unsullied in the midst of a surrounding
near-pagan Protestantism, and representing the pure pre-reformation
faith which, by unflinching uniformity of practice, education, belief, and
with unlimited births, eventually would prevail as the sole Christianity
of these islands. In Ireland the same myth was complicated by another,
sedulously propagated by the Church, by which it appeared as the guar-

dian of the nation's identity and folk-values.

This self-image has been eroded by suggestions such as that, until recently in England, '... the communities of Dissent could be presented as a series showing Unitarians at one end and Particular Baptists at the other; Catholics would come somewhere between Unitarians and Quakers'[2]; that the 'God of the latter-day Irish was not in fact the God of Catholic tradition in Ireland or anywhere else. He was the God of Victorian puritanism, a British and Protestant God most unnaturally imposed upon a Latin Church which, while un-Irish in its externals, was unquestionably Catholic ... The stringent social norms of nineteenth-century Britain became entangled with a fervent and essentially non-intellectual form of Catholicism' (Louis McRedmond, p. 39 below), whereas English Catholicism, conversely, was re-characterized by the cohesive folk-religion of the Irish immigrants; and that for working-class people from the late 1960s onwards, 'It no longer seemed natural to settle even nominally into one's parents' religion, nor as a matter of course to initiate one's own children into it: there was no longer any question of community or loyalty being involved. There was no very evident reason for being a Catholic ...' (Antony Archer, OP, p. 158 below).

Undoubtedly, the changes promulgated officially by the second Vatican Council, which express formally the inevitable social transformation brought about by shifts of economic power, affected British and Irish, and especially English Catholicism, profoundly and irremediably. David Lodge in his recent novel *How far can you go?* (London, 1980) has described the metaphysic or world-picture of educated Catholics as recently as the late 1950s: 'Up there was Heaven; down there was Hell. The name of the game was Salvation, the object to get to Heaven and avoid Hell. It was like Snakes and Ladders: sin sent you plummeting down towards the Pit; the sacraments, good deeds, acts of self-mortification, enabled you to climb back towards the light. Everything you did or thought was subject to spiritual accounting. It was either good, bad or indifferent. Those who succeeded in the game eliminated the bad and converted as much of the indifferent as possible into the good. For instance, a banal bus journey (indifferent) could be turned to good account by silently reciting the Rosary, unobtrusively fingering the beads in your pocket as you trundled along. To say the Rosary openly and aloud in such a situation was more problematical. If it witnessed to the Faith, even if it excited the derision of non-believers (providing this were borne with patience and forgiveness), it was, of course, Good — indeed, heroically virtuous; but if done to impress others, to call attention to your virtue, it was worse than indifferent, it was Bad — spiritual pride, a very slippery snake. Progress towards Heaven was full of such pitfalls. On the whole, a safe rule of thumb was that anything you positively disliked doing was probably Good, and anything you liked doing enormously was probably Bad, or potentially bad — an "occasion of sin" '.[3] But: 'At some point in the 1960s, Hell disappeared. No one could say for certain when this happened. First it was there, then it wasn't. Different people became aware of the disappearance of Hell at different times. Some realized that they had been living for years as though Hell did not exist, without having consciously registered its disappearance. Others realized that in fact they had ceased to believe in its existence long ago. By Hell we mean, of course, the traditional Hell of Roman Catholics, a place where you would burn for all eternity if you were unlucky enough to die in a state of mortal sin. On the whole, the disappearance of Hell was a great relief, though it brought new problems.'[4]

In 1980 the British and Irish Catholic Churches not only find themselves encumbered with remnants of all that Lodge's 'Hell' stands for, but they have surrendered (in obedience to official edicts), and are asked to go on surrendering (in obedience to new theological ideas and the general secularization referred to above), their 'national' and specifically Roman Catholic features: 'The Catholic theologian will always start out from the fact that the gospel has not left itself without witness to any nation, any class or race, and he will try to learn from other Churches. However deeply rooted he may be in a particular local church, he will not tie his theology to a particular nation, culture, race, class, form of society, ideology or school. Precisely in his specific loyalty, the Catholic theologian is interested in the *universality* of the Christian faith embracing all groups ... Does this affirmation of what is Catholic in time and space, depth and breadth, mean that you have to accept more or less *everything* that has been officially taught, ordered and observed in the course of twenty centuries? ... Even on the part of the institutional Church, it is now scarcely disputed that momentous and even theologically "justified" errors have occurred in the history of Catholic teaching and practice and have been corrected (most tacitly) up to a point even by the Popes. The list is immense ...'[5] Some would even go so far as to say that; 'By and large, and for most of its members, the Church in Britain and Ireland is set on a path that will make it just another Christian denomination, without any very outstanding characteristics of its own, primarily middle-class in compositon, unable to make effective any particular demands as to belief or practice, and through its unquestioning acceptance of the rightness of the way things are arranged giving its support to the prevailing social ethos' (Antony Archer, OP, p. 160 below).

And: 'Those particularly vulnerable to the pressures of secularism are adolescents generally, and members of the educated middle-class which has emerged from the old industrial proletariat. For both there is a temptation "to show that Catholics are just the same as other people", to conform to the current social, political or cultural fashion, to try not to be noticed as Catholics, or indeed as Christians' (Anthony Ross, OP, p. 28 below).

In this state of affairs, at a time of curiously mixed impulses and tendencies in British and Irish Catholicism, it seemed necessary to ask committed Catholic experts in various academic and practical disciplines to present for general reading, in a comprehensible yet intellectually respectable form, the recent history, actual practice, self-images, and prospects of Catholicism in the British isles; to give something approaching a truthful picture of it, so that we might discover, in Küng's words from *On Being a Christian*, which Lodge uses to preface his novel: 'What can we know? Why is there anything at all? Why not nothing? What ought we to do? Why do we do what we do? Why and to whom are we finally responsible? What may we hope? Why are we here? What is it all about?'

No such survey of British and Irish Catholicism has ever appeared, though symposia have been devoted either to specialized topics or to quasi-triumphalist commemorations of survival and growth as a community. And, in spite of (perhaps because of) all the secularization and acculturation referred to above, 1980 is the year in which English Catholics at least seemed to bid to take over the rôle once held by the Dutch Church, but ignominiously abandoned after the papal trouncing of its hierarchy. In May 1980, 2000 delegates gathered in Liverpool for a National Pastoral Congress which, as Cardinal Hume said, was 'a new and rather complex initiative. For the first time, the whole Church — bishops, priests, religious and lay people — has been asked to take stock of its life and work, to deepen and renew its prayer and spirituality and then to suggest a way forward for the future ... It will mean that there is a real and growing partnership among all members of the Church'. Inevitably, this call to democratic accounting called from another member of the English and Welsh hierarchy the comment that the main reason for going to the Congress should not be to 'clamour for new structures, more changes of laws that can't be changed, because they are not our laws, but God's, more resolutions, more surveys ... This is not a new rash of democracy in the Church, a new heresy of the divine right of 51%, or a new example of the tail wagging the dog. It is quite simply a fresh attempt by the episcopal body to find out why the tail is, or isn't wagging, or even why it is sagging, or why we, as bishops and priests, are failing to get across to a sagging tail the good news of the Gospel'. Sad to say, apart from the quaint mixed metaphors, the appalling notion of the laity as the tail and the anti-democratic assumption behind this distasteful pronouncement are characteristic of the attitude of many members of the clergy at all levels (and of some laity). They are apparently unaware that, as Antony Black points out (pp. 71-2 below),

'The present system for electing parish priests and bishops flagrantly violates centuries of early (and, in the case of bishops, quite recent) Catholic tradition. When all bishops are appointed by Rome, collegiality becomes a sham ... A social vision can only be translated into practice by means of known and effective rules. The Church is built of stones. If papal, episcopal and pastoral authority are to be brought into line with the collegial vision of Vatican II, the rules will have to be changed'.

The Pastoral Congress did indeed make proposals that were a rebuff to Archbishop's Murphy's insulting statement. They required, among other things, active, open and representative councils at parish, deanery and diocesan levels, consideration of the admission of married men to the priesthood, reconsideration of the papal teaching on contraception, and above all entry of the Roman Church into the British Council of Churches. They put forward the lines of a programme for the greater participation of the Church in questions of social reform, stressed the indecisiveness of much religious education, and generally asserted the vitality of the lay Church. The Congress was a 'courageous' experiment in lay participation. But the inadequacies and requirements of the Church in these islands obviously go beyond, lie deeper, and demand more detailed and general consideration than such a Congress could provide (of course it should have met in the 1960s rather than the 1980s — a fact which is in itself a measure of the degree to which the official Church still lags behind the lay and indeed the clerical reality).

In the present volume our authors describe, and offer proposals for the redress of, a wide area of Catholic life. The contributions range over an accounting of the state of English-language theology, moral theology and Christology in these islands; the Church's attitude towards sin, crime and social responsibility; the possibilities of democratic church government, law and organizations; the functions of a creative liturgy; an education system designed to satisfy the appropriate Catholic lay-and educationally-assessed demands of children nowadays; the responsibilities of a hitherto pusillanimous Church in the test-case situation of Northern Ireland; the loss of the working-class; the demands of the changed parish and the training of new priests; ecumenical endeavour; an informed and understanding attitude to marital problems and sexual development; and a new notion of the functions of religious orders in education and elsewhere. These contributions are buttressed by general surveys of the particular church situations in England and Wales, Scotland and Ireland, and by a survey of the statistics of the Church. Together they will, we hope, provide information on and a blueprint never before available for the Church of the future in the British Isles.

Inevitably, some gaps will be found, and some areas of overlap — the pastoral and moral need to revise *Humanae vitae*, for example, becomes a *leit-motif*. The contributors themselves may not always agree with one another; their brief has been to write from their own experience, conviction and expertise, not to try to force themselves into any common mould. Some, indeed, may not like the conceptual company in which they find themselves; if so, the editors can only hope that *in omnibus, caritas* will prevail. They have not tried to impose their own views on any of the contributors, nor have they changed any views with which they might happen personally to disagree, believing that an essential unity of purpose emerges from the healthy variety of attitudes expressed; for all of us, this book says, there is work to be done.

London, May 1980   J.C.
                                                                      P.B.

Notes

1. Jean Delumeau, *Catholicism between Luther and Voltaire: A new view of the Counter-Reformation* (London, 1977), pp.230-1.
2. John Bossy, *The English Catholic Community: 1570-1850* (London, 1975), p.401.
3. David Lodge, *How far can you go?* (London, 1980), pp.6-7.
4. *Ibid.*, p.113.
5. Hans Küng, *The Church Maintained in Truth* (New York & London, 1980), pp.82-3.

The Church in England and Wales

ROBERT NOWELL

VATICAN II took English Catholics rather by surprise. So much stress had been laid on the unchanging nature of the Church, in contrast to the fickle mutability which Catholic apologists saw in the Church of England and the Free Churches, that the idea that the Church could and should change simply in order to remain true to its original mandate came as something of a novelty. Yet English Catholics adapted themselves to the new order with remarkable ease. The misgivings that find expression in the potentially schismatic movement led by Archbishop Marcel Lefebvre are confined to a tiny minority of perhaps three thousand followers in Britain — who tend to come from the better-off classes of society. Given that the outward sign that marks this rebellion off is insistence on celebrating the Mass in the old Tridentine rite and in Latin, one might expect it to gather a more substantial following in a country where before the Council the official line was that support for a vernacular liturgy was confined to an eccentric minority.

With the publication in 1980 of the long-awaited survey of English Catholic opinion conducted by Michael P. Hornsby-Smith and Raymond M. Lee of Surrey University on the basis of fieldwork carried out by Gallup Poll in 1978, confirmation was provided of the judgment that the liturgical and other changes brought about by Vatican II had on the whole been welcomed. Even if a startling 46% of English Catholics had apparently never heard of the Vatican Council, 46% thought the changes it had brought about were about right and 23% would have liked it to have gone further: only 16% thought there had been too many changes. The Mass in English won the approval of 62% (77% of those aged between 15 and 24), and such an allegedly un-English custom as the 'kiss of peace' (actually a handshake) at Mass was approved by 60% of all English Catholics (i.e., people identifying themselves as Roman Catholics when asked their denominational allegiance) and by 71% of weekly Mass-goers. Yet as recently as December 1969 the late Cardinal John Carmel Heenan was warning his clergy of the need for great caution in introducing this gesture on the grounds that the British were not given to hand-shaking as were the French, Dutch and Germans and that 'some genuinely pious people might find it embarrassing to have to

shake hands and smile at strangers'; the kiss of peace could be a subject
for experiment in small groups, but until more experience had been
gained and people had been fully consulted it was not to be introduced
into ordinary Sunday parish Masses.

On the face of it, it would seem that Cardinal Heenan misjudged the
temper of his fellow Catholics. Yet it could merely be that he was taken
by surprise when it came to assessing the speed and the intensity of the
change that had come over English Catholicism. What is not quite clear
is the extent to which this represents a genuine change in attitudes or
whether it merely means that views are now being openly expressed that
formerly Catholics would have felt guilty and disloyal over admitting.
Vatican II, after all, brought to an end a rather artificial period in the
Church's history when a far greater degree of unity within the Church
was claimed than would be either likely or proper. One particular set of
local customs and attitudes — those of papal Rome — was imposed on
the Church; and at the same time the truth which it is the Church's
business to serve and to preach was thought of as something the Church
was in possession of and merely needed to point to, not something which
it had to struggle to attain by the normal human procedure of trial and
error, though in its case with the guarantee that it would not seriously
and consistently go astray. These pretences were fairly abruptly ended
by Vatican II. For England it meant the conclusion of that period of
Romanization which began with Wiseman frightening the natives with
his pastoral 'from out of the Flaminian gate' in 1850. English Catholics
reverted happily to being Englishmen and Englishwomen who happened
to be Catholics. It was the same kind of development as had taken place
in a much more obvious and dramatic way in the Netherlands. Dutch
Catholics were better poised to grasp at once the implications of Vatican
II and far more energetic and quicker off the mark in putting them into
practice: they were also helped by the social self-sufficiency they had
developed and the institutional resources and the assurance this provided.

What is not yet clear is whether the slower but similar shift of attitudes
among the more sluggish English will generate the same kind of creative
disaffection or whether it will merely peter out in self-indulgent grumb-
ling. What is likely to be critical is not so much the actual course taken
by the National Pastoral Congress held in Liverpool in May 1980 — the
first attempt at something like a democratic representation of the
Catholic population of England and Wales — but the extent to which
whatever emerges from the Congress is allowed to shape official policy,
and whether the need is recognized for such an exercise in consultation
to take place at regular intervals. What is also important is how far
English Catholics wish to take opposition to the intransigent line Pope
John Paul II has laid down on such issues as clerical celibacy, birth con-

trol, and theological dissent. It is, however, doubtful whether loyalty to Rome can again be used to smother disagreement with official policy after the failure of appeals to loyalty in the controversy aroused by Paul VI's encyclical *Humanae vitae* in 1968.

The dispute over birth control can in fact be seen as the turning point in the evolution of English Catholicism following the Council. When in 1964 and 1965 it became possible to discuss the question openly and honestly within the Church, many Catholics came to realize that a teaching which had always been presented as a matter of the natural law — in other words, a teaching the reasonableness of which was apparent to any person of good will, whether Christian or not — could be defended only by an appeal to the Church's authority. The process was spurred on by a clumsy and intransigent statement from the hierarchy trying to squash the debate before it had got properly under way: once again there was an official misjudgment of how Catholics felt. With the setting up of a papal commission to examine the question there developed a widespread expectation that the only course the pope could take was to reverse Pius XI's condemnation of artificial birth control. This was an attitude shared by a number of bishops who instructed their priests to take a lenient and sympathetic line in the confessional, and in a pastoral letter Cardinal Heenan, who was a member of the papal commission, hinted fairly clearly that change was on the way. When in *Humanae vitae* Paul VI rejected the advice of his commission and reaffirmed Pius XI's condemnation, English Catholics felt they had been betrayed. This helped to create a new maturity of outlook, a realization that they could not look to any outside agency to make painless decisions for them but had to work out for themselves, in the light of the Church's teaching (and in the knowledge that it was not always so clear precisely what the Church's essential teaching was), what was the right thing to do.

It is on practical issues such as birth control that the Surrey survey has found most divergence from 'official' Church teaching; on more theoretical matters such as belief in God and in the resurrection and acceptance of the papal primacy English Catholics show a high degree of orthodoxy, apart from a certain unwillingness to believe in hell and eternal punishment and apart from a slight tendency to entertain the idea of reincarnation. The survey found that 74% of all Catholics and 59% of weekly Mass-goers saw nothing wrong in married couples using 'artificial' methods of birth control, and this finding was confirmed by the preparatory discussions at diocesan level for the National Pastoral Congress. These showed that people regarded as dishonest the confusing situation in which contraception was forbidden in principle but could be justified by the informed conscience. Another area of dissatisfaction with official teaching and policy is provided by divorce. The preparatory discussions for the National Pastoral Congress revealed that Catholics were puzzled why remarriage after divorce should be the one unforgiveable sin, and that they were unable to grasp the fine distinction between divorce and annulment. (This distinction may well be blurred by the fact that in England and Wales a civil divorce is normally required before the Church courts will consider a petition for nullity. The sequence is that a marriage breaks down, a divorce is granted, and then the Church's marriage tribunal may in some cases decide that it never was a marriage in the first place). The Surrey survey found that 63% of all Catholics, though only 37% of weekly Mass-goers, thought Catholics should be allowed to divorce; 65% of all Catholics, and 47% of weekly Mass-goers, thought there was nothing wrong in two people in love marrying even if one of them had been divorced. Nor, suggested the survey's authors, were Catholics any less prone to divorce than the rest of their fellow countrymen.

The picture thus emerges of a community that is compassionate rather than censorious, tolerant rather than intransigent, prepared to stretch a point in the face of practical difficulties. Another example is that only 34% agreed, and 46% disagreed, that it was wrong for an engaged couple to have sexual intercourse before they were married — almost the same proportions as agreed (36%) and disagreed (44%) that, because the government wastes so much of our money, it isn't really wrong to cheat a little on one's income tax. There was even divergence on an issue which in some quarters has been elevated almost to become *articulus stantis aut cadentis ecclesiae*, the article of faith by which the Church stands or falls: abortion. On this, 24% disagreed with the statement that, except where the mother's life is a risk, abortion is wrong. Euthanasia showed even greater divergence: 44%, though only 21% of weekly Mass-goers, agreed that, if a person in his right mind is suffering from a painful disease which can't be cured and if he wants to die, termination of life should be permitted. Of course, such a view may merely indicate a healthy reaction to the grisly suffering some doctors inflict on their dying patients, as exemplified by the treatment accorded to Franco and Tito.

On broader social and political issues the survey revealed a commendable concern linked with a certain suspicion of the Church getting directly involved in politics. Thus 67% of English Catholics thought the Church should be more involved in issues like housing, poverty and race relations, but only 34% thought the Church should take active steps to promote social justice if this meant getting involved in politics. This suggests an understandable wariness of the Church as a clerical institution turning into a pressure group giving powerful backing to one particular political machine or party, and there would seem to be a hint of the same kind of distinction being drawn between the conditions for the political and social involvement of the individual Christian and those for that of the Church as a whole, as has been drawn by Hans Küng in *On being a*

Christian (London,1977, p.568).

On internal Church matters the survey showed an interesting blend of apparently 'conservative' and apparently 'radical' attitudes. Fifty-four per cent would acccept married priests, while 41% would accept the idea of married ex-priests coming back to serve as part-time priests: these proposals won the support of around a third of weekly Mass-goers (35% and 30%). There was greater support for the idea of short-term vocations — in other words, priests serving for only five or ten years: 58% overall and 49% of weekly Mass-goers. This would in fact institutionalize what, until the advent of John Paul II, had been happening in the case of the small but steady number of priests being laicized each year. Women priests won the backing of 25%. But lay people distributing communion — normal practice in quite a number of parishes — was approved by only 26%; reducing the number of 'old-fashioned' devotions like novenas and Benediction was approved by only 35%; and nuns in lay clothes by only 46%. On the other hand, communion under both kinds — a growing practice and one the desirability of which has been brought out by the vernacular liturgy — was approved by 52% overall and 55% of weekly Mass-goers, while admitting non-Catholics to communion was supported by 43% overall and 36% of weekly Mass-goers.

Whether these attitudes represent genuine change or merely the revelation of what was always there under the surface, they certainly suggest a shift from a closed to an open community, from an inward-looking, defensive one to one that is outward-looking and more self-assured. In keeping with this, Catholics are now increasingly likely to marry outside the tribe: mixed marriages, virtually forbidden in some dioceses in the 1950s, now form roughly two-thirds of all Catholic marriages. And this new assurance is reflected in attitudes towards and relations with other Christians, and particularly with the Church of England. Before the Council, Catholics were tempted to define themselves in negative terms: they were what Anglicans were not. Catholics worshipped in Latin, the 'language of the Church' (though in fact only of the Western Patriarchate), Anglicans in English; Catholics regarded contraception as sinful, Anglicans did not; Catholics had celibate priests, Anglicans had married ministers; Catholics had a valid Eucharist and valid orders, Anglicans did not; Catholics knew what they believed, Anglicans gloried in comprehensiveness and seemed to tolerate all sorts of weird and heterodox notions. Vatican II removed some of the surface differences, such as the language of worship, and pointed the way to change on others, such as birth control and married clergy. The development of ecumenical dialogue, and particularly the work of the Anglican/Roman Catholic International Commission, demonstrated the unreality of what had previously been imagined to be unbridgeable doctrinal differences over the Eucharist, over ministry and ordination, and to some extent over authority. Catholics could no longer glibly deny the validity of Anglican sacraments in the way they used to, even if Leo XIII's bull *Apostolicae curae* of 1896, in which he pronounced Anglican orders absolutely null and utterly void, has neither been formally abrogated nor subjected to the kind of 'development' which enabled the Church to endorse religious freedom at Vatican II a century and a quarter after Gregory XVI had condemned it as raving lunacy in 1832.

Catholic self-assurance has also benefited from the decline in the Church of England's fortunes. It may remain the residual Church of the English, but despite a fall in Catholic Mass-attendance there would still seem to be more Catholics than Anglicans in church on a Sunday: about a million and a quarter Anglicans, between a million and a half and a million and three quarter Catholics. Despite the Church of England's central rôle in the nation's pomp and ceremonial, its claim to be the Church of the nation is increasingly questioned from both inside and outside its membership, and in any case can no longer be upheld in any proud and triumphalist sense. Among all the Churches there is a new readiness to listen to the other denominations and at times to accept their leadership. Particularly noticeable was the way in which, when Dr Donald Coggan was Archbishop of Canterbury, people tended to look increasingly to Cardinal Basil Hume at Westminster to articulate the Christian view on matters of national concern.

Structurally, however, there has been little in the way of dramatic change. Like the Catholic Church in other countries, the Church in England and Wales has suffered a decline in vocations to the priesthood accompanied by a steady trickle of existing priests leaving the ministry, leading to a slight fall in clerical manpower. Ordinations to the diocesan priesthood dropped from 135 in 1963 to 77 in 1976, 68 in 1978, and 84 in 1978, and in these last three years they were not even enough to balance the number of deaths among the diocesan clergy (80, 81, and 97). The number of laicizations of diocesan priests reached a peak of 44 for the whole of Britain in 1973, but from 1974 to 1977 averaged between 23 and 24 a year; presumably laicization affected a similar proportion of priests belonging to religious orders. The Church thus faces the problem of fewer (and increasingly elderly) priests coupled with greater demands on their services, though the decline in vocations may have bottomed out: students at major seminaries, 899 in 1963 and 1964, fell to 472 in 1977 but rose to 481 and 480 the two following years. A number of married men have been ordained as deacons, the first in 1971, and by the end of 1979 there were 46 permanent deacons in England and Wales (not all of them married); but many people wondered what useful purpose was served by clericalizing some of the more active laity and hedging them around with institutional requirements (including a ban on remarriage should a deacon's wife die).

Despite the evidence revealed by the survey of a desire among lay Catholics for a greater say in the Church's affairs, little progress has been made. The development even of parish councils has been patchy, while the five diocesan pastoral councils in existence by 1970 (and two diocesan laity commissions) had only been joined by two more by early 1980, even if the widespread expectation was that the process of consultation and discussion needed in preparation for the National Pastoral Congress would leave permanent structures of this nature behind in all the two countries' twenty dioceses. In keeping with Vatican II's teaching on the rôle of the bishop, there was a move towards smaller and more manageable dioceses or at any rate subdividing dioceses into smaller units so that the bishop could genuinely act as a focus of the local community. Proposals published in 1974 to double the number of dioceses from 19 to 37 ran into some opposition because of the strain they imposed on existing loyalties: the plan was for dioceses to number between 80,000 and at the most 200,000 Catholics, in contrast to eight dioceses with more than the latter total and one (Liverpool) with over half a million Catholics. However, one new diocese (East Anglia) has come into being, one or two others are being considered, while some of the bigger dioceses (most notably Westmenster) have in effect been split up by a team of auxiliary bishops each being given responsibility for a particular area.

In the appointment of bishops, consultation is accepted in theory even if its implementaion in practice may still leave quite a lot to be desired. (Since *Herder Correspondence* was killed off in mid-1970 no other periodical has continued the task that journal began of monitoring successive appointments to the episcopate.) But those consulted rarely if ever know what weight has been given to their views, and officially the whole business is still surrounded by the requirement of secrecy, which makes it difficult to check whether people's views have been adequately reflected. Certainly the most imaginative and inspiring appointment of recent years — that of Abbot Basil Hume to succeed Cardinal Heenan at Westminster — might well not have been brought about by a democratic process within the diocese.

Until the National Pastoral Congress met in May 1980 the only democratically-elected assembly within the Church in England and Wales was the National Conference of Priests, which for the ten years from 1970 provided the nearest thing English Catholics had to a national representative forum. In many ways it offered a pretty accurate reflection of English Catholicism with its strengths and its weaknesses. It has consistently called for a more open and accountable system of Church government. In its early years especially there were frequent demands

22 THE CHURCH NOW

for a survey of Catholic opinion, something that has now been met by
the Surrey survey, even if that resulted from private benefaction rather
than official initiative on the part of the bishops. At its second meeting it
called on the bishops to set up a national pastoral council. That is what
the organizers of the National Pastoral Congress have been at pains to
explain the Congress is not: the suspicion and hostility with which Dutch
efforts have been greeted in Rome and some other places have created a
marked unwillingness to be seen following in Dutch footsteps. But certainly the idea of holding a national pastoral conference was put forward
by the joint working party established by the bishops' and priests' conferences to work out future pastoral strategy, and in that way the Congress can claim the priests' conference as its only begetter.

The priests' conference has also advocated the ordination of married
men. It has lobbied vigorously for justice not merely to be done but to be
seen to be done in internal Church disputes. It had called for more open
and effective consultation in the appointment of bishops. But its style
and approach are not based on confrontation. Bishops are welcome
guests at its annual meetings, and its resolutions are formally submitted
to the bishops' conference each year for action: there is little the priests
can do on their own. It did indeed come into existence at the instigation
of the bishops, who were embarrassed to find in meetings with their
European colleagues how little they knew about how their priests' minds
were working.

But at the same time the priests' conference has occasionally shown
signs of degeneration into a neurotically introspective talking-shop. It
can indulge in anguished debate about how representative it is: in
several dioceses there has been a shockingly low turn-out for elections of
delegates. It can be frightened of admitting it is split down the middle on
controversial issues. Procedurally its meetings can sometimes be a
disgrace. What everyone hoped was the lowest point in its history was
reached at its tenth meeting in September 1979 when it opted for an
embarrassed silence on the question of ordaining married men to the
priesthood; a procedural impasse had brought with it the risk of the conference reversing its previously established policy on this issue. But,
from its third meeting on, it has welcomed the press to report its
deliberations, and its members have learned not to be alarmed by the attention their activities attract in both the national and the Catholic press.

In all these developments and shifts of opinion practical issues have
been in the forefront. This fits the image of the English as concerned
primarily with practical rather than theoretical issues. But at the same
time there has been a marked revival of theology. This is shown both by
the standard of the work being done and by the way Catholic theology
has moved out of its splendid isolation towards co-operation with and
integration into English academic life, rather than seeing itself as pro-

viding an outpost for the Roman schools. How things have developed is well illustrated by the twists and turns in the fortunes of the Jesuit house of studies at Heythrop, in the depths of the Oxfordshire countryside. In 1965 this was established as a 'Pontifical Athenaeum' with non-Jesuits like Charles Davis on its staff; the idea clearly was to set up a centre of theological studies within reach of Oxford, but the term 'university' was studiously avoided. In 1970 it moved to London to become a recognized college of the University there. Similarly St Edmund's House in Cambridge has been transformed from a nature reserve to keep priests safe from contamination while they were studying for degrees into a house of studies attached to the university and making its contribution to scholarship there. At Canterbury the Franciscans have set up a study centre in association with the University. Meanwhile seminaries have realized that there is no point in them doing badly what universities on their doorstep are doing well; close links have, for example, developed between Ushaw and Durham, while in 1974 the Westminster arch-diocesan seminary, Allen Hall, moved into London from Old Hall Green north of Ware in order to be able to take advantage of the presence both of Heythrop and the predominantly Anglican theological department of King's College. In this way Catholic theology has become more or less integrated into the English academic system instead of rigorously maintaining a separate system of Roman degrees and qualifications.

At the Council the outstanding English theologian was Charles Davis, but in 1966 he shocked his many friends by announcing he was leaving the Church because of its lack of concern for truth and its lack of concern for people. His departure, however, challenged English Catholics to think out why they stayed in the Church despite its obvious defects — the Dominican Herbert McCabe got himself suspended for eight days from the exercise of his ministry and for three and a half years from the editorship of *New Blackfriars* for remarking that 'the Church is quite plainly corrupt' — and how the Church should exercise whatever authority it might possess. Meanwhile the fact that English academic theology is conducted on a largely non-denominational basis has made possible such appointments as that of Hamish Swanston at Canterbury and Nicholas Lash to succeed Donald MacKinnon in the Norris-Hulse chair at Cambridge.

Catechetics, however, has proved a more neuralgic field than theology — no doubt because catechists have to say what they mean in plain language and theologians are apt to shelter behind a breastwork of carefully-drawn distinctions (while a theologian noted for plain speaking like Hans Küng falls foul of the former Holy Office in Rome). Corpus Christi College was set up in London by Cardinal Heenan in 1965 to provide a national centre for religious education. Tensions came to a

head in 1971 when the resignation of the vice-principal and one other
priest from the staff because they felt they could no longer maintain
public silence over their disagreement with *Humanae vitae* was followed
by Cardinal Heenan's suggestion that invitiations to five eminent
visiting lecturers should be withdrawn, and that in turn by the resignation *en bloc* of the rest of the staff. The college reopened with a smaller
and different staff, but closed finally in 1975. The former principal, Fr
Hubert Richards, left the ministry that year because in the three years
since his resignation he had not been able to obtain a post teaching
theology in a Catholic establishment.

   In all this I have spoken mainly of English Catholics and English
Catholicism. To this there are two obvious objections. The first is that
English Catholics are surely predominantly Irish. The answer is that
they may well be so (and so too may be a surprising number of their non-
Catholic fellow countrymen) but that for the most part they have become
so thoroughly assimilated as to retain little positive sense of Irish identification. This helps to explain the extreme slowness of the Church in
England and Wales to take much official notice of the rekindling of sectarian warfare in Northern Ireland and so on. Because of its Irish roots
and British attitudes the Catholic Church in Britain was uniquely well-
placed to mediate between at least two of the many sides to the Irish conflict, but is was an opportunity that was let slip.

   The second objection is that I have ignored the Catholics of Wales —
some 140,000 of them. The tragedy is that in Wales the Catholic Church
tends to be yet another of the pressures towards Anglicization. Catholics
in Wales form only 5% of the population as opposed to between 10%
and 12% in England, and they are overwhelmingly English-speakers,
the descendants of Irish immigrants who in some cases had been brought
in as blackleg labour to break strikes. In these circumstances Catholics in
Wales have until recently been slow to identify with the host community,
though that now seems to be changing, and Catholics now seem to be
becoming consciously Welsh. If Welsh-speaking Catholics were in proportion to the number of Catholics in the Welsh population as a whole
they would number some 28,000 — Welsh-speakers have declined from
50% of the people of Wales in 1901 to a mere 21% in 1971; but the
informed estimate of J.P.Brown in 1976 was: '*Our* Welsh-speaking
numbers are negligible (perhaps one thousand)' (*Clergy Review*, March
1976, p.87). The number of Welsh-speaking priests seems to have risen
of recent years, particularly (and paradoxically) in the archdiocese of
Cardiff which convers the largely Anglicized industrial south: one
estimate put their numbers at only about a dozen in the whole of Wales
in 1976, but in 1980 there were more than that in Cardiff alone. Nevertheless, despite the existence of a handful of centres where Mass is said
regularly in Welsh, life for Welsh-speaking Catholics can be bleak and

the Church can too easily appear an alien intrusion. In an article in the *Clergy Review* (April 1976, p.157) Harri Pritchard Jones explained what it meant to come home a Catholic: 'When I returned to live in Wales, to the Anglesey village where I had spent much of my childhood and where my parents lived, I had to go to the only place of worship where Welsh was not the medium of communication with God. This was the horror of coming home a Catholic'. For members of this minority within a minority there is thus a tension between loyalty to their language and culture and loyalty to their Church. Yet, paradoxically, the founding father of Plaid Cymru and the inspiration behind Cymdeithas yr Iaith Gymraeg, the Welsh Language Society, is a Catholic convert, the veteran poet Saunders Lewis. For him, understandably, the linguistic imbalance was yet another reason to regret the passing of the old liturgy: Latin had at least been impartial between Welsh and English.

The Church in Scotland

ANTHONY ROSS, OP

DISCUSSION of religion in Scotland often becomes a wrangle about dubiously relevant statistics of membership or attendance at Sunday worship. How fast is Church of Scotland membership declining? Is Roman Catholic membership now creeping up sufficiently to challenge long-established Presbyterian privilege? In fact such discussion is out-of-date, an expression of social rivalry which avoids the real issue, which is that increasingly Scots of all kinds have lost their fear of Hell and that teenagers rarely know the word even as an expletive. Catholic and Protestant alike were motivated tragically often by fear, fear not only of Hell but of painful social consequences if they stepped out of line in religion.

It has been estimated that in 1901 the Church of Scotland could claim 46.2%, the Roman Catholic Church only 9.9%, of the adult population of Scotland. In 1977 the estimates were 28.4% and 13.7% respectively. Catholics have often taken comfort from such figures but, as James Darragh has pointed out (*Modern Scottish Catholicism*, Glasgow 1979, p. 226), 'the Catholic statistics offer no grounds for satisfaction since their recent trend is due to changes in structure — fewer children, more adults — and they conceal deeper and more lasting losses'. The estimated Catholic population of about 823,000 would have been much greater today but for a long-continuing drift from the Church. Religion in Scotland, as we have known it, is in decline and the difference between the Catholic community and the Protestant is that the rate of decline is perhaps slower in the former. For many people God is not dead, but distant; Churches are no help in finding him, 'and most of them are pretty dead anyway!' It might be granted that there are signs of life in the Roman Catholic Church but to many these signs are dangerous. They fear the monster of ancient myth, the Mother of Inquisition and Index (both presided over by fornicating prelates), who still threatens intellectual freedom, and lays impossible burdens on the world's poor now that she has achieved sexual respectability herself. In Scotland distrust of the Catholic Church lingers among those who have long given up any ecclesiastical attachment; it is strengthened by a conviction that Catholicism and social problems go together.

These preliminary remarks must be followed by a caution, which is that generalizations about the Church in Scotland must be qualified by reference to the two ecclesiastical provinces into which the country is

divided. One consists of the archdiocese of St Andrews and Edinburgh
and the dioceses of Aberdeen, Argyll and the Isles, Dunkeld and
Galloway, with a total population of just over 250,000, more than half of
which is in St Andrews and Edinburgh. The other province consists of
the archdiocese of Glasgow and the dioceses of Motherwell and Paisley,
with estimated populations of 293,000, 190,000 and 89,000 respectively.
In the first there are great variations between counties such as Caithness
and Berwick with less than 2% Catholic representation, and Stirling-
shire (12.4%) and West Lothian (16.2%). Only in the city of Dundee
does the Catholic percentage of population approach that found in the
Glasgow Province where the 1971 figures show Lanarkshire with
28.3%, Dunbarton 24.9%, and Renfrew 24.5%. In certain districts the
Catholic percentage is even higher, over 30% in four districts of Strathclyde Region, one being the City of Glasgow itself. Broadly speaking the
St Andrews province is dominated by Scottish recusant tradition, the
Glasgow province by immigrant Irish tradition. Representatives of the
two traditions have not always understood or appreciated each other but
have been showing greater mutual understanding in recent years. The
Church in Scotland cannot afford mistrust or rivalry between them. The
Glasgow province has not only numbers but great vitality and it is there
that hope for the future must mainly lie.

The Church in the Glasgow province, and in the industrial areas of
the other province, has close contact with large numbers of working-
class people. There is occasionally a self-consciousness about this among
some of the clergy and more highly-educated laity, straining to avoid
charges of being middle-class, not quite sure where they stand in the old-
fashioned social classification. They are aware often that the most
serious threat to the Catholic community is no longer from the Protestant Churches, for ecumenism has made good progress in Glasgow, but
from secular materialism which is making inroads among the Church's
own members. Those particularly vulnerable to the pressures of
secularism are adolescents generally, and members of the educated
middle-class which has emerged from the old industrial proletariat. For
both there is a temptation 'to show that Catholics are just the same as
other people', to conform to the current social, political or cultural
fashion, to try not to be noticed as Catholics, or indeed as Christians.

In the eyes of many, especially the Scottish bishops, the great safe-
guard against religious decline is the system of Catholic schools, as
established by the Education (Scotland) Act 1918. Scottish Catholics are
free from the financial burdens carried in the field of education by the
Church in other parts of Britain; the total cost of schools and two
teacher-training colleges is carried by the Scottish Education Department. Teachers appointed to these institutions must be approved by
both Church and State. In principle non-Catholic students must be

admitted, if Catholic demand is not sufficient to take up all the places in a school and if parents wish to send their children there. In practice non-Catholics are almost unknown in Catholic schools, where solidarity in religion is frequently stigmatized as a cause of religious bigotry, usually by those whose own position is firmly anti-Catholic. In fact there is scanty evidence to suggest that Catholic schools encourage bigotry. Indeed the senior schools employ a striking number of non-Catholic teachers who enjoy excellent relations with their Catholic colleagues. In 1978 non-Catholics accounted for 22.7% of teaching staff in secondary schools. The proportion varied locally from 11.3% in Lanarkshire, to 62.1% in Fife. In the Strathclyde region it was 17.4%. Such figures are often dismissed with the suggestion that only 'secular' subjects are taught by non-Catholics. There is some ground for this assertion, for what the distinction in subjects is worth, but, in a large Catholic comprehensive school, the principal teacher of history for many years was an active member of the Salvation Army whose appointment caused no trouble when it was made, and whose subsequent teaching caused no complaint. Generally, it may be argued, nominally Catholic teachers do more damage to the Church in Catholic schools than any of their non-Catholic colleagues. In some instances head-teachers of mediocre ability and superficial religious practice have been appointed, immovable until the compulsory retirement age and doing harm to education and religion alike. Many Catholic teachers are too insecure in their faith to tackle religious education classes; many others in the senior schools have accepted responsibility for such classes but have not discharged it honestly, frittering away religion periods most of the time. The critical significance of what goes on in schools is emphasized by the fact that nearly a quarter of the total Catholic population was at school in 1977, and of that 41.2% was in secondary schools — a total of 81,725 pupils. It is not possible to say how many of those are now at universities. What can be said is that while the rate of minimal orthodox practice among Scottish Catholic students is high, perhaps over 70%, the standard of religious knowledge is poor and their Christian witness in the universities is weak, notwithstanding Glasgow students' keen opposition to abortion. In general members of the Church in Scotland, and not only students, lack a firm theological basis for action and fail accordingly to give that lead in the community of which they are potentially capable.

Theology has not flourished among Scottish Catholics in the twentieth century, although there are some hopeful signs of growing interest since the second Vatican Council. But it was a Scottish bishop who declared on television, not so many years ago, that crocodiles were created by the Devil, and another Scottish bishop who rebuked a priest who had echoed St Jerome's reservations about the Pauline authorship of the Epistle to the Hebrews, with the words: 'We want none of your continental

theology here!' Both these men have gone to their reward but they were
symptomatic of the milieu in which the older generation grew up. Many
problems were not faced, intellectually or practically. Bishops, with few
exceptions, did not want to hear unpleasant truths and there were
enough priests, teachers, and pious laity to encourage an unrealistic
vision of 'our good ordinary Catholics'. The latter were to be known by
their regular attendance at Mass on Sundays and holy days of obligation, their presence on certain pilgrimages, a sufficiency of children, and
submissiveness to creeping infallibility whether local or international.
'The Boat should not be rocked' would have been an appropriate motto
for the Church in Scotland, carefully trimming the balance by adjusting
the crew's weight now and then, and hoping that God would make the
waves be still. The waves are higher; the boat is making heavy weather,
and the crew seems less than it was. There are more bishops than before
the Council, eight diocesan and three auxiliaries; but vocations to the
priesthood are fewer. The Church still maintains four senior seminaries,
two at home, and two abroad, and a junior seminary at Blairs, near
Aberdeen. Seminaries are to the Scottish bishops what schools are to
their English brethren, a financial burden from which there seems no
easy release. A community of 823,000 people with a yearly average of
perhaps 130 students, excluding juniors, hardly seems to require four
major seminaries; but ancient bonds with Spain and Italy (and useful in-
vestments) guarantee the existence of two, and provincial rivalry and
difference in outlook preserve the other two from that union which
education, economy and fraternal charity would suggest is desirable.

There have been important changes in the seminaries, however.
Biblical studies are tackled in greater depth by the students than they
used to be; there is more reading of theology; there is more openness to
the world. The Church believes in inoculation of young clergy rather
than strict segregation from the world in which they will have to work.
One of Scotland's oldest priests used to sing 'Old Man River' occasionally, at functions arranged by the Catholic Young Men's Society,
accompanying himself at the piano and sounding rather like Paul
Robeson. The product of the modern seminary may be found with his
guitar in the local youth club, or as chaplain in a comprehensive school,
sounding like a redundant member of 'The Who', or maybe reminiscent
of Cliff Richard. The seminaries at home have frequent contact with
schools and parishes and, less often, with clergy and students from other
churches. There is a danger of over-estimating the effect of such con-
tacts. They help to prepare students for simple pastoral work among 'ordinary' Catholics, and for fraternal social mixing with the separated
brethren, but not for encounter with the sociopathy which takes the
place of early nineteenth-century typhus and cholera in modern
Scotland, not least among Catholics. The guitar-playing student is in a

privileged position, sheltered by clerical status and by youth. It remains to be seen how he will stand up to pastoral drudgery, how much he will prove able to communicate with the growing numbers of the lapsed and not simply with the more reassuring members of the flock.

What of the 'flock', from which priests and bishops come? Some light has been thrown on it recently by Gallup Poll, commissioned by Archbishop Winning of Glasgow and Bishop Thomson of Motherwell in a courageous effort to discover truth however daunting it might prove to be. The poll was nation-wide. Some of its findings might be modified slightly as between the central industrial belt which lies between the estuaries of the Forth and Clyde, and the dioceses of Argyll and the Isles, Aberdeen and Galloway. A sample of 989 Catholics was interviewed, of whom 88% were Scottish-born, 6% Irish-born and 3% English.

There was massive emphasis by respondents on the importance of being baptized and confirmed — 95% of the sample; as against 78% on going to Sunday Mass, 75% on the importance of sending children to Catholic schools, and 51% on the importance of being politically aware and interested. The old saying in the Highlands that Catholics are good neighbours seems to be supported by the 93% who stressed that Catholics should be actively concerned for others. Many of them, 83% of the total sample, believed that the Church — by which no doubt they meant the hierarchy and the clergy principally — should be concerned with housing, provision of caring services, and social improvements in general. This concern for the corporal works of mercy is expressed concretely by the work of the St Vincent de Paul Society and the Legion of Mary, particularly among alcoholics and the homeless and destitute. It finds expression also through Catholic participation in the work of such non-denominational bodies as Telephone Samaritans, the Simon Community and the Gay Christian Movement. Such sharing of concern with other people in joint action is not as new as is sometimes thought, for over a century ago Catholics and Protestants united in Father Matthew's Temperance Movement, and in support of Bishop Gillis's 'Guild of St Joseph' which tried to ameliorate life in the Edinburgh slums. Among some of the socially and politically conscious young people in the Church there is a feeling that not enough is done in Scotland in the cause of social improvement. There is a Commission for Justice and Peace, as there are other commissions reflecting the ideas of Vatican II — but, 'what do they *do*?' is the cry? The answer is 'very little usually, except to hold meetings and produce reports'. Scotland is a land of committees, grinding more slowly than the proverbial 'mills of God', and the Catholic Church can match the established Church of Scotland any day in the art of setting up committees with high-sounding titles, and a fine standard of annual window-dressing reports.

Where the impact of Vatican II is most impressive is in liturgy. There is nothing yet approaching England's National Pastoral Congress, and priests' councils and parish councils still seem to be suffering acute growing pains. But liturgical change has taken place remarkably smoothly and quickly on the whole, partly because there was little liturgical movement in Scotland before the Council. The Gallup Poll indicated a weekly Mass attendance of 54%; only 22% said it was at least a year since they had been to Mass. There was evidence that many people stopped going to Mass between the ages of 18 and 30 but returned to Mass attendance in later life. Of regular Mass-attenders, now, 63% want Mass only in English, 19% want a choice of language, and 15% show desire for the Tridentine Latin Mass. 56% registered disagreement with such changes as the reduction of devotional services, such as benediction, recitation of the rosary and novenas. Younger people were less concerned about these changes. Curiously the very young and the very old were united in approving the giving of a sign of peace at Mass — 70% of the total sample approved. There are in fact parishes where there is continuing reluctance to give even a hand-shake, and even great unwillingness to receive communion in the hand. Only 60% of all respondents approved of folk music during Mass, and about 70% of the regular Mass-goers. Here again there is an age difference, not surprisingly; but there appears to be considerable support for traditional hymns and it is interesting to find how often nineteenth- or eighteenth-century favourites are sung. Congregational singing varies greatly, and what can happen depends very much on the parish priest.

What must have given comfort to the bishops who commissioned the poll was the evidence of the continuing importance of prayer in most people's lives, whether or not they went to church regularly. Since the poll was conducted, in 1978, prayer groups have multiplied and the charismatic movement has gathered impressive strength in Scotland. There have been large gatherings of clergy and laity, and some strong feelings expressed for and against 'the charismatics'. The renewal of devotion to the Holy Spirit perhaps alarms the canny Scot who dislikes the idea of being blown about even by the winds of God. All ages are involved in the movement, whose leaders are well aware of the dangers of 'enthusiasm', in the late Mgr Ronald Knox's sense of the word. Scotland has had its share of revivalism, to shake up dourness from time to time; and although there has been heady excitement which evaporated quickly, there have been conversions and a total commitment to God, for some. Three religious communities in particular can give evidence that there is in the Church in Scotland a strong concern with prayer, charismatic or otherwise in name, which gives hope for the future. The Cistercians at Nunraw, the Benedictines at Pluscarden, the Passionists at Coodham, the Dominican Sisters in Glasgow, the Poor Clares in Edinburgh, and various Carmels, know that there is a spiritual hunger among people of all ages eager to learn how to meditate and pray. Nor is such hunger confined to visible members of the Church — it can be found everywhere, and it turns many towards oriental teachers offering knowledge. There is hope of an opening to the Holy Spirit which will enable the Church in Scotland to become an effective minister to the universal needs.

The difficulties in the way are considerable. One is mental confusion, illustrated by any group of students questioned about belief and again by the Gallup Poll which showed that a quarter of those who go weekly to Mass do not believe in life after death. There was more belief in papal supremacy than in life after death; and 67% of all respondents declared belief in papal infallibility, whatever they understood it to mean. The Devil's existence has been denied by 78% of Britain's population, but is maintained by 79% of Scottish Catholics who are, however, less sure about Hell. Only one-half think it probably exists, but only 45% of the 15 – 24 age group. In view of the positions illustrated with reference to the Pope and the Devil it is surprising to find that only 41% declared the Catholic faith the most important thing in their lives; only 20% of those in the 15 – 24 age group. There is a need for extensive religious education for adults and for specially trained teachers in school. There is a move in Scotland in favour of specialist religious teaching. The Church could give a strong lead here, especially if it were to shake off timidity and with stronger faith in the Holy Spirit offer to integrate its secondary schools completely with the others in the state system.

Marriage continues to be a vexed subject, the Protestant Churches objecting to Catholic conditions for inter-church marriages, especially the undertaking required from the Catholic partner that he or she will do his or her best to bring up their children in the Catholic faith. The conditions for mixed marriages have been eased considerably but the Established Church is hard to satisfy with anything other than unconditional abandonment of Catholic requirements, although in practice much depends on individual ministers. Significantly, the Church's more lenient demands in mixed marriages have resulted in a large drop in the number of converts. Tensions within marriage seem similar to those experienced outside the Church and a majority of Scottish Catholics think divorce should be allowed. There is a Catholic Marriage Advisory Council, but there is evidence that some Catholics prefer to go for advice to clinics unconnected with the Church.

Politically the Church has attempted to appear neutral among the various parties. The Labour Party appears to enjoy support from about 60% of the Catholic members of the electorate; the Scottish National Party a poor second with 15%. In Glasgow and Dundee, and in some of the large Lanarkshire towns, the Catholic Labour vote is significant in local elections and is reflected in a succession of Catholics as Lord

Provost of Glasgow. There is nothing to suggest that Labour programmes are influenced by the religion of party members.

Irish politics have little influence now on what happens politically in
Scotland, although there are centres of IRA support here and there, as
there are of its opposition. The Church in Scotland does not want to be
involved in Northern Ireland, in so many ways the product of an earlier
Scottish bigotry. There is bigotry to face in Scotland today but it is
localized and individualized and is best met by the Church keeping a low
profile and showing a dedication to Christ and to the service of all God's
people. The opportunities are vast for service. Scotland has immense
economic and social problems and an uncertain political future. It is increasingly differentiated from England politically, its traditional
radicalism impatient with English Conservative domination. Devolution
will clearly become an issue again, and may re-awaken fears of religious
discrimination between Catholic and Protestant. Within and without the
Church's membership there are severe social problems to be tackled —
in growing alcoholism, violent crime, civic and industrial corruption.
Catholics by baptism and confirmation are well represented in those
areas — it may be doubted whether Gallup took samples from prisons
and model lodginghouses — but are not totally beyond contact with the
Church. It has the means of helping to make a just and peaceful society,
and in so doing fulfil the commandment of Christ. In an age of transition and crisis there is room for hope. The Church is losing some
ground, but there are signs of growth, not least among the young. The
prayer must be for leaders to stimulate that growth, and with the
courage to strip off dead wood.

The Church in Ireland

LOUIS McREDMOND

THE RAG BALL is the social event of the year at University College in Dublin. It takes place on the Saturday before Shrove Tuesday and goes on until five o'clock on Sunday morning. At the end of the 1980 Ball some half-dozen youngsters, boys and girls, adjourned to the home of one of them for a cup of coffee. Then, still in evening dress, they went to early Mass at a nearby church. After Mass the parish priest came down from the altar to the conspicuous little group and thanked them for coming. The gesture says a lot for the perception of the priest, who thereby greatly pleased the students and in human terms made them feel that their effort was appreciated. It says a lot more about the state of the Irish Church. Twenty years ago young people in party finery, together with policemen and night nurses, were stock components of the congregation at early Sunday Mass in Dublin. Today the party-goers have become so rare that the priest can spot them at once and rejoice at their presence.

The implication that young people are less diligent in Mass-going, and therefore in general commitment to religion, may be countered by those who recall another Sunday Mass some months before, the Youth Mass celebrated in Galway by Pope John Paul. The quarter-of-a-million singing, dancing, ecstatically-happy under-twenty-fives, many of whom had spent the night in tented encampments and who came from every diocese in Ireland, certainly made it an impressive occasion. Their spontaneous explosion of cheering and unscheduled songs of joy, sustained for a full twelve minutes in response to the Pope's declaration 'Young people of Ireland, I love you', was perhaps the most heart-warming event of the entire papal visit. For any who chose to read it so, Galway massively confirmed the strength of faith among Irish youth. Cool assessment modifies the picture a little. In the first place, the attendance was made up for the most part of parish-organized delegations — that is to say, of young people who regularly went to church and accordingly were in the way of receiving the invitation to Galway. Secondly, most went to see the Pope, a motivation which at its widespread best meant that they felt the urge to link themselves with the universal Church, unlimited in its depth and its breadth by narrowly Irish dimensions; the same motivation at its worst, which also existed, meant no more than the attraction of a Woodstock-like carnival of pop.

It would be churlish and unjustified denigration of a marvellous happening to allow these realities to erase the truly religious significance of Galway. They merely constitute a salutary caution against making too much of any manifestation of religious attitudes, or of attitudes which suggest that religion may be in decline. The same caution applies to the story of the party-goers at Mass. Subject to this caution, the parish priest's surprise upon finding the students in his church serves to underline the mid-seventies estimate of 9% non-practice among Catholics in Ireland. The greater part of this percentage were aged under twenty-five and living in the city of Dublin. The papal Mass in Galway can stand as verification of the million-and-half Irish people in the same age group who continue to be practising Catholics with degrees of commitment varying from superficial conformity to deeply-held conviction. However rough these statistics and however generalized the understanding of 'practice', the figures matter because Ireland is the 'youngest' country in Europe. Half its population is under the age of twenty-five. On the attitude of these young people depends the future of the Irish Church.

One attitude can be discerned in the feature common to the two very different Sunday Masses which I have mentioned. In each case the celebrant went out of his way to indicate his regard for the young, his acceptance of them as they were. In each case the young reacted positively to the open-armed welcome, to the essential message 'you are wanted' from the minister of Christ, priest and Pope alike. This welcome contrasted with the disapproval so often voiced in Ireland for youthful tastes, interests, dress, modes of behaviour and expression. The young may have a growing numerical weight but their standards cause much argument still, based on the entrenched values of the past. It is necessary to distinguish. The generation-gap distaste for hair-styles and jeans has virtually disappeared, aided by a certain moderation in Irish youngsters who stopped short of the more exotic and bizarre fashions prevailing elsewhere. Modern popular music still provokes apoplexy in older citizens ignorant of, and not caring about, the myriad schools of country, soul, pop and rock: if the youngsters are winning here, it is less because of conversion than because the relentless beat of the transistor dulls the edge of protest. This adoption of international taste provokes a paticularly Irish resentment, which sees the young turning their backs on national culture, and a kind of moral resentment which sees them falling victim to commercial exploitation. Well-intended and possibly well-grounded, the resentment amounts to an adverse judgment on the young. Alienation puts up its shoots. The rearguard spurns the new values with the futile assertion 'not wanted here', futile because those to whom it is addressed will be running the country in ten years' time. Meanwhile, to be told that they are wanted, that their presence is appreciated, soothes the tender-skinned juvenile awareness of the society to which they belong.

I describe a mood, unresearched and all the more difficult to pinpoint with words like 'alienation' and 'rejection' which in their normal usage imply simmering revolt. Nothing goes as far as that in Ireland. What we have, rather, is a degree of incomprehension between the generations, hardened by a measure of intolerance on both sides. It would be of little consequence, no more than a pale reflection of more serious clashes in other countries, were it not that the Irish confrontation shows itself most clearly within the Church. Social phenomena like tastes in dress and music wilt with maturity. Whether it be sad or desirable, the young people who acquire jobs and responsibilities acquire with them more sober clothes, a wider spread of interests, less extreme opinions and a dislike for the ghetto-world of the discotheque. This is evident in Ireland and, indeed, has been delineated in a number of newspaper features of the genre 'Where are the young tigers of 1970?' What is equally evident is that those who become alienated from the Church in their youth are no longer likely to 'come back'. This single phenomenon of youthful behaviour survives, carries over into marriage and bids fair to be the most effective stimulus to religious indifferentism in the Ireland of the 1980s and beyond. Its causes and its nature demand analysis, for this drift away is neither mainly nor even in large part a reflection of international tendencies. It is rooted in Irish circumstances. To understand, we need to delve a little into the past.

A German diplomat told me in 1971: 'I have never been in a country where people talk so much about national identity as they do in Ireland'. He was right twice over. At the immediate level of that troubled year, with Northern Ireland collapsing into an anarchy which Dublin and London seemed powerless to prevent, Irish men and women took to much agonized examination of their own preconceptions to see in what they might have been the agents of disaster.

These preconceptions in turn embodied the self-appraisal, or more properly re-appraisal, through which the majority had arrived over the previous century at a sharply-outlined definition of what made for Irishness. The definition was compounded of elements in Irish social and political history, both of which it distorted. Because the independence of what is now the Republic of Ireland had been achieved in arms, the true Irishman was expected to be a nationalist of the root-and-branch separatist persuasion. Because an aspiration to revive the old Celtic language had been a powerful motive force among the revolutionaries, the true Irishman was expected to be a Gaelic enthusiast. Because the vast majority of the majority were Roman Catholics, the true Irishman was expected to be a Catholic also. Few, of course, put the compendium of *desiderata* as crudely as that but none who grew up in the independent Ireland of the 1940s can deny that the nationalist-Gaelic-Catholic ethos was all-pervasive. In majority eyes, to be a Southern Protestant was to be out of the mainstream of national life. To be a Northern Unionist was to be a mutated Irishman who would some day see the truth. To have had an uncle who died on the Somme or a cousin who flew with the RAF was a fact which did not have to be hidden away but which somehow rarely came up in conversation. Yet these were not insubstantial categories. There were 175,000 Southern Protestants and a million Northern Unionists. Some 30,000 Irishmen died in Flanders and during the second world war *Southern* Irishmen alone won 780 decorations in the British service. As for the Irish language, perhaps 100,000 people spoke it as their first or favoured vernacular. This left nearly three million in the independent state, or four-and-a-half million on the whole island, speaking English — using it, often enough, to praise the beauty of the ancient tongue and to urge its adoption as the vehicle of communication by all!

It sounds obsessive, in-grown, a little hypocritical and blind to reality. It was all that and yet that is not all it was. This vision of Irishness represented a genuine pride of place, origin and destiny. It was not imposed and not borrowed from abroad. It was home-grown in the hearts and minds of most of the people, the Catholic people, of the island. Its defects were their defects, its virtues theirs also. It was kindly in a way which no bald recitation of its characteristic elements conveys. The late Jack White, chronicler of Southern Protestantism, wrote of the manner in which independent Ireland dealt with its religious minority: 'It is not easy to think of another case in which a defeated ascendancy has been treated with such exemplary generosity by a victorious people. An Irish democracy converted a privileged minority into an equal minority, not into an underprivileged or subservient minority'. This was true not only in the application of ordinary law but in the sharing out of scarce resources like financial aid for schools and in the distribution of offices under the state from judgeships to the Presidency itself (twice held by Protestants). In short, the majority image of itself was not invoked as an instrument of oppression. It was rather a formula for phrasing what seemed to be immutable facts and ideals which set the truly Irish apart as a chosen race.

I say 'chosen race' deliberately because the sense of being a light in the darkness was never far removed from the Irish vision. By some miracle it failed to produce any racialism of the pejorative kind but a conviction of righteousness in a wrong-headed world permeated the Catholic majority. It sprang directly from their Catholicism. *Their* Catholicism must be stressed. I have said that the majority vision was not imposed. Nobody imposed the Catholic faith on the Irish; on the contrary, they had held to it despite centuries of discrimination and occasional persecution. However, although few of its practitioners knew it, the mid-twentieth century form of Irish Catholicism was actually an import scarcely a hundred years implanted in the country. It was the Catholicism of the anti-liberal papacy, brought to Ireland by the Archbishop of Dublin, Cardinal Cullen, from the Rome of the embattled Pio Nono. Its distinguishing marks, apart from cassocked priests and Latinized devotions like the Corpus Christi procession and the French Mission, were Roman authoritarianism and legalism untempered by the Roman appreciation of human frailty. This Irish version of continental Catholicism made no concession to frailty. Substantial observance of the rules on fasting or Sunday Mass attendance or 'Easter duties' was not enough. Only obedience to the letter of church decrees could save an Irish Catholic from eternal damnation. His life was governed by the God of Justice and not by the God of Love or Mercy.

The God of the latter-day Irish was not in fact the God of Catholic tradition in Ireland or anywhere else. He was the God of Victorian puritanism, a British and Protestant God most unnaturally superimposed upon a Latin Church which, while un-Irish in its externals, was unquestionably Catholic. In straight historical terms what happened, for reasons which do not concern us here, was that the stringent social norms of nineteenth-century Britain became entangled with a fervent and essentially non-intellectual form of Catholicism. The resultant mix became the religion of the Catholic Irish who, in their innocence, imagined it to be the faith of Patrick, Brigid and Columcille. Foreigners were more perceptive when they saw little difference of rigidity between Irish Catholics and Scots Presbyterians. How far the tensions of Northern Ireland can be related to a clash of look-alike attitudes, held with equal certainty or righteousness, is a field of study demanding investigation. It could be that Britain has been the author of Irish misfortune in deeper ways than national sentiment comprehends for holier-than-thou righteousness is a Calvinist conviction, and in these parts a British conviction, which had no place in the pre-Cullen Irish Church or in the old Gaelic tradition. Whatever about that, it remains a great tragedy that Irish Catholicism lost, in its Cullenite transformation, the liberal instincts — the concern for what we would now call human rights — which through Daniel O'Connell it first promoted within the universal Church. But this also is a story for another day.

What needs to be noted here is that the Catholic element in the self-awareness of the majority during recent times implied this form of Catholicism. To be a true Irishman was to be a Catholic of the type described, believing that in matters of faith and morals all had been settled for all time; that no scope for argument existed; that discussion was limited to the resounding defence of every *obiter dictum* of the Pope as interpreted by the local Church leadership. Here it is important to say that the Irish bishops had little enough to do. They had only to promulgate literally the often subtle pronouncements from Rome. Contrary to popular belief, based on a few over-publicized cases, they rarely tried twisting the arm of the secular authority. Out of 1800 statutes passed between 1923 and 1970 the historian of Church-State relations in modern Ireland could find a mere 16 on which the Catholic bishops, publicly or in private, had made representations. The corresponding proportion in England was probably greater. The difference was that in Ireland the bishops had no occasion to act. Bishops and legislators, priests and people belonged to the one stock, shared the one vision of Irishness, understood their Catholicism in the same way. The 'Catholic influence' in Irish laws dating from this period should therefore not be attributed to episcopal interference. It was crudely democratic: crudely, because minority wishes were not consulted; democratic, because these laws embodied the ethos sustaining majority standards. The ethos itself smacked of puritanism, which was scarcely surprising in the light of its origin.

Hence to the sometimes beneficial but frequently silly censorship of books and films. Hence to the prohibition of contraceptives. Hence to the Constitution of 1937 with its obeisance to the nationalist and Gaelic ideals, its ban on divorce and its sermonizing on fundamental rights drawn word-for-word from the social encyclicals. Hence, finally, to the confrontation of today, for the young have distanced themselves from the old vision of Irishness and especially the understanding of Catholicism which it embodied; at the same time most bishops, many parents and sufficient legislators cling to the vision still and rush to bolster it up against the assaults of materialism, the media and degenerate foreign fashion. It rarely occurs to these good people that fashion (or taste) can be international and thus be native rather than foreign to the place where it is found, that materialism panders to fashion more often than it shapes it, that the media reflect the world in which they function more often than they influence it. Canute-like, those who cling to the old vision try to stop the tide where they should be learning to swim. Tragically, they waste their energies in keeping alive a *form* of Catholicism which repels the new generation of young Catholics. Either the Irish Church must redefine itself or run the risk of diminution to a fringe status in Irish society over the remaining years of the century.

Once again we must beware of defining a blurred picture too precisely. I have said that the young distance themselves from the old vision. This does not involve total rejection. Separatism in the south, or rather the fully independent Republic which is separatism incarnated, meets with unquestioned approval. The Irish language probably has the support of

more young revivalists than it had twenty years ago. The difference today is that young people holding such beliefs do not see them as badges
of superiority, the necessary attributes of a fully-rounded Irishman. The
obnoxious *gaeilgeoir* (Irish-language enthusiast), who made himself a terror to small children and a tiresome bore to their parents by addressing
them in Irish regardless of their preference to converse in English, no
longer goes about inspiring an inferiority complex in his neighbours.
Instead, Irish-speakers now use whichever language they know their
listeners want them to use and — by their ability to do business with one
another in Irish, for example — provide the spur for others to take down
from the shelf of memory their rusting store of Gaelic words and
phrases. In the same way, English visitors need no longer fear to allow
the conversation to drift away from the subject of horses: the danger is
minimal today that they will have to endure a recital of some ancient
perfidy attributed to their ancestors which they themselves can never
hope to refute for want of the maddening precision of the Irishman in
possession of a grievance. The sense of grievance rooted in history has
all but died, except in Northern Ireland where its survival (for reasons
sometimes understandable) leaves the Southern Irishman more and
more with the feeling that he has stepped into a foreign country or into a
time-machine which has whisked him back to childhood. Obsessions are
needed no more to prop up the Irish awareness of national identity. In
particular, the young have no need of them.

So what has happened to the old vision? It has become less a vision
than a statistical average: the average Irishman is nationalist, Catholic
and probably, in some sentimental way, Gaelic. Since nobody goes to
the stake for a statistic, nobody worries about an Irishman who deviates
from the average. An Irishman who happens not to be a Catholic, who
has no thoughts one way or the other about the language and who har-
bours the eccentric belief that the Republic should re-join the United
Kingdom will not be considered inferior nor even noticeably different
from his neighbours if he is active in community affairs or is a cheerful
workmate, if he has a knowledgeable interest in some popular sport or
devotes his spare time to the charitable objectives of the Samaritans, the
Simon Community or Third World relief. Conformity to a prepacked
image no longer determines acceptability. Consequently, the image
looms less in people's minds. It is interesting to notice, in the two
categories of suburban householders and university students, that people
quite often do not know the religion (if any) of a neighbour or a regular
acquaintance. This would have been inconceivable twenty years ago in
Ireland, not because — or not merely because — of idle curiosity but
because a person's religion was part of the identification code by which
others recognized him or her.

What caused the change, this relegation of a formerly all-pervasive vision to the status of one point of view among several? Apart from factors common to most liberal democracies — the coming of television, the economic boom of the sixties and the questioning of authority (Ireland had its Days of May, appropriately scaled down but nonetheless real) — two developments had a special effect on the attitudes of Irish society. Northern Ireland punctured the superiority complex associated with the nationalist Gaelic ethos. The Vatican Council did the same for the Catholic ethos. What concerns us here is the Vatican Council, for which Irish Catholics found themselves singularly ill-prepared. The insights of the new theology, of a Church more concerned to enlighten the world than to preserve the minutiae of its inheritance, a Church which confessed itself less than perfect and always open to be reformed, a Church which could pursue Christian unity by means other than converting Protestants to Roman Catholicism, a Church which proclaimed its familiar liturgy to be inadequate and which recognized the human rights of men-in-error ... such a Church was far removed from the smugly self-confident and righteous Church, the puritan Church which had all the answers.

At first it seemed that the transition might be smoothly, if slowly, made from the old Church to the new. Irish Catholics took successfully, even enthusiastically, to the new liturgy — to the vernacular Mass, to the lay readers, eventually to communion-in-the-hand. Ecumenical gestures presented no serious problem: joint prayer services with Protestant neighbours, attending their funerals and weddings, dropping the language of diatribe. A fresh openness developed, so that Catholics on radio, television and in the press could question the attitudes and actions of Church authority. It was through this questioning that the *lacuna* in the post-conciliar Irish Church became apparent. What was missing was the spirit of the Council. The liturgical and ecumenical changes represented obedience to the letter. This, as we have seen, was a characteristic trait of Irish Catholicism. Paradoxically, therefore, the Irish Church accepted the Council in pre-conciliar terms. Word came from Rome to do this, to do that. The Irish did what was required of them. The local Church as a whole (many committed individuals must be excepted) failed to make its own the deeper message of the Council, the message of internal conversion. It failed to abandon its possessiveness, clutching the faith to its bosom as a miser clutches his gold, not seeing that it was given the faith for sharing: a pastoral issued by the Irish bishops in March, 1980, was entitled *Handing on the Faith in the Home,* and treated the faith throughout as a kind of heirloom for preservation rather than as a stimulus to action. Such an approach leaves the impression on critical minds (e.g., young minds) of a Church unable or unwilling to address itself to the problems of the age in contemporary language.

Some Irish Catholics have tried to speak with an adult sense of responsibility and in the light of the faith newly exemplified by the Council. They have agreed, for example, that on matters like contraception and the indissolubility of marriage the clearly phrased law of the Church must not be used to coerce those who in conscience reject that law. They have asked that the alleged virtues of church schools be examined with a critical eye, lest received attitudes may in fact be doing harm to Catholic and other children alike. They have protested that the rules on mixed marriages, in which the Catholic partner must still give an undertaking, drive a divisive wedge into the bond uniting the spouses and flout the human rights of the non-Catholic. They have championed those Irish theologians who dared to suppose that new approaches might be employed in probing the truths of faith.

The response of the church authorities to all this has been less than encouraging. They acknowledge, and this is an advance, that civil laws are the business of the legislators. But they also warn so much and so often about the hazards to society if the sale of contraceptives should be legalized or the prohibition of divorce be removed from the constitution that they must be supposed to believe still in the monolithic Irish Church, whose legistator-members could be counted on to reflect the views expressed by its bishop-members, with the approval of its like-minded citizen-members. The church leaders seem sadly unaware of the many Irish Catholics, especially young Catholics, who see a far greater hazard to the good of society in legislation which does offence to a fellow-citizen's conscience than in merely permissive legislation which nobody is obliged to invoke for himself. Senior churchmen in Ireland can still be heard to argue that because the country (meaning the Republic) is 95% Catholic, the Catholic view (meaning the churchmen's personal view) must prevail: as if the majority *wishes* are entitled to over-rule minority *rights*, as if the 95% are all of one mind, as if the debate touching legislation is not for the most part between Catholics of different opinions — i.e., a dispute within the local Church itself. An argument no more convincing, but equally insulting to Catholics trying to think their way through a dilemma of the modern age, hints darkly that relaxation on contraceptives will be followed by campaigns for abortion and euthanasia. Ironically, it was the unjust condemnation as would-be abortionists of persons seeking reform of the anti-contraceptive laws which introduced the subject of abortion into public discussion in Ireland. If the beginnings of a campaign can now be discerned, the blame must lie in part with those church leaders who went to inordinate lengths to denounce (and thereby draw attention to) what nobody had proposed.

The church leadership blew cool on other aspects of post-conciliar concern. The original thinkers among Irish theologians have by now all gone away, either to foreign countries or out of the priesthood. *Res ipsa loquitur* and the need was none too evident for the hierarchy's pastoral letter of February 1980, reminding the faithful that only the bishops can define what is authentic teaching, a claim which no Irish theologian had denied. The same pastoral expanded on the timely theme of conscience but left the unhelpful impression that the only *informed* conscience was one which *conformed* to the teaching enunciated by the bishops (unhelpful, because the people who suffer in the matter are those who have set out to inform themselves and find that, with the best will in the world, they cannot agree with official teaching). On mixed marriages a new initiative is promised, but its scope appears limited to achieving uniformity of practice throughout the dioceses of Ireland: this does not touch the core complaint that one Church, through direct coercion on its own member in a mixed marriage, indirectly coerces the other member and his or her Church contrary to conscience. Obedience to the Roman instruction on mixed marriages is, of course, pleaded by the Irish Church authorities. In the best Cullenite tradition, Roman flexibility (which actually permits wide dispensation from the rules) is overlooked. And the possibility of advising the Pope to relax the rules generally does not seem to have been considered at all, despite the special light which Irish experience can throw on this problem.

To seize on examples of recidivism invites, and in my experience receives, the rebuke that the Irish Church has many admirable features which a selective reading suppresses from view. True enough, in social concern, help for the Third World and a virtually total substitution of the God of Love for the puritan God of Justice, the modern Irish Church has its healthier aspects. But writing about the Irish Church, from within it and out of a profound sense of belonging to it, cannot be a mere literary project, a descriptive essay. If there are failings, especially failings which threaten the survival of the Church, they must be underscored. To do so is a mark of affectionate concern, not of malice.

Let me therefore try to sum up the perilous anachronism of official church attitudes in Ireland with two quotations from statements made as late as April, 1980. Both dealt with education. Resisting a proposal that the appointees of the Church authorities on primary school boards should be fewer than the present 60% of board membership, the monsignor-chairman of the Catholic Primary School Managers Association declared it to be 'imperative that the Church retain control of the schools' in order to ensure that 'the Catholic education of our children be preserved'. On a related subject, the involvement of religious orders in certain types of school, an auxiliary bishop of Dublin told the Association of Primary Teaching Sisters that 'because of its complexity it is an issue which will not be easily grasped by parents, teacher's associations and the media'.

The heart sinks before the antediluvian innocence of these concepts and their phrasing. Here is the preconciliar Irish Church in full bloom. Church control means clerical control. Only this clerical Church can be trusted to have a care for the religious upbringing of children. Indeed, only this clerical Church has the wisdom to understand a complex problem. This, in 1980! It is difficult to choose between outrage and hilarity by way of response. Perhaps sadness is most appropriate, sadness that such paternalism lives on after Vatican II has reminded us that we are all the Church, that the laity have competences which the ecclesiastical authorities are in duty bound to respect, that dialogue is to be preferred to *Diktat*. More serious than being merely out-of-date is the fact that this old self-righteousness slams the door in the face of the generation which expects a hearing for its views and answers to its questions, which renounces prepacked visions and demands participation as the price of commitment. It will certainly not be bought off by what passes for modernity in the Irish Church — promotion of safe activities which involve no questioning of authority, like marriage encounter, the charismatic movement and folk Masses. Nor will this new generation accept as lay participation in church affairs the high profile permitted by the bishops to beck-and-call organizations like the Knights of St Columbanus.

If the church authorities want to see the faith sustained through another generation of Irish Catholics, as they loudly proclaim that they do, they must learn to admit their own mistakes, to speak of modern topics in adult language and to listen to the laity on the many subjects about which the laity are better informed than the clerical establishment. It is a matter of attitude as much, and more so, than of content. Much modern thinking may be woolly-headed and some of it falsely reasoned. It would be dangerous to assume that the progressives are always right, the traditionalists always wrong. What has to be said is that the persistent ignoring, and even repudiation, of those who disclaim the old vision does harm to the Church itself. Pastoral letters which nudge the faithful consistently in the direction of old standards, old devotions, old loyalties and old concepts of authority alienate the young. The young cannot accept that the world in which they have to live the one life given to each of them is an undilutedly dangerous place, against the hazards of which they must batten the hatches and settle down to live by the norms of their forebears. Not accepting the proposition, they find it increasingly hard to accept the Church which proposes it. Thus, in Ireland, does the local Church sow the seeds of its own decline.

Northern Ireland

DESMOND WILSON

THE CHRISTIAN CHURCHES were given an opportunity in Ireland to construct two States which would reflect the best in their traditions and ideals, the Roman Catholic Church on one side of the border between Northern Ireland and the Republic of Ireland, the Protestant Churches on the other.

What we have in Ireland today then, is the end result of a conscious effort by the Churches to create States according to their own ideals. The result has been disastrous. Is it true that the Churches have failed in Ireland? Perhaps the truth is that they have succeeded — but what they tried to do was inadequate or even improper.

In Northern Ireland Christian clergy have considerable political power. The Unionist Party, which governed for fifty years, was under the influence of Protestant clergy through the Orange Order, a religious-military order which brought into Northern Ireland life a tradition of military-religious organization with roots in the Middle Ages. The origin of the Order was in the eighteenth century but the tradition of armed might in sanctified brotherhood was already centuries old in the Christian Churches. On the Roman Catholic side, the Nationalist Party, which had the allegiance of most of the Catholics most of the time, held many of its conventions under the chairmanship of the local parish priest. The Ancient Order of Hibernians and the Knights of St Columbanus were the weak Catholic counterparts of the strong Protestant Orangemen and Masons. There were other organizations as well, National Foresters, Ex-Servicemen's Associations and various religious and social groupings which reflected and strengthened the division of citizens into Protestant and Catholic and which in their strength or weakness fought out, gently most of the time, cunningly much of the time and corrosively all of the time, the struggle for power in Northern Ireland.

In education, during the half-century from the foundation of the two States in Ireland until the dissolution of the Stormont government (1972) Protestant and Catholic clergy had an ever-increasing power, influence and control over the structures. The founding fathers of the Northern Ireland State wished the people of Northern Ireland to become unified within the State and eventually some amicable arrangement to be made even between the 'North' and the 'South'; education would,

they hoped, be integrated. But the founding fathers met with determined opposition to integrated education; Protestant clergy and Orange
Order united in fighting a battle for separate denominational schools;
while the Roman Catholic clergy stood by, knowing that the cause of
segregated schools would safely win the day. By the end of the sixties
most of the children of Northern Ireland were passing through
segregated schools managed by committees which contained, on the one
hand, at least 50% of members nominated by the Protestant Churches,
on the other, two-thirds of members nominated by the Roman Catholic
Church. The hold of the clergy on education was firm, the control of
political processes at least well in hand.

One of the effects of recent events in Northern Ireland has been to un-
do some of this. The fall and disintegration of the Unionist Party left
Protestant clergy without the firm base in politics they had been used to.
Many of them sought a new political home in the Alliance party. The
new Protestant organizations which arose from the shambles of the
troubled years of 1969 – 72 had little regard for clergy. The Ulster
Defence Association, the Ulster Volunteer Force and such organizations
not only were reluctant to work within the old political-religious framework, but said so, at least in private. The fall and disappearance of the
Nationalist Party left the Roman Catholic clergy without even their
weak political base and no new one was available. The Social
Democratic and Labour Party under the leadership of Gerry Fitt and
John Hume had no desire for a return to the old days of a clerically-
influenced party. The Irish Republican Army continued in its old attitudes towards the Catholic Church, loyal but politically its own master
in face of abuse and condemnation from clergy which, if Irishmen were
really as influenced by clergy as they are thought to be, would have
destroyed the organization utterly. That clergy controlled political and
ecclesiastical structures in Northern Ireland was true. That they influenced people might be true or not, depending upon the importance of
the issue to an Irish mind. By 1980 however, Northern Ireland is once
again in the grip of clerical politicians, through Paisley's Democratic
Unionist Party.   .

Even as Northern Ireland left the chaos of the early seventies and advanced towards the eighties, clerical control of education still remained.
Most of Northern Ireland's children still attended schools over which
presided committees of which at least half were Protestant Church
nominees or two-thirds Catholic Church nominees. The government-
created Astin Working Party which suggested in 1979 that school
management should be shared equally by parents, teachers, local education authorities and Churches was quietly ignored while religious integration of schools was praised in theory, pushed far away in practice
by the Churches.

It would be wrong to say that Northern Ireland has simply suffered misfortune in recent years. Everything that has happened in politics, religion and economics has been the result of calmly-taken decisions for which leaders in Church and State must take full responsibility. The tortured Christian in Northern Ireland could well adapt the words of his Master by praying, 'Forgive them Father, for they knew what they were doing'.

The response which the Churches made to the Northern Ireland situation was to try to control it as far as possible. As we have seen, the political process was partly controlled by clergy, and carefully monitored by them. Education was virtually in their control in the vital areas of children's and young people's education (including teacher training to a considerable degree). Clerical influence extended into the field of public morality and culture. In the forties a theatre company in Belfast turned down an invitation to visit Moscow because a local church leader quietly sent word that they should not go. In the eighties the reform of divorce and homosexual legislation is being opposed mainly by clergy. If the Churches' control in politics, worship, morality, welfare and education was strong, it was argued, Northern Ireland (or the Republic of Ireland) would be safe from evil influences from abroad — let us then make this control as strong as possible in order to ensure maximum safety.

This strategy worked to the extent that control became so rigid that people were afraid to utter opinions which were contrary to orthodox teaching. Some of the bitterest of many public disputes in Northern Ireland were about Christian orthodoxy; there were even heresy trials within one of the Churches. In 1980, at the end of sixty years of this Christian experiment in State-building, it was found that, for example, school teachers were so afraid to speak in favour of integrated education that many of them refused to speak to television interviewers on the subject. Fear stalked the land and drove out love.

But the Churches' strategy of control of the vital sectors of political, social or cultural life was unsuccessful in that they did not keep the allegiance of their members to the extent that might have been possible had love driven out fear. During the mid-sixties there was a movement of concerned Catholics and Protestants towards each other, a movement with great potential. The potential for good was only partially realized, owing to a number of reasons, one of which was the rise of an anti-ecumenical movement stemming from fundamental Protestant groups and from severely orthodox elements within the Churches in general. In the course of discussions between these concerned Christians a picture of religious life in Northern Ireland emerged which was very different from that proposed by the Christian propagandists who said that Protestantism still maintained its tradition of home bible-reading among most of the people and that 95% of Roman Catholics went regularly every

Sunday to public worship. In fact the situation had changed dramatically from the heady days when Churches could validly make such claims. The political situation did not allow the truth to be spoken in public, but observers who looked quietly and closely at the Northern Ireland situation during the mid-sixties had the same kind of shock as those who looked at the French Churches in the mid-forties. Many of the churches had emptied without the churchmen appearing to notice the change.

In parts of Belfast for example one could expect in some churches 5 – 15% attendance of members of a particular denomination. Some City churches were supported by loyal members who had moved from the centre of the city to the suburbs but kept their connection with the church of their native area. Some of the churches had indeed as much as 50% of the men attending, although their official figures spoke of 95%. There was no sociological work to clarify the position and the worries which some Christians felt at the desertion of the churches remained for the most part private; public statements generally upheld the view of Northern Ireland as composed of Sunday-worshipping Christians for whom bible-reading, church-going and attachment to church were paramount. It is significant that even when worries were expressed openly there was still no attempt to use sociology to find out what was happening, and why. There was little therefore to go on except the observations of those with actual experience in dealing with congregations; some of the clergy, after some years of observation, came to the conclusion that of all the people in Belfast half might well be unbaptized.

If however the Christians' experience in Northern Ireland were to be the same as that of the French in the mid-forties, who at last awoke to the seriousness of their situation, then the Churches would in all probability go on losing support and loyalty until even their leaders could evade the truth no longer. There was no indication that in Northern Ireland church leaders would be more perceptive than their brothers in other countries. There has not been, however, any attempt seriously to define what a Christian community means in the context of Northern Ireland, or to discuss whether such a determined attempt to build a State on the basis of Christian orthodoxies could have been anything but disastrous.

What could the Churches have done to help their people in Northern Ireland? The Churches argue that they are poor. This is in a real sense true of the Church of Ireland, which has declined in a hundred years from a position of affluence to one of *comparative* poverty; it is not at all true of the Presbyterian Church, which enjoys the patronage of many prosperous citizens, nor of the Roman Catholic Church whose members, many of them poor, have sustained an ecclesiastical structure in considerable splendour during all the years in which Northern Ireland has been a distinct State. There has been no effort by the Churches as such to create industry in this area of high unemployment. Individual churchmen have created or helped to create industrial co-operatives both as an answer to the unemployment problem and as a social educational experiment, but they have, in general, worked as individuals without having use of the Churches' wealth. Pleas sometimes made to the Churches to use their considerable wealth in land, property and money to create employment — since the Churches are the only institutions which not only can afford to take risks but are in conscience bound to do so — have met with little response. For the Roman Catholics the priority was building their churches and maintaining their schools, after which there was little left over for the risks of industrial or commercial development. Roman Catholic church administrators in the seventies sold industrially valuable property to private developers because the Church's priority was to use its resources to finance schools rather than to create industry. 'Our people', said a church administrator, 'do much better when they are not too well off'. For the Protestant Churches there was no principle of social renewal which could rival that of sturdy individual effort.

The use to which the Churches have put their intellectual potential can be judged by their response to the armed conflict in Northern Ireland. Although much has been said and written by church spokesmen about the situation there has been little serious attempt to analyze it. Violence is frequently condemned but seldom defined; but a valid definition of violence is one of the most acute problems facing Christian theologians. Although there is a theology of war and revolution which has been painfully worked out within the Churches over many centuries, this theology is seldom invoked by the Churches in Northern Ireland. The Churches declare that they are in favour of peace and against war, but their history shows that this attitude is conditional. A close study of their own theology and history would make the Churches' stand against the use of arms in Northern Ireland seem highly questionable and even dishonest. Discussion about this war and this injustice among Christians in Northern Ireland therefore turns quickly into a discussion of how different the Protestant threat of revolution in 1912 was from the Ulster Defence Association's mobilization of the seventies; how different the 1916 revolution of Irish republicans was from the present IRA campaign. That is, Churches feel compelled to explain why they approved the threatened revolution of 1912 or the actual revolution of 1916 and yet condemn as sinful a revolution which is in the dangerous present rather than the safe past. The Churches are reluctant to say 'We were wrong then', or 'We are wrong now'. Political expediency has damaged theology.

The failure to use material resources for greater prosperity and intellectual resources to create a relevant theology has been disadvantageous not only for Christians in Northern Ireland but for others in other countries. By now, some Christians would argue, the Churches in

Northern Ireland should be giving the benefit of their experiences and insights to those in other countries who are also suffering. Instead, Irish churchmen travelling abroad tend to defend what they have done or not done, and plead for understanding from others. When help is offered from outside it has often been refused; churchmen in Northern Ireland have made it clear that they do not welcome intervention in their affairs unless on their own terms. Intervention, they say, may be well-meaning but useless, and if injudicious, may upset the delicate balance of relationships between Christians in Northern Ireland and even between Christian church leaders and those for whom they feel responsible! One Roman Catholic bishop in Northern Ireland said, with something approaching exasperation: 'We spend a lot of our time explaining to people from outside that the solutions they naïvely suggest would in fact be useless, or that we have actually tried them and they do not work'. Outside intervention is considered by churchmen in Ireland, it seems, as equally divided between the useless and the harmful.

This may not be because churchmen in Northern Ireland believe they have solutions for their problems — patently they have not — but because it is painful to have one's inadequacies laid bare, and because, in a strange way, the cure of one political problem could well give rise to the emergence of another. That is to say, there is no guarantee that the control of schools so carefully constructed over a period of sixty difficult years would survive if a new political structure came into being in Northern Ireland. There are more reasons to fear republicans or loyalists than because they bear arms. Once come to power they might feel compelled to take control of the education system.

In a troubled area like Northern Ireland it is easy to be adversely critical of the Churches. They have made themselves an easy and vulnerable target. It is not easy to say what they should do in order to bring the real Christ into view. There is no living theology to point the way.

The Churches need then to create conditions in which a fresh theology can emerge in Northern Ireland. In the episcopal Churches rivalry between bishops and theologians is an ever-present difficulty; in the others resources for encouraging study are meagre. But if not in each of the Churches separately, certainly in all the Churches united in real ecumenism there are sufficient intelligence, manpower, money and international fellowship to make it possible to give scholars all the time and help they need to discover what insights the Holy Spirit has given to the Christians during the past half-century. Whether the Churches will be generous in the matter remains to be seen; there are few signs of it.

In Northern Ireland the question of what the Churches should do is expressed in more everyday terms. Protestants blame the Roman Catholics for their discriminatory inter-church marriage requirements by which a Protestant may be forced to educate children in a faith he does not profess. This problem could be alleviated if the Catholic Church were to act generously even within existing Roman legislation; the difficulty is not just that Rome will not change its laws, but that when Rome does so, the Irish Catholic Church is slow to carry them out, thus leaving Protestants wondering what Roman Catholics mean by loyalty to the Holy See. Can it still exist even when one refrains from carrying out its liberalizing laws? For some, like Fr Michael Hurley, founder of the Irish School of Ecumenics, there is no question of *tolerating* mixed marriages — we should welcome them with open hearts.

Ecumenism has not flourished in Northern Ireland. If it did, there could be many generous symbolic gestures from the Churches, many courtesies which might not change the political situation much but whose example could well make it easier for politicians to act more generously towards each other than they do. It is beyond doubt now that Ulster politicians who wished to act generously — and there were more of them than is generally believed — always lived in fear of being deposed by their followers who had learned too well the lessons of segregation and distrust which political opportunism and theological incompetence had taught them. There is room now for a confessing Church, a group of people who will say, not 'This is what my Church teaches' but 'This is what I believe'. There are some Christians in Northern Ireland who wish that such a group would emerge, and if it did would thankfully be part of it. But in this kind of society the fear of doing anything unorthodox is very real because the penalties can be very real. Clearly the Churches must do something to remove fears which are largely of their own making.

Welcoming marriages between Christians of different traditions, fostering ecumenism and abandoning fear as an instrument of control and influence would transform the Churches in Northern Ireland from declining institutions into the leaven of society which they should be; it would certainly bring to life again the ability to compromise which is as much part of the Irish person's character as it is of anyone else's. If we are to have change the Churches should lead the way. There can be change without their help, but the change is less rich without them.

There are two other pressing problems in Northern Ireland which the Churches could do much to solve, while still being true to their mission. The problem of prisoners is one of them — for after all the Christians first faced the world with the claim that they would have a care for prisoners beyond what anyone else would offer; another problem is the isolation of political groups with whom for one reason or another the government refuses to speak. A government may well say: 'We cannot talk to members of armed groups'; but the Churches have no right to say the same. The Churches are the only associations with the duty, and

privilege, of talking to people whom others reject. In Northern Ireland
the Churches officially reject those whom the State rejects, accept those
whom the State accepts. They are the protectors of the State, not its
critics. If Irish churchmen were seen to act generously towards each
other, and mercifully towards those whom others reject, they would
become witnesses to the better way not only in Ireland but in other parts
of the world where other people also suffer through imprisonment, war
and revolution.

The tragedy of the Irish Churches is not that they have done evil.
That is hardly important now. It is that they are still so often paralyzed,
by fear, from doing good.

The statistics of the Church

MICHAEL P. HORNSBY-SMITH

1. Introduction

IN THIS chapter an outline of statistical indicators of the current position of Roman Catholicism in Britain and Ireland will be given and an attempt will be made to identify trends since the second World War. First, a brief review of various sources of statistics will be given. Second, the contribution of the Church's officially produced statistics will be discussed. Third, some of the more significant findings from a number of recent surveys will be reviewed. Fourth, the chapter will conclude with some reflections on the implications of recent trends and on the future needs for statistical services in the Church.

It is, perhaps, necessary at the outset to challenge two opposing errors in the use of statistics. In the first place it is necessary to reject the view that all statistics are either falsehoods or fabrications. It is true that statistics can be misused but so can any other human construction and the error is in their misuse and not intrinsic to them. An alternative error is to suppose that statistics are ends in themselves and will automatically throw illuminating light on some aspect of social reality. It is, however, naive to suppose that the collection of statistics will solve any problem or replace the need for policy decisions. Rather, the collection of statistics relating to the beliefs, attitudes, behaviour, resources and so on of a religious institution such as the Church is a necessary tool for the bishops and other pastoral decision makers and their advisers in helping to discern, identify and monitor new trends, to facilitate the interpretation of any changes and trends and the formulation of rational pastoral responses on the basis of knowledge. Church statistics, then, are useful indicators of the position of the Church as a social institution in a period of very rapid social and religious change.

2. Sources

Before commencing the task of summarizing the available statistics, a brief word on sources may be helpful. First of all a general overview of the purpose and scope of ecclesiastical statistics has been given by Spencer (1967). Secondly a range of comparative summary statistics is available in the *Statistical Yearbook of the Church* produced by the Central Statistics Office of the Church. However these combine the returns for England and Wales and Scotland.

In all three local Churches the major source of official statistics is the *Catholic Directory* which is published annually. All three Directories publish detailed information about the churches and parishes, secular and religious clergy, schools, organizations and societies and so on, by diocese. In addition a restricted range of summary statistics is presented in a way which enables some limited analyses of trends to be carried out over time. However, in general it is not possible to explore such salient issues as the age structure of the clergy or the types of marriage entered into by Catholic laity. With few (mainly Scottish) exceptions there are no commentaries on the figures given so that the impact and implications of the massive social and religious changes since the second World War remain unconsidered by the compilers of the Churches' official statistics. Apart from the national directories many dioceses produce their own directories annually but these have not been considered in detail for the purpose of this review.

In England and Wales the Catholic Education Council every two years publishes a Handbook which gives detailed information about all the Catholic maintained and independent schools in this country. In addition summary statistics indicate the current designation of schools by type, numbers of Catholic and non-Catholic teachers and pupils and an analysis of teachers by type of school and religious status. In recent years a number of working-party reports on various aspects of the pastoral concerns of the Church have also produced a range of additional statistics. Thus the Final Report of the Joint Working Party on Pastoral Strategy, *A Time for Building* (1976), included an analysis of the age structure of diocesan priests. Some detailed diocesan comparisons were contained in *Groundplan* (Lawrence Report, 1976). A number of other analyses of the age structure of the priests in England and Wales have also been given recently (Commission for Priestly Formation, 1979; Winter, 1979). When considering the interpretation of all social statistics it is important to note that they are the social products of their compilers who accumulate them for their own administrative (and rarely for scientific) purposes (Hindess, 1973).

Account must also be taken of a number of secondary analyses of the official statistics. Chief among these is the recent study of patterns of growth and decline of the various religious denominations in Great Britain and Ireland from 1700 up to 1970 (Currie *et al.*, 1977). In particular these authors examine the significance of external influences such as secularization, industrialization, urbanization, trade fluctuations, political changes and war. The data about Catholics are in the main derived from the various Catholic Directories. A number of international comparisons on such matters as the number of known Catholics per priest or per parish and the number of child and adult baptisms per thousand Catholics have recently been published for the later 1960s and early 1970s (Pycroft, 1977).

The foremost authority on the demography of Roman Catholics in England and Wales outlined the evidence relating to the size and composition of the Catholic population at the time of the collapse of the Newman Demographic Survey (Spencer, 1966) and has analyzed trends of involvement in the Church up to the mid-1970s (Spencer, 1975, 1976). An analysis of the CEC education statistics has indicated that with the general and rapid fall in the birth rate since the mid-1960s the Catholic schools system has declined in size since 1974 (Hornsby-Smith, 1978a). The increase in the proportion of mixed marriages was noted by Coman (1977).

In Scotland the centenary of the restoration of the Hierarchy in 1878 was marked by the publication of a major review of *Modern Scottish Catholicism* (McRoberts, 1979). In this volume Darragh has contributed an important analysis of the changing Catholic population of Scotland over the past 100 years. Included is an analysis of Catholic marriage and divorce statistics based on the *Annual Reports* of the Registrar General for Scotland.

The *Irish Catholic Directory* for 1968 included not only the usual church statistics but also a review of census data not only for Ireland (considering the twenty-six counties and the six counties separately) but for Irish-born emigrants to England, Wales and Scotland.

Apart from the official statistics produced by the Catholic community for its own purposes, the findings of sample surveys have thrown light on the beliefs, practices and attitudes of Catholics on a wide range of issues. Much of this material remains unworked but there is scope for the secondary analysis of the Catholic respondents in such major studies as *Relative Deprivation and Social Justice* (Runciman, 1972) and *Political Change in Britain* (Butler & Stokes, 1971) and of the Irish-born in such studies as the Oxford Mobility Project (Goldthorpe *et al.*, 1980) and the General Household Survey. In Scotland there is scope for the analysis of the academic outcomes of Catholic schools in the data collected by the Centre for Educational Studies, University of Ediburgh. A considerable amount of information relating to the social mobility of Catholics in four different parishes in the London and Preston areas was also collected in the mid-1970s (Hornsby-Smith, 1978b).

Apart from these university-based researches there has also been a number of surveys of religious attitudes, beliefs and practices by market research organizations, especially in the past decade. Some Gallup Poll statistics were reviewed in the late 1960s (Martin, 1968), and more recently general surveys of religion have been reported by Gallup (Social Surveys, 1978) and NOP (1978). Early in 1977 the *Catholic Herald*, the *Scottish Catholic Observer* and the *Catholic Standard* (Dublin) between them obtained nearly 20,000 responses to a postal questionnaire of their readership on attitudes to change in the Church.

Partly as a response to the lack of representativeness of such polls, the Scottish bishops commissioned their own survey of a representative sample of Catholics in Scotland (Social Surveys, 1979). An even more ambitious survey of Catholics in England and Wales was sponsored privately by some Catholic laity and the report *Roman Catholic Opinion* (Hornsby-Smith & Lee, 1980) was made widely available to various groups preparing for the National Pastoral Congress.

3. *Official statistics*

The analysis of the official statistics of three local Churches comparatively is complicated by the fact that they are not collected or presented in a uniform way. However in Table 1 estimates have been given for three points in time: the mid-1940s: i.e., at the end of the second World War; the mid-1960s: i.e., at the end of the second Vatican Council; and the mid-1970s: i.e., the latest period for which all the statistics are available.

Broadly speaking, it can be seen that in the three decades since the second World War the estimated Catholic population has increased by more than two million. One must recognize, however, that part of this increase may simply result from improvements in the accuracy of the estimates which continue to be much lower than those based on sample surveys of the total population. Child baptisms have generally followed the trends in the birth-rate though it appears that Catholic baptisms (in England and Wales) have declined more rapidly since the peak year 1964 than the birth-rate generally. It is possible that this indicates the greater recourse to contraceptive practices since this time. At the end of the 1970s child baptisms were taking place a little over half as frequently as fifteen years ago.

Confirmation statistics do not appear to have been collected systematically. For England and Wales the latest figures indicate a 42% reduction in the past twenty years. For both England and Wales and Scotland the figures fluctuate wildly from year to year. One must infer that the illness or availability of bishops is a major factor here.

The marriage figures have not varied to the same degree though, again, the indications are that these reached a peak in the 1960s but have since declined by about one third (in England and Wales). What is significant, in England and Wales at least, is the big increase in 'mixed' marriages. Whereas in 1960 the number of mixed marriages was the same as the number of marriages where both parties were Catholic, the latest figures for the late 1970s show that there are twice as many mixed marriages as marriages between Catholics.

Although there are some three thousand more priests now than thirty years ago, there are indications that the numbers are beginning to decline. Indeed the *Cherwell Report* observed for England and Wales that

TABLE 1: SUMMARY OF OFFICIAL STATISTICS (1945-1975)

ESTIMATES	PERIOD	E. & W.	SCOT.	IREL.	TOTAL
Catholic	mid 40s	2.39	0.67	3.24	6.30
Population ($\times 10^6$)	mid 60s	3.96	0.82	3.17	7.95
	mid 70s	4.16	0.82	3.49	8.47
Child Baptisms	mid 40s	7.34	1.87	na	na
($\times 10^4$)	mid 60s	13.41	2.38	na	na
	mid 70s	7.58	1.46	7.93	16.97
Confirmations	mid 60s	6.97	2.91	na	na
($\times 10^4$)	mid 70s	7.40	0.91	na	na
Marriages ($\times 10^4$)	mid 40s	3.66	0.57	na	na
	mid 60s	4.61	0.69	na	na
	mid 70s	3.47	0.61	2.68	6.76
Total Priests	mid 40s	6.20	0.94	4.67	11.81
($\times 10^3$)	mid 60s	7.81	1.28	5.98	15.07
	mid 70s	7.51	1.20	6.00	14.71
Parishes ($\times 10^3$)	mid 40s	1.91	0.30	1.13	3.34
	mid 60s	2.32	0.43	1.17	3.92
	mid 70s	2.60	0.46	1.27	4.33

if the present rate of intake and perseverance remains unchanged then in twenty years time there will be a 25% decline in the number of secular priests. Others have emphasized that the priestly work force is aging rapidly (Winter, 1979). In spite of this the number of parishes continues to increase by about 10% each decade. One recent development is the steady increase in the number of permanent deacons in England and Wales, from ten in 1975 to forty-six in 1980,

A number of other statistics are collected but not published. There are also differences between the local Churches. For example the standard Parish Register Returns for England and Wales request information about receptions into the Church, first communicants, Mass attendance on a specified Sunday, the numbers of lay catechists, catechumens under instruction and members of Catholic associations. Receptions reached a peak of 16,250 in 1959 but declined to one third of that level throughout the 1970s. First communions have declined from around 2.1 million in the mid-1960s to around 1.7 m. in the late 1970s. The estimates for members of Catholic associations have remained around 125,000 to 14,000 during the past decade. It is too early to interpret a reported increase over the past four years, and in any case in making the estimates parish priests are asked to 'count people who are members of more than one society once for every society they are in'. If one estimates the Catholic population on the basis of opinion survey findings, then very roughly it seems that about 86% of Catholics are known to the parish clergy, 35% attend Mass on the survey Sunday, and around 1-2% are known to be members of Catholic associations whose objectives 'are apostolic, pious or charitable, or which include the spiritual formation of their members'.

For England and Wales the Catholic Education Council collects statistics annually on the numbers and type of Catholic schools; the age, sex and distribution of pupils; the religious and professional qualifications of teachers; and the numbers of non-Catholic pupils and teachers. An analysis of post-war trends up to 1977 was given by Hornsby-Smith (1978a) and the latest figures for 1979 confirm the earlier analysis. The number of Catholic schools and pupils reached a peak around 1974. Around 85% of pupils in maintained secondary schools are now in comprehensive schools compared to 15% in 1968. The decline in the number of clergy or religious teachers has continued, as has the rise in the proportion of graduate teachers and non-Catholic pupils and teachers.

In Scotland the decline in the birth-rate since the mid-1960s has been accompanied by a decline in the proportion of baptisms to live births from an average of 17% in the 1960s to under 15% in the mid-1970s. Other statistics regularly reported for Scotland indicate a decline in the numbers of students in major and minor seminaries since the mid-1960s but at the same time an increase in the numbers of religious houses for both men and women. The 1971 *Catholic Directory for Scotland* included a useful analysis of trends and concluded that 'the present position is not one of dramatic decline but rather of a slow and almost imperceptible, downward movement in all the indices of baptisms, marriages and estimated population' (p. 367).

The 1968 *Irish Catholic Directory* contains useful summaries of population change and migration patterns based not only on Irish census returns but on the analyses of Irish-born persons in Britain in 1951 and 1961. In 1961 95% of the Irish Republic was Catholic and 35% of the six counties of northern Ireland. Overall 75% of the population of Ireland was Catholic. The 1979 Directory estimates this to have increased to 77%. A fuller analysis of Irish Catholics in England was given by Hornsby-Smith (1978c).

4. Survey findings

There is no official Church research institute charged with the task of monitoring the religious attitudes, beliefs, practices and identification in any of the three local Churches. What is known about these matters is largely accidental (for example in the case of abortion or contraceptive practices) and the result of investigations pursued for other purposes, or the result of the routine monitoring of public opinion by market or opinion researchers, or the result of private initiatives. For example, Cartwright (1976) has reported that 43% of Catholics held restrictive views with regard to abortion compared to 32% of Church of England and other Protestants and 65% of Moslems. The proportion of Catholic mothers who said that if they found they were pregnant again they might try to get an abortion was 13%, the same as the proportion of all mothers in her sample. Martin (1968) reviewed some Gallup Poll statistics on a range of social, moral, political and religious issues up to the mid-1960s and more recently a number of market research organizations have surveyed the religious beliefs and practices of samples of the adult population.

The 1977 Survey of the *Catholic Herald* and its sister papers in Scotland and Ireland not only indicated that there was a substantial measure of agreement among the Catholic respondents to the three papers but suggested that the children of Irish immigrants differed little in their religious attitudes and practices from those born in England and Wales. More recently considerable interest has been generated by the two surveys of Catholics in Scotland and in England and Wales. The findings reported in Table 2 show that while in some respects Scottish Catholics are more traditional than English Catholics, a fact which reflects to some extent the higher working-class representation among Scottish Catholics, nevertheless in general the results are remarkably similar. There is evidence of higher levels of agreement on the key dogmatic beliefs of Catholicism but at the same time substantial divergence on moral issues. Recent changes in the Church are given solid support and there is evidence that there would be a strong measure of acceptance even for such radical suggestions as the ordination of women priests. Catholics in both local Churches overwhelmingly stress the importance of Christian unity. Both these surveys also indicated high levels of satisfaction with Catholic schools even though in England and Wales under two-fifths (compared to two-thirds in Scotland) agreed with the education of Catholics in separate schools. In the study of Catholic schools in England and Wales the two studies by Fr Andrew Greeley in the United States were replicated with broadly similar results. Whereas there was a consistent positive relationship between the proportion of Catholic schooling and a wide range of adult religious belief and practice, the magnitude of the effect was small, especially when set against the impact of the religiosity of the parental home or of the respondent's spouse.

TABLE 2: SELECTED RELIGIOUS BELIEFS AND PRACTICES

BELIEF OR PRACTICE	E. & W.	SCOT.
1 Mass attendance weekly or more (%)	37	55
2 Pray daily (%)	48	52
3 A married couple who feel they have as many children as they want are not doing anything wrong when they use artificial methods of birth control (% agreement)	74	55
4 Catholics should be allowed to divorce (% agreement)	63	58
5 Except where the life of the mother is at risk abortion is wrong (% agreement)	65	77
6 Jesus directly handed over the leadership of his Church to Peter and the Popes (% true)	83	84
7 Under certain conditions, when he speaks on matters of faith and morals the Pope is infallible (% true)	62	67
8 Women priests (% acceptance)	25	25
9 Recent changes in the Church (% about right)	46	62
10 Saying the Mass in English instead of Latin (% approval)	62	72
11 The 'handshake of peace' at Mass (% approval)	60	71
12 Christian unity (% extremely important)	52	50

(Sources: *A Survey of Scottish Catholics*, Gallup, 1979; *Roman Catholic Opinion*, University of Surrey, 1979)

TABLE 3: MARRIAGE TYPE BY YEAR OF MARRIAGE (ENGLAND AND WALES)

MARRIAGE TYPE	YEAR OF MARRIAGE					ALL
	Up to 1939	1940-49	1950-59	1960-69	1970-77	
Valid non-mixed	68.5	64.6	68.5	51.6	30.2	52.8
Valid mixed	22.2	19.5	20.8	28.3	33.5	25.7
Invalid non-mixed	3.7	3.7	1.5	1.2	3.2	3.0
Invalid mixed	5.6	12.2	9.2	18.9	33.0	18.6

(Source: *Roman Catholic Opinion*, University of Surrey, 1979)

Another major finding from this survey was that among recent marriage cohorts there has been since 1960 a dramatic increase not only in the proportion of mixed marriages, but also in the proportion of invalid marriages (Table 3). Since the survey demonstrated a significant relationship between type of marriage, religious practice and the baptism and religious upbringing of the children, the long-term demographic consequences for Catholicism in this country are potentially very serious.

Finally, on almost every religious variable these surveys indicated very large differences between the different age groups. Generally the older Catholics more strongly conform to the official teaching of the Church while the younger Catholics are more likely to diverge from it. Since these surveys were both cross-sectional 'snapshots' at one moment in time, no *direct* evidence of trends over time is available. The probability is, however, that young Catholics will substantially carry through life their present attitudes and practices. If this turns out to be the case then the Church of 2000 will be very different. Indeed, in a number of recent analyses Spencer (1975, 1976) has suggested that there has been a dramatic alienation from the Church since the late 1950s. With the ending of massive Irish immigration since this time it has become clearer that the supposed ability of the Catholic Church to retain the allegiance of the working class was largely spurious and attributable to Irish immigration. Paradoxically, the liturgical reforms of recent years and the emphasis on lay participation have both favoured the more articulate and assertive middle class, so that for the first time the Catholic Church is faced with the same problems as the other major religious bodies.

5. *Future needs*

The three local churches differ from a number of continental countries in having no significant research institute, not only for the collection of routine statistics in order to identify trends and monitor pastoral developments, but for the serious study of religious phenomena and their meaning in the highly secular culture of advanced industrial and urban societies. In retrospect it is tragic that the Newman Demographic Survey (Spencer, 1964) collapsed. Perhaps it was ahead of its time; perhaps it overstretched itself; perhaps it was asked to do too much with limited resources. Whatever the reasons, there are growing indications that some such continuing research and statistics unit is necessary , and that there is now much stronger support among church leaders for such a body. The National Conference of Priests, for example, has been urging such developments for a number of years.

Recent developments have indicated at least six areas where serious research appears to be necessary to inform pastoral strategies. First, variations between different age groups point to the need to monitor and attempt to understand the changes in religious identity and meaning which appear to be taking place. Second, comparative studies of

Catholic schools are necessary in order to identify those aspects which contribute to the development of life-long religious commitment. Third, more research needs to be undertaken to understand recent marriage patterns, and in particular to identify those factors which are conducive to stable marriage and those types of community support which are necessary at different stages in the life-cycle. Fourth, there is a need to monitor new developments in the Church such as the charismatic movement, the redeployment of resources (e.g., parish sisters in inner-city areas), inter-church schools, new forms of ministry in response to the decline in the traditionally defined rôle of the clergy, and so on. Fifth, there is a need to understand more clearly the processes of assimilation of immigrant groups to host societies. In particular, the case of Irish emigrants to Great Britain and their experiences of social mobility require more attention than they have had hitherto. Such studies would also contribute much to the clarification of what it is that constitutes the Catholic identity. Finally, the recent National Pastoral Congress indicated that one cannot meaningfully talk about pastoral strategies without first carrying out a full inventory of all the available resources of the Church in terms of clerical, religious and lay skills and financial, material and cultural resources. However, it is perhaps important to stress again that in general such research will only provide a more informed basis for the development of pastoral strategies; it is not an alternative to decision-making. The distinction between problem-identifying and problem-solving must be made clearly.

All the signs suggest that the Church is in a period of very rapid change in the light of the industrial and democratic revolutions and the enormous social and technological changes of the past two hundred years. The shift from a 'mechanistic' to an 'organic' Church and from uniformity to pluriformity, the new theological emphases on the people of God', collegiality and participation, the decline of ritual and the stress on relationships, and the development of new interpretations of authority are all likely to create strains in the transitional period between the old model of the Church and some new emergent model. In meeting the challenges of this period the social sciences and statistics have their proper contribution to make.

Acknowledgments

I would like to express my gratitude to Br Alan of the Catholic Central Library, London, Philip Blake and Norbert Winstanley of the Catholic Education Council, London, Mrs Sandra Rowe of the Catholic Press Office, Glasgow, and my colleague Raymond M. Lee, for their generous help in the preparation of this chapter.

Selected bibliography

Cartwright, A., *How Many Children?* (London, 1976).

Coman, P., *Catholics and the Welfare State* (London, 1977).

Commission for Priestly Formation, *The Cherwell Report: A Working Party Report on the Future Training of Priests* (Abbots Langley, 1979).

Currie, R., Gilbert, A., & Horsley, L., *Churches and Churchgoers: Patterns of Church Growth in the British Isles since 1700 (Oxford, 1977).*

Hindess, B., *The Use of Official Statistics in Sociology: A Critique of Positivism and Ethnomethodology* (London, 1973).

Hornsby-Smith, M.P., *Catholic Education: The Unobtrusive Partner* (London, 1978a).

Hornsby-Smith, M.P., *Tradition and Change in the Roman Catholic Community in England: Final Report to the S.S.R.C.* (Guildford, University of Surrey, 1978b).

Hornsby-Smith, M.P., 'Irish Catholics in England: Some Sociological Perspectives', in Irish Episcopal Commission for Emigrants, *Irish Catholics in England: A Congress Report* (Dublin, 1978c).

Hornsby-Smith, M.P., & Lee, R.M., *Roman Catholic Opinion: A Study of Roman Catholics in England and Wales in the 1970s* (Guildford, University of Surrey, 1979).

Joint Working Party on Pastoral Strategy, *A Time For Building* (Abbots Langley, 1976).

Lawrence Report, *Ground Plan: A Suggested Scheme for Roman Catholic Diocesan Boundaries* (Abbots Langley, 1976).

Martin, B., 'Comments on some Gallup Poll Statistics', ch. 10 in Martin, D. (Ed.), *A Sociological Yearbook of Religion in Britain* (London, 1968).

McRobers, D. (Ed.), *Modern Scottish Catholicism: 1878-1978* (Glasgow, 1979).

NOP Market Research Ltd, *Church Going: A Report on a Survey: 13-19 July* (London, 1978).

Pycroft, F., *Catholic Facts and Figures* (London, 1977).

Social Surveys (Gallup Poll) Ltd, *Religion Study: 22 February-17 April* (London, 1978).

Social Surveys (Gallup Poll) Ltd, *Survey of Scottish Catholics* (London, 1979).

Spencer, A.E.C.W., 'The Newman Demographic Survey, 1953-1964: Reflections on the Birth, Life and Death of a Catholic Institute for Socio-Religious Research', *Social Compass* (1964), XI (3-4), 31-7.

Spencer, A.E.C.W., 'Statistics, Ecclesiastical', *New Catholic Encyclopedia, 13* (New York, 1967), pp. 672-6.

Spencer, A.E.C.W., 'Demography of Catholicism', *The Month, 8* (1975), (4) , April, 100-5.

The government of the Church[1]

ANTONY BLACK

IN NO AREA has Vatican II, in what it said and did and in the image it projected, produced more creative turmoil than in the government of the Church. But, while it is easy to exaggerate what is going on elsewhere, the general feeling is (to put it rather mildly) that the British Isles have been less affected by this than most other countries.

First, the ecclesiology of Chapters 1-4 of the *Dogmatic Constitution on the Church (Lumen Gentium)* emphasized the caritative and communal aspect of 'the people of God', the ministerial nature of all clerical offices, and the apostolate of the laity. It proclaimed the collegiality of the universal episcopate. Second, the Council recommended collegiate organs of church government: a periodic 'Synod of Bishops ... acting in the name of the entire Catholic episcopate' (*Decree on the Bishops' Pastoral Office in the Church*, ch. 1); 'episcopal conferences' on a national basis, whose decrees were to have 'juridically binding force' under certain conditions (*ibid.*, ch. 3); and councils including lay people 'in dioceses' and 'on the parochial, interparochial, and interdiocesan level as well as in the national or international sphere' (*Decree on the Apostolate of the Laity*, ch. 5). Third, the Council's ecclesiology and ethos gave rise to fresh doctrinal and moral sentiments, summed up in the word 'collegiality'.

It has thus come to be widely believed that decision-making in the Church ought to be a collaborative work among several persons of appropriate rank and ability, undertaken in a spirit of consensus with those likely to be affected. In a general way, the charismatic movement has proclaimed group participation: every baptized person is the direct recipient of the gifts of the Spirit. This swing in opinion has had its effect on the ethos of church government: the more that people think of themselves as 'the people of God' and as vehicles of the Holy Spirit, the more they will — unless carefully advised otherwise — apply this belief to matters of organization.

Yet when we turn to practice, the effects of all this have been very uneven. This is largely because the Council itself, due to its 'anti-authoritarian' mood but also for other reasons to be discussed later, stopped short of putting its recommendations in the form of binding rules. The Synod of Bishops was formally set up as an advisory body by

a papal *motu proprio*, and this central organ of collegiality has been one of
the least effective. The greatest success has been episcopal conferences,
which have become a regular feature of church life; but again, how effectively they operate and how much their existence affects believers,
depends entirely on the energy of the local episcopate and on their taste
for collegial procedures. They are supposed to formulate Christian
responses to local problems; but one would be hard pressed to find a
single issue on which the British or Irish episcopal conferences have
made a real impact in Britain or Ireland or contributed anything distinctive to the debates of our time.

The implementation of collegiality at the diocesan level (that is, the
functioning of diocesan commissions comprising laity and clergy, and
the participation of all clergy in diocesan affairs) and at the parochial
level (that is, parish councils) is, in effect, left to the initiative of the individual bishop or parish priest. It is extremely patchy. There are
dioceses in Britain which remain in this respect virtually untouched by
Vatican II. It was brave and right of the Council to leave so much to
local initiative; but its drive appears, in many parts of Britain and
especially most of Scotland, to have come up against firm obstacles, or to
have become embedded in torpor. It is indicative of the present mood at
Rome that the Netherlands and not Scotland has been singled out for
corrective treatment by a Pope who clearly thinks he is implementing
Vatican II.

The new organs have been less than adequate and the new sentiments
have begun to evaporate, or to be turned aside from the stony task of
realizing the Council's ecclesiology in practice. There is a temptation for
the charismatic to stop short of applying his or her beliefs to the actual
structures of the Church, out of misplaced pietism; and for all of us to
forget that the actual method by which the Church organizes its public
life and takes decisions makes a powerful impression, sooner or later, on
the self-awareness and spirituality of Catholic individuals and groups, let
alone on non-Catholics. In short, collegiality remains fragile. Great
numbers of people in Britain who were set on fire in the 1960s have been
quietly disillusioned. There is a general stagnation, a growing sense of
'plus ça change ... ' In larger historical perspective, one may still marvel
at what has been achieved and look with reasonable hope to the future.
But this hope can remain reasonable only if we recognize how far we
have *not* travelled, and face up to what remains to be done.

There are two stony problems: to what extent are the presently
authorized church leaders prepared to implement Vatican II's recommendations, and how can collegiality be brought into the authorized
structures of the Church themselves? The reasons for failure in Britain
and Ireland are, first, the generally 'conservative' stamp of many
bishops, and, secondly, the defensive and often equally 'conservative'

spirituality of congregations, which is still in many areas being actively promoted by quite young clergy. Collegiality is not something that can be easily be imposed; like all forms of responsibility, it has to be grown into. It requires a whole spiritual formation that is liberated and reasonably activist — there are parallels with secular democracy. Nevertheless, when a priest has been prepared to open doors and lead the way, the results have been considerable. It is not true, in my experience, that the great majority of Catholics are so absolutely wedded to authoritarian modes of government, any more than they were to the Tridentine liturgy, that they would not be willing to try new ways. Hence the problem lies rather with the leadership. *If* bishops and priests were generally as devoted to collegiality as they are to (say) the Eucharist — and the two are ultimately inseparable — the way would be easy. But they are not.

Let us take a down-to-earth example. A certain parish in Scotland, founded in 1963 on a new housing estate, had an amiable parish priest and a curate with a dynamic 'Vatican II' vision. It developed a lively liturgy, a strong sense of social responsibility, and an elected parish council with committees for education, liturgy, missions, and so on. Young people attended in large numbers. In 1977 a visiting priest of considerable experience called the parish a beacon for the Scottish Church. (Incidentally, the only recent vocation to the priesthood in the diocese came from this parish). But the bishop (also an amiable man) was conservative in the sense that he would make no change unless explicitly instructed 'from above'; as a man trying to sleep is disturbed by a power-drill, so he found this parish a constant source of irritation. First, he tried to remove the curate. Then, having received a letter from the parish council asking him to bear in mind the parish's nature when considering a new parish priest, he installed in rapid succession two ultra-'conservative' parish priests with mandates to reverse matters. The second of these instantly abolished the parish council and appropriated its funds. When challenged, both these men asked in what way they were violating their office as defined in canon law.

Those who supported collegiality (and the parish soon became divided) first appealed to the bishop — what else could they do? Then, with some hope, they approached the Apostolic Delegate. The eventual reply was illuminating: 'The whole issue ... is surely well-known to the bishop', but in any case 'while the laity have a specific rôle to fulfil in the Church, as it is clearly and repeatedly stated in the Vatican Council's documents, they are not called upon to guide and govern the Church, which is the reponsibility of the bishops with the collaboration of their priests, who have been appointed to lead the particular churches as vicars and legates of Christ'. Parish councils 'can operate ... as consultative bodies'; but, having stated their case 'with clarity, but also with humility and respect', they 'must be willing to accept the decisions of their Pastors, and to obey in a spirit of faith ...'[2]

So much for Vatican II in practice. A single appointment, made 'from above', can change overnight the public worship and life of a parish; appeal can only be made to the person who made the appointment; and the representative of the universal Church can give a small-minded lesson in (pre-Vatican II) canon law.

Similarly, at the diocesan level, more than one bishop has effectively shelved the organizational recommendations of Vatican II; there are dioceses in which all commissions and collegiate procedures languish through the inactivity of a single leader. At the national level, the Scottish hierarchy at least have shown themselves collectively incapable of implementing the Council's message: they have not been summoned to a special synod at Rome.

What our little story reveals is that Vatican II did not effectively resolve the question of *power* in the Church. The question of who has legal authority in terms of canon law turns out, after all, to be of crucial importance. The truth is not only that there is no law *enforcing* the recommendations of Vatican II in matters of church government, or imposing sanctions on those who flagrantly violate its intentions, but also that there are actually *contrary* laws in force. One may contrast the liturgical area and conclude, I think, that the Vatican *and the actual popes* Paul VI and John Paul II have quite consciously held back from what the Council expected of them in matters of organization. This is presumably because they believed, first, that the existing system adequately represents ecclesiological truth (*pace Lumen Gentium*), and, second, that once they introduce — or allow to be introduced — effective collegiality, things will never be the same again for the *curia Romana*. It will lose that ultimate ecclesiastical power which has been our curse; it will be liberated; it will have to place more trust — and not in word alone — in others. None of this, however, would violate — indeed it would realize — the basic premiss of Petrine-papal doctrine, that all Christians must be in communion with one another and with the Roman see.

Anyone who reads *Lumen Gentium* will be struck by the great disparity between its general vision of the Church, which is a marvellous exposition and development of Catholic tradition in all its creative richness, and the constitutional *norms* actually in force today. There are clear reasons for this. First, at the doctrinal level the relationship between papal infallibility and collegiality was not satisfactorily resolved. Second, canon law has not been changed: it continues to enforce a monarchical form of government at every level of the Church's life (whenever, that is, anyone chooses to invoke it). However strongly collaboration and a fraternal ministry may be recommended, anyone familiar with the way large, powerful institutions work must know that omelettes cannot be made without breaking eggs, that law is the only effective restraint upon power — or, more precisely, is essential if *any* restraint is to operate. This is not to say that moral and spiritual factors are unimportant in the Church, as they are in any society. It is to say that they require careful implementation, and that in this case this can only be achieved through structural changes ('faith without works is dead').

A further reason for lack of success in realizing collegiality has been that Vatican II's ecclesiology of renewal remained steeped in — not to say drugged with — the social philosophy of German romanticism, typically transmitted by the great Karl Rahner. The Church was said to be 'really' collegial and fraternal; the relation between Peter and the Apostles was conceived as 'ontologically' collegial; and a charming picture was drawn of the mystical, caritative union betwen leaders and led. But precise constitutional provisions for the realization of all this were left out. Emphasis on the distinction between the 'caritative' and the 'institutional' Church provides all kinds of excuses.

One can only conclude that the very structure of the Church, its public life and law, must be transformed in the light of the collegial ideal. Neither social romanticism nor constitutional rationality are on the same level as revealed truth. But, taken together, they may well be the appropriate vehicles for expressing the core of the Gospel in ecclesiology today; certainly more appropriate than the sad vestiges of oriental despotism transmitted by Roman law, with which Roman Catholics are still forced more or less consciously to live their organizational existence.

One may instance two areas in particular: elections plus accountability, and decision-making. The present system for electing parish priests and bishops flagrantly violates centuries of early (and in the case of bishops, quite recent) Catholic tradition. When all bishops are appointed by Rome, the very notion of episcopal collegiality becomes a sham. Appointment of priests should combine an element of congregational choice with an element of diocesan approval; the bishop, with advice from his clergy, could draw up a short-list, from which the parish chooses, or vice versa. Appointment of bishops should combine diocesan preferences and the views of clergy and laity, with advice and consent from the national hierarchy; there is no need for Rome to be involved. Complaints against a parish priest could be heard by a diocesan group; complaints against a bishop, as in the early Church, would go to the regional episcopate. To make such procedures workable is not beyond the wit of man, and accords with tradition. It would involve some confrontation and clash of opinions; but at least a true marriage between pastor and people would result.

Above all — to put a crucial point very briefly — *parish councils, diocesan synods and so on should be given a formal place in canon law as necessary partners with priest or bishop in the formulation of policy*. The alternative, of abolishing altogether the 'public-law' aspects of canon law, may sound romantic and might even be an improvement on the present situation. But its anarchistic consequences are obvious, and could only seriously be contemplated by someone who had ceased to believe in the visible universality of the Church.

Without some such measures, there will still have been some progress in the realization of the mystery of the Church on earth following Vatican II. But it will have been slight, and always subject to reversal at the whim of a superior. Ecclesiology has for too long been drugged by quasi-mystical formulae. No human society can live without morale and a sense of community that cannot be translated into law; one is reminded of Hegel's *dictum* that when the law enters family relationships these have already begun to dissolve. But, similarly, no human society can live by ideals alone. A social vision can only be translated into practice by means of known and effective rules. The Church is built of stones. If papal, episcopal and pastoral authority are to be brought into line with the collegial vision of Vatican II, the rules will have to be changed.

Notes

1. I am extremely grateful to Tony Robb, one-time chairman of a one-time parish council, for his comments.
2. The words are those of Mgr Mario Oliveri, *chargé d'affaires*, later confirmed by Archbishop Bruno Heim, Apostolic Delegate to the UK.

The parish and the priesthood

DAVID FORRESTER

IT IS OFTEN difficult for many of us to appreciate that for young Catholics the second Vatican Council is akin to ancient history. Even for someone of twenty, it can only be a faint memory. After all, the Council concluded its deliberations in 1965. And yet how many Catholics of all generations in England and Wales today are truly familiar with the constitutions, decrees and declarations of Vatican II, let alone appreciate why the Council was called and what was its purpose?

Not long ago I gave a lecture to a large group of concerned and serious-minded Catholics on the rôle of the laity in the Church. At the conclusion of the talk a woman present stood up and asked if the ideas I had put forward were my own, since they seemed rather novel. Two sentences in particular had caught her attention. These were: 'An individual layman, by reason of the knowledge, competence, or outstanding ability which he enjoys, is permitted and sometimes even obliged to express his opinions on things which concern the good of the Church'[1] and 'The laity should accustom themselves to working in the parish in close union with their priests, bringing to the church community their own and the world's problems as well as questions concerning human salvation, all of which should be examined and resolved by common deliberation'.[2]

When I replied that, apart from a few strategically-placed conjunctions throughout my lecture, all that I had said could be found written down in the documents of Vatican II, there was an audible gasp of astonishment throughout the audience. This was immediately succeeded by a universal demand to know: Why have we never been told? And the truth is that, as Catholics in these islands, in many areas of life we haven't even begun to implement the enactments of Vatican II. (It is to be hoped that implementation in England and Wales will be speeded up as one of the fruits of the National Pastoral Congress held in Liverpool).

We may also be unaware that the Council was concerned above all with renewal. But, as Cardinal Hume informed the National Conference of Priests in 1979: 'In the years since Vatican II have we been concerned with restructuring rather than renewal? Do we yet know what "renewal" means? We haven't begun fully to implement Vatican II'.

And that most certainly would seem to be very much the case in many instances when we think of how actually we experience the realities of parish and priesthood in contemporary Britain and Ireland. We have been instead, and to a lesser degree still are, mesmerized by the notion of 'restructuring rather than renewal. This distinction is vital but not always understood.

In 1973 Michael Winter published his book *Mission or Maintenance*, subtitled 'A study in new pastoral structures'. Winter himself fully understood the distinction between restructuring and renewal; indeed, he would possibly claim that his emphasis on the former was precisely to enable the latter to occur more effectively. In the moderate stir that the book made in ecclesiastical circles, however, many readers concentrated solely on his criticism of the institutional aspects of the Church and of the diocesan and parish systems in particular. Such remarks as 'The parish is of an unworkable size. It is either too large or too small for the functions which the Church requires of it' inevitably raised eye-brows. Others, such as 'Authentic mission will not start again until the parish structure has been superseded by something more dynamic', occasioned considerable comment, particularly among priests. And Winter's stated four objectives of achieving what he termed 'satisfactory worship, witness, apostolate and charity', as well as his ideas on how they might be attained within a new system which included emphasis on small worshipping comunities and clergy living together and working as teams, became talking-points for some considerable time. Whether *Mission or Maintenance* had a lasting effect, however, is open to question.

The document *The Church 2000* appeared in the same year as Michael Winter's book. The authors were a joint working party set up by the Bishops' Conference of England and Wales and the National Conference of Priests. Over 25,000 copies were circulated among the Catholic population. Deliberately termed an 'interim report', the document invited public discussion on what its authors considered the major issues of Christian life and witness and how the Church could plan to meet them. Three years later, in 1976, a final report, entitled *A Time For Building*, was published with a circulation of 20,000. Among other things *A Time For Building* specifically urged the restructuring of the basic Christian communities on the basis of shared interests, professions or neighbourhoods, each with its own 'eucharistic leader'. Much more remarkable than the contents of either of the two documents was the extraordinary paucity of the response they each provoked, compared with the numbers of copies sold. In response to *The Church 2000* only 400 or more letters were received, and in response to *A Time For Building* only 350 replies were sent in. The correspondence which followed both documents was compiled and selected by David Miles Board, the National Co-ordinator of Catholic Information Services, and published in Holy Week 1980. It makes sober and often depressing reading. Why did Winter's book on the whole evoke little more than animated conversation and ultimately simply gather dust on presbytery shelves? Why did so few people respond to *The Church 2000* and *A Time For Building?* We can only guess at the answers and what follows must be a purely personal assessment. In my view the poor response of Catholics to ideas about restructuring voiced in the first half of the 1970s does not mean in the least that as a people we are apathetic or unconcerned. The main reason for the poor response has been a failure on the part of most of us — clergy and laity — to educate ourselves in the teachings of Vatican II. We are therefore often extremely ignorant concerning our mission as members of the Church. A second reason might be that restructuring the Church's institutions, particularly in regard to the parish and priesthood as they have always been known, does not feature high on the average Catholic's list of priorities. A third reason is that both Pope John Paul II and Cardinal Hume in their different ways have undoubtedly struck chords closer to the hearts of the average English and Welsh Catholic than any amount of well-intentioned, highly-skilled and sociologically-orientated, committee-minded people: 'I have a dream of a new form of exercising the priesthood', said Cardinal Hume in 1979. 'It has two characteristics which I have learned from young priests and strangely, from men who had thought of offering themselves for the priesthood but decided against it. They say something about prayer — about a need to pray, a deep life of prayer. And this is essential. And they say something about community. These two values are primary'.

It is this kind of approach which the average Catholic understands and has always instinctively sought. It is because such a Catholic shares the Cardinal's chief priorities that he is then prepared to follow when the Cardinal goes on to say: 'But, thirdly, this new form of priesthood must not be so churchy, so ecclesiastical. There is a need to be more radical and more prophetic ... I am looking for young men who are ready to be radical in their approach to their Christian life and deeply committed to renewal'. It is interesting to note, incidentally, that the Cardinal was addressing the delegates to the National Conference of Priests in 1979. They were debating the themes of prayer, preaching and community in the lives of priests; themes rather different from those which preoccupied the minds of their colleagues in the early 1970s. The difference possibly reflects a change in outlook among Catholics generally; a change in the direction of seeking to get to the roots or fundamentals of our faith and then seeking a renewal on the basis of Vatican II. Such a radical review necessarily includes taking a hard look at the parish and priesthood in this tail-end of the twentieth century. Until we are conversant with the outlook of Vatican II on both, however, restructuring would seem premature. Our priority must be that of the Council, namely renewal.

In the *Constitution on the Liturgy*, article 42, the *raison d'être* of the parish as most of us know it is expressed succinctly: 'Because it is impossible for the Bishop always and everywhere to preside over the whole flock in his Church, he cannot do other than establish lesser groupings of the faithful. Among these, parishes set up locally under a pastor who takes the place of the Bishop are the most important: for in a certain way they represent the visible Church as it is established throughout the world'.

The parish system has existed in Britain since the seventh century. It exists because the bishop (head of the local Church or diocese) is unable to minister directly to eveyone in his care and he is obliged to ordain priests as his 'co-workers' to share in his priesthood and mission. It is the common experience of most of us to find ourselves living in an area to which a priest (either alone or with assistants) has been assigned to take upon himself, as far as he is able, those duties and concerns which in the very early Church the bishop would have been able to discharge himself. 'As they sanctify and govern under the bishop's authority that part of the Lord's flock entrusted to them, they make the universal Church visible in their own locality and lend powerful assistance to the upbuilding of the whole body of Christ'.[3] It is not generally known that parishes nevertheless may be one of two kinds, either territorial or personal. In the latter, membership is not defined by residence but by sharing in common ties such as those of language, nationality or even occupation — as for example being a member of the armed services. *The Constitution on the Liturgy* speaks only of the establishment of 'lesser groupings of the faithful'. Even so, the important thing is whether the 'lesser groupings of the faithful' within the local Church do effectively represent the visible Church. In practice this means establishing whether the parish makes incarnate God's salvific work, especially in the proclamation of the Word; and in the celebration of the Eucharist. It is at the Eucharist above all that the parish represents the fellowship and unity of the People of God. The eucharistic sacrifice, defined as 'the fount and apex of the whole Christian life', must be at the centre of the parish community's life. It is a sign of the community's place within the local Church. It takes no account of social differences and integrates all the baptized into the family of God. It should be the source of all the pastoral concern and charity of everyone — clergy and laity — within the community and beyond its confines. If fittingly celebrated, it is the highest vehicle of Christian education and formation. In the average parish in Britain and Ireland today, however, whether the parish authentically represents the visible Church is still largely dependent on the person of the parish priest. This is so because, despite the passage of fifteen years since Vatican II and apart from exceptional places, most parishes are still wedded to pre-Vatican II attitudes. This is not a criticism of the clergy, the majority of whom are dedicated, hard-working and caring pastors.

Most parish priests indeed had been labouring long and hard in the Lord's vineyard years before Vatican II was first mooted; more than a few were ordained before some of us were born. But in what sense were they prepared for Vatican II or even given in-service training after it to enable them to adjust to it? If this is true of the majority of parish priests, is it small wonder that the laity — apart from a minoriy — are simply unaware of their rôle as members of the people of God? Very few of them indeed have heard of, let alone read, the *Decree on the Apostolate of the Laity*. Because of this, no amount of physical restructuring of the parish system *at this time* will improve matters. It may be blatantly obvious from the sociological point of view that the present system is inadequate in the face of the spread of urbanization, the increased mobility of our population, the impact of industry and technology, the changed pattern of family life and so on. John Harriott's words in 1972 are probably as true today as they were then: 'The worlds of businessmen, artists, politicians, or hippies, sportsmen, coloured immigrants, dockers and communicators are all remarkably self-contained — and the claim I wish to make is that in most of them the institutional Church, especially through its official representatives, is no longer present. Not merely without prophetic or moral influence, but physically absent. As for the men of power who set the goals of society and steer it towards them, the politician, the trade unionist, the financier, they can go for years without meeting anyone who represents the Church. It has become a side-show, occasionally putting on a firework display which catches the eye but without any direct bearing on the shaping of society.'[5]

Even so, what is needed most urgently in view of this state of affairs is not a change in the parish system, but a radical review of and renewal in our training of priests — the future leaders of our Catholic community. In the Vatican II *Decree on the Training of Priests* (article 4) major seminaries are described as necessary for priestly training. The document goes on to say 'In them the whole training of the students should have as its object to make them true shepherds of souls after the example of Our Lord Jesus Christ, teacher, priest and shepherd. Hence they should be trained for the ministry of the Word ... They should be trained for the ministry of worship and sanctification ... They should be trained to undertake the ministry of the shepherd'. But are they so trained?

Today no serious-minded Catholic can doubt the inestimable contribution that English seminaries at home and abroad have made over the years to the Church in these islands. The number of priests (ultimately, in more than a few instances, canonized saints) who, after formation and training, have emerged from such institutions and have subsequently worked vigorously here is beyond question. This remains so whether one is thinking of the Venerabile in Rome, Ushaw in County

Durham, Oscott College in Birmingham, Allen Hall in London, the English College at Valladolid in Spain, the Beda College for late vocations in Rome, St John's College, Wonersh in Surrey and, until fairly recently, the English College in Lisbon, to name only the English houses.

Today, however, when seminaries in, say, England, such as Ushaw, increasingly have connections with the theology departments of English Universities, when Maynooth is a college of the National University of Ireland, and such establishments as Heythrop in London and La Sainte Union College of Higher Education in Southampton offer degree courses in Catholic theology; when opportunities for long-distance travel in vacation time are no longer rare; when greater emphasis is placed on the value and importance of the local Church; when ecumenism is a serious matter; and when the cost of sending students abroad is inevitably high, questions are sometimes asked about the usefulness and value of seminaries on the continent for British and Irish students. This is particularly so when one considers the field of pastoral training.

Whereas, for instance, English colleges in Italy and Spain may continue to train their students excellently as ministers of the word and of the sacraments, as required in the *Decree on the Training of Priests*, it is often asked how they measure up to the Vatican II requirement that their students should also be well-trained in the pastoral field. Put more bluntly, one is sometimes asked how a student, who lives and studies in community in a foreign country for perhaps six years, can understand and adequately cope with the needs and outlook of the lay men and women he will one day serve at home.

When one attempts to evaluate the training received at a seminary outside one's own country, it does not seem difficult to fault it on pastoral grounds, especially in regard to involvement with the laity. Those who do criticize it in this way usually point to differences concerning language, culture and national customs, or the subtly different ways in which nowadays the various local Churches are organized and function or individually apply the enactments of Vatican II. It is obvious that the English, Welsh, Scottish and Irish outlooks on the one hand and the Italian and Spanish on the other are different and therefore manifest or give rise to differing approaches to particular pastoral problems, in spite of unanimity in doctrine.

Seminarians being trained abroad are themselves not slow to question the pastoral experience they receive in such matters as marital breakdown, alcoholism, drug addiction, delinquency, sexual permissiveness, racism and how to minister to the handicapped, the deprived, the aged and the dying; all matters which may be treated differently on the practical level in their own countries.

In other instances it is not unknown for them to ask how much they know of British or Irish parochial life. What experience do they obtain of parish visiting, youth activities, and Catholc schools in these countries? How do they discover what is entailed in living in a presbytery? Should they learn how to organize parish prayer groups, bible study groups and catechetics? What should they know of parish committees, councils, finances, societies and communication? How will they even get to know their future fellow diocesan priests or learn the differences between being a 'shepherd' in an industrial town, suburbia, a seaside resort or a rural area? Are they trained in the different techniques required to convey the good news to the affluent on the one hand and to the poor on the other? Most important, do they learn how to relate effectively as celibates to the men and women they will encounter daily once they are ordained? Do they understand the preoccupations and pressures which are the common lot of lay people living in contemporary British or Irish society?

To those opposed to the continuance of seminaries abroad these criticisms or questions are not answered by placing students in parishes just when they are home for the summer, or by giving them crash courses during the holidays on especially chosen topics such as catechetics, the uses of the media, school and hospital chaplaincy work and the place of group ministries. Even so, it is important to ask whether students trained at home are better equipped in the pastoral sense. Are they necessarily better qualified 'to undertake the ministry of the shepherd'?

Many if not all criticisms of the abovementioned kind and usually directed at English seminaries still existing on the continent tend to ignore a vital factor: namely that, until he is actually at least a deacon, no amount of immersion in pastoral matters anywhere will enable a future priest to bring his sacramental powers to bear on any problem. Until ordination to the diaconate, such a person's service, as distinct from his obedience to the injunction to love his neighbour which is incumbent on all Christians, will be little different from that of a voluntary social worker — and an unqualified one at that! It may well be the case that too much interest or involvement in social problems and parochial administration during his pre-diaconate training will only confuse him as to what is to be his essential future task.

This is not to say that a church student being trained either at home or abroad should be kept deliberately ignorant of the problems of society, but during his training clear distinctions in and emphases on his particular place within the people of God should always be made. It is too simplistic to concentrate on the pastoral rôle of the priest and not see it as fundamentally stemming from his function as a minister of the word and of the sacraments.

Being a shepherd today, more than ever before, also includes knowing one's specialist sphere and limitations. If this is achieved, after his ordination a priest should rarely confuse his function with those of equally-qualified and highly-trained lay people in other walks of life and vocations, such as doctors, psychologists, social workers, probation officers, school teachers and so on. He and they will the more readily understand that: 'Though they differ from one another in essence and not only in degree, the common priesthood of the faithful and the ministerial or hierarchical priesthood are nonetheless interrelated. Each of them in its own special way is a participation in the one priesthood of Christ'.[6]

Pastoral training nowadays is unquestionably more than simply a matter of learning what to say to the bereaved, how to instruct converts, how to counsel couples contemplating marriage, and how to prepare parents for the baptism of a child or children for confirmation — crucially important though each of these matters remain.[7] It is vital too for a future priest to have studied the root causes of such social issues as alienation from institutional religion, the causes of poverty, injustice, unemployment, lack of housing, deprivation in our inner cities, the question of disarmament, and the quest for human rights. Even so, such study should always have the aim of enabling him to see how as a priest he may bring Christian values to bear on these matters, and how the Gospel, unlike so many transitory secular solutions, is perennially relevant.

Part of our problem in the recent past — the time when one heard so much of crises of identity among priests, the shortage of vocations and the large numbers of priests seeking laicization — was that of determining precisely what the rôle of the priest should be. This was complicated by the fact that, as Raymond Brown pointed out in his book *Priest and Bishop* (1970), 'The priesthood represents the combination or distillation of several distinct rôles and special ministries in the New Testament Church' (Brown summarized these as the disciple, the apostle, the presbyter-bishop and the celebrant of the Eucharist). Nevertheless, it is clear what the majority of the laity in our country are seeking from their priests, no matter how differently the priesthood may be required to be exercised according to the particular needs of different local Churches. What they are seeking is a priesthood obviously rooted in and shot through with continuous prayer.

In the first week of Easter 1980 the Sacred Congregation for Catholic Education in Rome published a circular letter concerning some urgent aspects of spiritual formation in seminaries, following the post-conciliar turmoil. It offered four main guidelines for the spiritual formation of future priests:

1. They should be encouraged to develop a profound love of Christ as the Word of God, 'to which end it is necessary to cultivate a feeling for true inner silence'.

2. They should learn to share in the paschal mystery of the death and resurrection of Christ and 'to instil in him (the future priest) a sense of his inalienable responsibility to see that the faithful participate in it worthily'.

3. They should be taught to realize that communion with Christ requires asceticism and a spirit of penance.

4. They should be encouraged to develop an unsentimental filial love for the mother of Christ.

Is this in any way different from the first priority laid down and mentioned earlier as being looked for by Cardinal Hume? Indeed, only when this is achieved, together with a deep commitment to Vatican II, will it be possible for us all — clergy and laity together — to judge such structures as the parochial system. The latter may be inadequate but renewal must take precedence. What we must avoid at all costs is the state of affairs in a parish known to me in which a fourteen-year-old once said: 'This parish is efficient but it is lacking in love'.

Notes

1. *Dogmatic Constitution on the Church*, art. 37.
2. *Decree on the Apostolate of the Laity*, art. 10.
3. *Constitution on the Church*, art. 28.
4. *Constitution on the Church*, art. 11
5. John Harriott, 'Apostolic Presence', *The Way* (1972).
6. *Constitution on the Church*, art. 10.
7. This need for the widening of pastoral training was recognized in the *Cherwell Report on the Training of Priests* (London, 1979).

Worship

NICHOLAS KENYON

No FEATURE of Roman Catholic life in Britain and Ireland was more visibly changed by the work of the second Vatican Council than its form of public worship. To a disconcerting extent, it was possible for us to ignore the insights of the Council on ecumenism, justice and peace, evangelism, and so on; but every time we entered our parish churches after the beginning of Advent 1964, something was different. Historically, the renewal of the liturgy took us by surprise. When the Council gave its massive endorsement to the Constitution on the Liturgy (2162 *placet*, 46 *non placet*) on 14 November 1962, the Council was barely a month old and its mood had not been sensed; reports from Rome still contained rumours of the rearguard action fought by curial cardinals against the proposals of the liturgy schema. A year later, the Constitution was ready to be promulgated, but the Church in Britain and in Ireland was scarcely ready to receive it. True, the ideas which it embodied had been circulating in the Church in these islands since at least the end of the second World War; but those enthusiasts who had argued the case for a pastoral and flexible (rather than a rubrical and historical) approach to liturgy had always been somehow suspect as 'out-of-line'. Quite recently, after all, Pope John XIII had reasserted the central place of Latin in the Church's worship. So there were few in these islands ready enthusiastically to explain the thinking behind the Constitution. Two priests active in the liturgical movement for many years should be mentioned: Fr Clifford Howell, SJ, produced a fine translation of the Constitution almost instantaneously, and Fr J.D. Crichton wrote, almost as quickly, *The Church's Worship*, a commentary that was to be invaluable in helping many worried clergy and people in the years ahead to interpret the changes which followed so quickly.

Looking back over fifteen years, it is difficult to avoid the conclusion that the situation was bungled. In their enthusiasm to follow the agreed methods of implementing the Constitution, the bishops of England and Wales, for instance, began almost at once to introduce the vernacular into the celebration of Mass. Bits of the Catholic Truth Society's *Simple Prayer Book* English translation were lifted into a liturgy that was still mainly in Latin (Advent 1964); then on Palm Sunday (of all Sundays) 1965, a second stage brought the vernacular into command from the start of the Mass up to the 'Secret'; extraordinary confusion prevailed at the end of Mass, where the communion and postcommunion were in English but the *Ite missa est* and blessing in Latin. All this occurred before any except the most attentive clergy had had the opportunity to work together, or attend courses, or read extensive material in English on the purpose of these changes. Inevitably the detailed, tricky instructions were treated in exactly the same rubrical spirit that had characterized the performance of the old liturgy. For too many congregations, the experience was like being told how to fill in a new type of income-tax form.

Not until Advent 1969 was the situation clarified, with the introduction of the new order of Mass (which became obligatory in England and Wales from 15 February 1970). By then, post-conciliar bodies had taken the reforms in the liturgy far beyond what many people thought the Constitution had spelled out. Therefore this *Novus Ordo* or *Missa Normativa* (as it was always called by those who tried to discredit it) became a rallying-point for people who were convinced that the Church had run off the rails of reform onto the never-ending track of revolution. Moreover the efforts of liturgists were devoted to rebutting charges of heresy rather than to explaining the spirit of the new liturgy. But the spirit in which the new order of Mass was conceived precisely reflected the thinking of the Constitution: 'Even in the liturgy, the Church has no wish to impose a rigid uniformity in matters which do not implicate the faith or the good of the whole community; rather does she respect and foster the genius and talents of nations' (art. 37). 'Provision is to be made, when revising the liturgical books, for legitimate adaptations and variations to different groups. . .' (art. 38). 'The rites should be distinguished by a noble simplicity; they should be short, clear, and unencumbered by any useless repetitions' (art. 34). These pastoral guidelines were expanded and explained in the most important yet the most disregarded document of liturgical renewal, the general instruction on the Roman Missal which accompanied the promulgation of the new order: 'The pastoral effectiveness of a celebration depends in great measure on choosing readings, prayers and songs which correspond to the needs, spiritual preparation and attitudes of the participants'. But this document was not published for English-language readers, except with the revised missal, until it appeared from the Catholic Truth Society at the end of 1973, more than four years later.

It was scarcely surprising, then, if the celebration of the renewed liturgy in Britain and Ireland was all too often characterized by mumble and missalettes. Nevertheless Ireland worked much harder to catechize its people and to educate its clergy; it is no coincidence that the most valuable collection of liturgical documents and discussion was published by Scepter Books in Dublin under the title *Vatican II: The Liturgy Constitution*, and later revised and enlarged as *Liturgy: Renewal and Adaptation*. In England and Wales there were isolated pockets of adventurous activity: in Liverpool, Sebastian Moore and Kevin Maguire were experimenting with the form of Mass before the introduction of the new order, and Oliver and Ianthe Pratt wrote an influential book, *Liturgy is what we make it*, which provided a background for the adaptation and celebration of the liturgy for small groups. The Society of St Gregory, which had developed liturgical thinking in England before the Council, continued to hold summer schools which took on a new lease of life as clergy, nuns and parish musicians came to discuss and take part in the revised form of Mass. The Church Music Association, whose work was for a time supported financially by the hierarchy, set up a network of diocesan branches and organizations.

But all this work hardly impinged on the mainstream of Catholic parish life. There, one somewhat pessimistically suspects, the pace was made by the publishing houses. They were far more energetic at promoting their wares than the National Liturgical Commission or diocesan liturgical commissions were at providing guidance. When a publisher came up with the handy notion of a disposable sheet containing all the options of the day's liturgy, pre-selected so as to avoid the necessity of creative choice, easily packaged so as to run straight through from the start of Mass to the finish, and seasoned with a few irrelevant hymns, the glorious age of the missalette was ushered in. Any new hymnal enjoyed good sales, on the basis that hymns were the best thing to 'get people to join in' (a recurring, mindless chant of the late sixties and seventies); a plethora of people's Masses — the most popular, by Dom Gregory Murray, adapted from his old Latin people's Mass — came on the market; and enterprising new firms such as Mayhew-McCrimmon flooded the country with so-called 'folk' music in idioms nicely described by one commentator as 'the pop, the plush, and the twee'. Not infrequently, alas, one encountered culturally-sensitive people outside the Church who thought that the main purpose of Vatican II had been to introduce guitars into the liturgy.

Where are we today? In spite of all the chaos and miscalculation of the early years of renewal, a great deal has been achieved: more than even the most optimistic onlooker would have thought possible in 1964. We now have a framework for worship which is clear in its structural outlines, full of possibilities for adaptation, rich in scriptural content, closely bound to the continuing tradition of the eucharistic liturgy, not needlessly unintelligible either to Catholics or to other church-goers (the convergence with the Anglican Series III Communion service is an important subject which cannot be considered here). The work of the International Committee on English in the Liturgy, and the more recent associated body, the International Consultation on English Texts, has given us clear language in which to celebrate the liturgy. In time, no doubt, we will do better, making translations which capture more of the resonances of the ancient texts while not being bound by their grammatical constructions. But (in spite of, or even because of, the violent controversies in the Catholic press) I would date back to the introduction of the ICEL Roman Canon, and the subsequent translations of the three new eucharistic prayers, a feeling that liturgical renewal in this country had moved decisively forward.

The perfect blueprint for a liturgy, however, does not give us a sense of renewal in our worship. If our liturgical practice can remain independent of other vital areas of renewal in the Church since Vatican II, what is the valuable result of all this praiseworthy effort? I suspect that most people think we have now 'done' liturgical change: the new order of Mass has become a comfortable routine; and that, for the time being, is it. Yet we have only just stopped worrying about the *means* of renewal: what about its *end*? Lest a mere layman be thought unduly critical of the clergy's rôle in this undertaking, I quote an English priest's recent appraisal of the situation ('Task Unfinished' by Fr Christopher Walsh, in the collection of essays *English Catholic Worship*: London, 1979): 'The principal problem, indeed crisis, facing liturgy in this country is that of credibility... attendance at the liturgy has become the only criterion of practice and expression of faith; all else is optional, supererogatory. Worse still, only one form of liturgy is offered and required, the Sunday Mass which, in its form, presupposes a prior catechesis which has not happened...' Fr Walsh says that the homily at Sunday Mass 'is intrinsically incapable of bearing the weight put up on it. We have all experienced... major scriptural and theological themes that are avoided, trivialized or moralized upon; preaching suspended altogether for a pastoral letter or appeal of quite extraneous content, or because of summer heat or winter cold or the bus company's timetable, or Father's holiday; sermons from the backs of envelopes, from the tops of heads, from the filing cabinet; diatribes, ferverinos, jeremiads, vaporizings, moralistic anecdotes. The Sunday homily is little short of a lottery...'

These comments support the broad thesis of this chapter, which is that liturgical reform in these islands has run faster than pastoral life can keep up with it. Bridging the gap between the two is a most urgent priority for the Church in the eighties. Otherwise, the liturgy will seem progressively remote from life, because it has no implications for action. It will not change our own lives, because the life of the Church is unaffected by it. Perhaps I am unwise to label this task 'urgent', for it is clearly a gradual process dependent mainly on personalities and organizational structures. Until a new generation of clergy grows up, who no longer think of their function mainly in terms of dispensing the sacraments; until we change our own notions of 'the Church' as an institution from which we receive those same sacraments; until then, little is going to change.

In some places, a change of heart has already become evident. It is difficult, for example, to enter a parish church over which Fr Michael Hollings presides without becoming aware that activity and worship have been thrown into balance; that one complements the other, one expresses the other. In his splendid book. *The Fantasy of Human Rights*, another parish priest, Fr Patrick O'Mahony, has described how, in his community in Shirley, West Midlands, he attempted to 'alter the stance and commitment of the majority of people'. He involved them in projects relating to the Third World, prisoners of conscience, medical supplies for underdeveloped countries, local race-relations, Help-the-Aged, and so on. The celebration of the Eucharist 'which teaches that, in spite of the standards of a consumer society which is dominated by possessions, everything we have is on loan for a short time. . .and that as God our Father shares his daily bread with us, so we should share with one another, whoever we are and wherever we live' was the focus of his mission. This was a long task: he said it took three or four years before anything worthwhile was achieved. But it represents the kind of activity which should be essential to the Church's work, one which must be undertaken if the liturgy is to take on its true significance.

Essentially, the question is one of education: of drawing out the commitment which most Catholics feel keenly and turning it into action. In Britain and Ireland there is a desperate need for continuing liturgical education, yet this is something that official bodies have shied away from since the first days of liturgical reform. Of course some diocesan liturgical commissions have been active in running courses for their clergy; these continued through the period when the liturgical texts were being revised into that of the far less appreciated but even more radical changes in the sacramental rites. But these have been optional, and often preached to the converted. And opportunities for laymen who might take leading rôles in bringing parish liturgies to life have been severely limited. A thriving, active and pioneering institution like the St Thomas More Centre for Pastoral Liturgy in North London, which serves the diocese of Westminster and, informally, a nationwide network of liturgists and musicians, is all the more outstanding for being exceptional. The foundation of a National Liturgical Institute has been discussed and nearly put into action for many years now; some may feel that the time for such a major organization is past, but I think that if it were properly conceived and run, with an emphasis that was really pastoral and not merely academic, it could provide the foundation for the work of renewal that is needed, especially in England, Wales and Scotland. Liturgical institutions in Ireland are more active than those in Britain.

Areas associated with the liturgy also need far more attention than they have so far received. All too often the revival of church architecture,

which could so fruitfully serve and make explicit the ideals of community, of joint celebration between clergy and people and of the links
between liturgy and life, has been confined to the 're-ordering' of a
church sanctuary so that it looks like a chess game in which the players
have been shifted surreptitiously. The work of Wilfrid Cantwell and
others, and the insights of the Anglican movement of modern church
architecture (led by such important figures as Gilbert Cope) have scarcely begun to impinge on the Catholic Church. The arts of movement and
dance, which in the Methodist and Free Churches have begun to contribute to the celebration of worship, are beginning to make an impact in
small Catholic communities — colleges of education, schools, young
people's Masses — but there is still a long way to go if they are to
become part of our liturgical culture. Finally, the art of church music, on
which so much of the success of a living liturgical celebration depends, is
at a very, very primitive stage in Britain. The National Music Commission, since it ceased to 'censor' new settings of the ordinary of the Mass,
has been among the least active of the national commissions; it has done
little to stimulate the work of composers, text-writers and practical musicians. Once again, the impetus in this field has too often come only from
publishers, and they have now become worryingly inactive. We need
new theoretical research into the function of church music, and a whole
range of practical instruction for cantors, directors, organists and most
of all choirs — who seem to think that there is little place for them and
their music in the reformed liturgy.

Changes have been made; the renewal is only just beginning.

The religious life

DAVID LUNN

1980 is the 1500th year since the conjectural date of the birth of St Benedict of Nursia, the founder of western monasticism, and much of the development of the religious life during that millennium and a half has happened either by inspiration from his life and work or by reaction against it. Of his life, little is known, and most of that is of dubious historical value: how, in his early teens, his hopeless infatuation for an older woman drove him into a hermit's life in a cave and thence, when a vision of the woman appeared, naked into a bed of old stinging nettles; how, impressed by his valour, a group of like-minded men asked him to be their leader; and how, as the fruit of many years spent in the difficult task of ruling these and others, he wrote a little book of instructions and advice for future generations. Like the works of Shakespeare, the authorship and the originality of this book have been the subject of much learned and earnest questioning, but whether Benedict or someone else of the same name was the book's author, there is no doubting its genius. The book's genius and the secret of its enormous influence lay in the author's ability to harness, in ways that were acceptable to the Church's authorities and manageable by ordinary mortals, the wild individualism of the previous monastic tradition: heroic hermits, who were canonized by popular acclaim after living for years in caves or atop pillars without benefit of clergy or of the sacraments, spiritual athletes who engaged in a kind of early Christian one-upmanship, vagrant monks and small, evanescent communities. With the practical wisdom of late Roman law and society behind him, Benedict made his monks acceptable to the hitherto fearful and suspicious authorities of Church and State: like soldiers of the period, the monks were bound by lifelong vows; like the Roman *paterfamilias*, the abbot presided over them with enlightened despotism; and together they lived the self-contained life of a Roman country estate. Stripped of its contemporary origins, this basic structure of vows, superior and community has survived changed circumstances and the chief adaptations which resulted: the friars, product of medieval urbanization, and the Jesuits, who met the challenge of individualism in the early modern period, both of them adaptations which loosened the structure without scrapping it. Curiously, it looks as if we have had to wait until Benedict's fifteenth centenary for a wide movement that seeks to return the religious life to the tradition of wild witness, with all its attendant risks, which preceded him.

In composing this survey of the religious life in the Catholic Church in the British Isles in 1980 and the changes that have overtaken it since the second Vatican Council, necessary limits of space, time and scope have been imposed. Within these limits, however, I have drawn on my knowledge of the history, ancient and modern, of the religious orders, congregations and societies, and I acknowledge my debts to the many documents, published and unpublished, that these bodies have produced in response to the Council; to those religious with whom I had conversations; and to those who answered my questionnaire. While some religious superiors and others politely declined to answer my questions, I received enough answers to cover a cross-section of men and women from the diverse traditions of monasticism, both active and contemplative, the friars, canons regular and modern societies, engaged in a wide variety of work, from home and foreign missions to teaching and nursing. I am grateful to those who gave time and thought to this task, and I have tried to preserve anonymity, even when I received explicit permission to cite names.

Changes did not, of course, begin with Vatican II. Change and decay, reform and renewal, have been constant themes in the history of the religious life. But official intimations of a desire for reform can be seen in the 1944 commission for reform set up by the Sacred Congregation for Religious and in the statement by Pius XII in 1951 that 'The nun's task in the world today cannot be accomplished without certain modifications in the customs of the classical type of religious life'. At the first congress of the committee of general superiors in 1957 Fr Lombardi SJ said: 'There are too many of these institutes that proceed at the same old sedate trot, with no idea of how urgently the rapidly changing conditions of our time call for new efforts and new methods in apostolic work and spiritual life. They work to rule ... ' There were some changes: nuns, for instance, were allowed some relaxations of the rules governing visits outside the convent walls, and lay brothers in Benedictine houses were brought more closely into line with the status and obligations of the choir monks.

Direct influences on these changes were the important works of Bishop Huyghe, such as *Religious Orders in the Modern World*, and *The Nun in the World* by Cardinal Suenens, but behind these there were the recognition of the secular institutes by the apostolic commission *Provida Mater Ecclesia* in 1947, the example of the recently-founded Protestant community at Taizé and the philosophy behind the Little Brothers of Jesus; both of these have forced religious to look hard at the traditional concept of religious poverty and to think about the importance of contemplative prayer. Also of significance is the foundation in 1958 of the Kurisumala Ashram in Kerala, India, by a French Cistercian and an

English Benedictine in an attempt to integrate the Christian and Hindu ways of religious life. Other, more secular, factors working upon the religious before and after the Council, and contributing towards a yearning for a new goal of enterprise and a new security, have been the horrors of war and oppression, the disappearance of familiar landmarks in science and ethics, all the mingled opportunities and frustrations of a complex new world in crisis, questing for solutions. War, that great locomotive of change, introduced a generation of religious who knew more than their predecessors about Marx and Freud, Sartre and Teilhard; and, more recently, humanitarianism, often in the form of organizations such as Voluntary Service Overseas, has forced the religious world into a new awareness of its relationship to the social gospel.

The chief documents of Vatican II concerning the religious life were the dogmatic constitution on the Church, *Lumen Gentium* (1964) and the decree 'De Accommodata Renovatione Vitae Religiosae', *Perfectae Caritatis* (1965). A comparison with the text of the preparatory commissions makes clear how new were some of the elements in these documents and how fruitful for the future. One should not forget, however, that the documents also marked the culmination of a long evolution. Nevertheless, although some conciliar theology, for instance on the states of life in the Church, is still far from having been universally accepted and is still in the process of formation, the main lines of the *aggiornamento* of the religious life have to be thought of in conjunction with the renewal of the Church at large, as chapters 5 and 6 of *Lumen Gentium* in particular make clear. The decree *Perfectae Caritatis* set out certain guidelines for renewal: the return to sources (Scripture, the spirit of the founder and the best traditions of the particular religious body); the organization of life, prayer and work according to the physical and psychological condition of the religious; and adaptation of the apostolate to cultural, social and economic circumstances. Rules and constitutions, therefore, 'custom-books, books of prayers and ceremonies and other similar volumes must be revised accordingly and brought into line with the documents of this sacred Council, by the suppression of anything obsolete'. This revision was to take place only after full consultation of all members, and it was not to be a purely legal change but one which incorporated evangelical and theological principles relating to the religious life. These documents were completed by post-conciliar papal pronouncements between 1966 and 1971, which, together with statements from the Congregation of Religious, aided the religious bodies in their search for identity in these years of uncertainty.

These replies from the Congregation of Religious were so numerous that they created some uncertainty about the right interpretation of the conciliar documents and how to put them into practice. This uncertainty

arose not so much from any obscurity in the documents but rather from
the efforts by the Congregation to give a reply to particular questions
taking into account both the origins of the religious life and its subsequent evolution. It had to be left to national conferences of religious
superiors, in consultation with episcopal conferences, to make decisions
that would suit regional variations and then to pass the task to specialized commissions. In England and Wales the Conference of Major
Religious Superiors was set up. It was open to all major superiors in
those countries, and most superiors have availed themselves of the
chance to join, attendance at recent annual general meetings being in
the region of 120. The Conference has no authority to make policies for
religious or to bind members to follow any decision, but it is hoped that
the quality of suggestions is itself persuasive, and a considerable amount
of collaboration and exchanged information is achieved, all on a voluntary basis.

Response by orders, congregations and societies in Britain seems to
have been universally enthusiastic and energetic, and although the pace
of change may sometimes seem slow to observers, it has continued
steadily. Centralized bodies such as the Dominicans and the Jesuits were
relatively quick to send out questionnaires to find out what each member
thought should be done. A great deal was then done at provincial and
local levels, though many religious, if asked, would now have to confess
to individual or collective amnesia about what happened some fifteen
years ago.

Women, it is generally agreed — not just by women — responded
more fruitfully than men to the Council's call for change, possibly
because women had more to gain. The lifting of papal enclosure, for instance, has favoured the collaboration of women religious in the work of
renewal and has opened the way to new and fruitful tasks. The belief
that women are born as a result of a weakness of the generative principle
(St Thomas Aquinas) and the habit of treating nuns like ecclesiatical
chars persisted in the Council in the absence of adequate female
representation; and, despite the fact that women outnumber men in the
religious life, nuns still have no way of communicating with the Holy
See except through men. Although, of course, many nuns have hung on
to their traditions as to a kind of security, and feel threatened by change,
others, especially those whose institutes were based in France, benefited
from the continental movements of renewal in the 1950s, and they were
prepared for change.

Changes were in fact adopted in so thoroughgoing a fashion by so
many monks and nuns in the 1960s that it seemed to many observers
that the baby had been thrown out with the bath water. David Knowles,
an exclaustrated monk, in *Christian Monasticism*, and Geoffrey
Moorhouse, an agnostic Anglican, in *Against all Reason*, books which

were both published in 1969, seemed to share this view. Knowles wrote of the 'enthusiasm of forces released from bondage' and 'a profound malaise and questioning', which, he thought, had been produced by the same forces that lay behind the summoning, deliberations and decisions of Vatican II. 'Nowhere is this more apparent than in the monastic sector of the Church's life, where, for the moment at least, there is a keen sense of landmarks lost and of low visibility on the road ahead'. Moorhouse entitled one of his chapters 'Towards a New Dissolution', and he quoted the prediction by Bishop Huyghe than 'half the convents of religion which now exist will have disappeared by 1980'. This prediction has not proved to be correct, though the pre-conciliar note of quiet satisfaction is demonstrably absent in 1980, and many feel that the religious life is still lurching around a bend more acute than that which Benedict navigated fifteen hundred years or so ago.

The return to sources, so vital a part of the process of renewal and the rediscovery of landmarks, has been a continuing part of the annual or triennial chapters and conferences of many religious bodies, together with changes in rules and constitutions and adaptation to new conditions. This was a constant theme in the replies to my questionnaire. *Consider Your Call*, a theology of the monastic life published by the English Benedictines in 1978, began life as a commission set up by the English Benedictine Congregation in 1969. Though late in the field, by comparison with, for instance, the Swiss-American Benedictines and the Anglican religious bodies, who published their statements in 1969 and 1970 respectively, *Consider Your Call* may be thought to have its own advantages of 'a longer perspective, the test of post-Conciliar experience and the closer influence of the monastic workaday world'. Likewise, the Mill Hill Missionaries (an 'Institute of the Common Life' and a member of the Council of Major Religious Superiors) discussed the documents of Vatican II when they first appeared; the updating of the ideal of their founder, Cardinal Vaughan, has been a continuous concern in the triennial general assemblies; and a more permanent revision of the laws and constitutions will be dealt with in 1982. One respondent, however, felt that a tremendous amount was taken for granted about the intentions of the founder of his religious order; though another member of the same body thought that much had been done to make the language of the constitutions more flexible, more descriptive and less declaratory. Contemplative, as well as active, religious orders have been engaged in the process of re-writing their constitutions. A Carmelite nun, for example, is now allowed out of enclosure to visit a close relative who is ill, and scholarly nuns are able to leave Stanbrook, a house of contemplative Benedictines, in order to do research or to give talks. There was general agreement, however, that while the constitutions might be changed, the founder's rule ('seven hundred years old and very evangelical and simple', wrote one respondent) was unchangeable.

Evidence from constitutions which have already been approved by the Holy See and from statements by chapters and conferences make it possible to note certain characteristics in common, which, incidentally, correspond in part to those of the communities set up by some of the Protestant Churches, such as Taizé. One characteristic is the insistence by the Council on the nature of the religious community as a local church; a theological principle which finds strong support in the conciliar documents and in a tradition going back to the New Testament. This insistence is not intended in any way to exclude the aspect of personal conversion and the special gifts of the Spirit in the religious calling, an aspect which finds support in Pauline theology of the Church and in the nature of the first Christian community at Jersusalem. Replies from religious indicate that they are well aware of the emphasis on the community as a church, though they do not think that it has always had entirely happy results. One wrote: 'We have closed all our independent establishments, and the Sisters are working in existing structures, e.g., state schools'. Such adaptation to the needs of the local church and the wider community is not always acceptable to the beneficiaries: parish priests are sometimes wary of well-meaning attempts to help them, though a team ministry which includes women religious can often be made to work well, and the vast majority of Catholic laity would prefer to see religious continuing to run their schools and nursing homes, and so on as the recent survey by Surrey University showed. Some religious, male and female, who are already heavily involved in parish work prefer to drift with the prevailing wind rather than rock the clerical boat.

Quite apart from the conciliar emphasis, personal experience of small communities and prayer groups, together with some unease about religious 'poverty', has led some to question the existing structure. Fruitful contemplative prayer and real poverty have been the hallmarks of Taizé and the followers of Charles de Foucauld, the Little Brothers — and the Little Sisters especially — of Jesus. One young religious left his order, though not the priesthood, because he found 'such a prevailing attitude of suspicion and patronizing humour from many who are made insecure by new currents of ideas and practices'. It is perhaps significant that a member of the same order wrote: 'We have been involved in this (adaptation) for seven hundred years'. Possibly as a result of this kind of attitude, one observer has commented that 'the most significant form of adaptation has been the departure of many of the more interesting brethren. They apparently had been a lot of good monks as good monks go, and as good monks go they went'. Some communities became split over the issue of adaptation, and at least one has happily resolved this by institutionalizing the situation, with two groups now co-existing peacefully in the same buildings, one active and progressive, the other contemplative and traditional. It is interesting to note that the very old found it easier than the middle-aged to understand what was happening.

The paradoxes of religious poverty seem to have caused more agonized discussion among religious after the Council than they do now. It would probably be difficult, if not impossible, to find a story in 1980 to cap the one told by Bishop Huyghe of the nun travelling from Paris to Lyons who was obliged to take two sisters with her — one as her chaperone, the other as the chaperone to the chaperone on the return journey. Possibly the religious agonize less now because their buildings are more fully used than hitherto. The taboo against inviting members of the opposite sex into the cloister is less powerful than it used to be, and it is now a common sight to see women disturbing these previously exclusive male clubs: eating in the refectory, sitting in the choir and sleeping in the guest house. What was once outrageous at the Cistercian monastery of Boquen, where monks and lay people, married and single, happily lived together, is now a commplace, with lay communities established in several religious houses. Poverty, even if understood in the Benedictine sense of community of goods rather in the Franciscan sense of actual penury, will probably always present a problem, because more or less hard-working men and women will continue to reap the rewards of their labours, and there will always be a reluctance to give away what a benefactor has given. But the insistence at Taizé on leasing, not owning, and the lessons of Roger Schutz's books such as *Living Today for God*, will continue to exert an influence. Rather than attempt a vow of poverty, some religious now make a promise to try to observe 'simplicity of life', and some bursars are publicly concerned to invest what money they have in corporations which do not appear to be immoral in their dealings.

Sex is a nettle that few religious in 1980 seem to grasp as firmly as St Benedict once did. However, although the benefits from a more relaxed attitude have been enormous, no one would claim that all problems have been solved, and the vow of chastity is a subject on which it is still difficult to extract unembarrassed opinions from religious. Actually, many religious prefer to take a vow of celibacy, to distinguish them from married people, who also have to try to be chaste. Some indication of changing attitudes can be glimpsed by comparing the one solitary religious whom Geoffrey Moorhouse could find in 1969 expressing the view that life vows ought to be scrapped in favour of a kind of short service commission, with the more frequent occurrence of this suggestion documented in 1976 by Marcelle Bernstein in her book, *Nuns*. It has been argued that secular institutes and lay apostolates are attracting such comparatively large numbers because their members promise celibacy only for as long as they are with their group. Fewer people than ever are prepared to commit themselves to lifelong celibacy, as the low vocation figures and the continuing stream of those leaving to get married in-dicate. For those, however, who wish to remain celibate or who wish to attempt this calling, the amount of sensible advice that they can obtain seems to grow every year. Terminology has something to do with this, as one sister says: 'We used to call it particular friendship and it was frown-ed upon. Now we call it personal relationships and it's all right'. Some of the most useful insights in *Consider Your Call* are contained in the foot-notes, such as the distinction between repression, 'a blind, unconscious, desperate mechanism triggered by pre-rational fear', and suppression, 'a free and intelligent act or series of acts, motivated by some higher love'. The authors go on to say: 'A man who has not wholly faced and accepted his own sexuality cannot relate in a Christlike way to women ... the immature, non-integrated celibate either takes refuge in shyness, awkwardness, and withdrawal, or else he converts the adult man-woman relationship which he feels he cannot handle into one which he thinks more tractable and less dangerous, namely a father-child relationship ... Of course, this can be just as much her fault'. Acceptance of oneself, the book continues, should include recognition of primary heterosexuality or primary homosexuality, where they occur, though in every person, except in pathological cases, there is a male-female continuum. If this is so, and all relationships are basically sexual, it does not have to follow that they are genital; and religious, now that they mix more freely with members of the opposite sex than hitherto, are more aware of their own feelings, and are readier to accept that they may fall in love without hav-ing to fall into bed.

In general it seems that the essence of the vows has not changed, but that they have changed in emphasis and practical expression. The vow of obedience is now seen less as an abdication of will and more as an ex-pression of loyalty to the common good. Vatican II abolished the use of the word 'inferior' to denote any religious who was not in a position of chief authority; and superiors see their rôle more in terms of service than of paternalism, the first among equals; while in some small communities the office has disappeared, and the concept of shared responsibility has taken its place. The superior's task, like that of the religious life in general, is now much more complex than hitherto.

Changes have come to the public prayer of the religious as a corollary of Vatican II's insistence on religious communities as local churches, which could not escape from the adaptation and the greater degree of participation that the Church at large was experiencing. As in all aspects of modern religious life, these changes were an aspect of the de-monasticization that has affected even the monastic orders, a backlash against the monasticization of the clergy and the devout laity that began in the eleventh and twelfth centuries and lasted, with modifications, until Vatican II. The liturgical movement, which began with the aim of pruning monastic accretions from the Church's public worship, has had the effect of lightening not only the burden of set monastic prayers placed upon the secular clergy but also that of the religious and the monks themselves. Busy religious used to fulfil their quota of seven doses of set prayers by cramming several of the them together, as if, to quote one superior's comment, 'a man should kiss his wife good morning and goodnight at the same time, in order to get it over'. Now even the monks rise later in the morning than they used to do, and recite fewer prayers.

Personal prayer was considered to be important in the monk's life in St Benedict's time, but a disproportionate emphasis was placed on it by the revivalists of mysticism in the sixteenth and seventeenth centuries, and it is now generally recognized that a taste for mystical or contemplative prayer belongs only to a small minority of religious with eremitical tendencies. On the other hand, contemplative orders have had a small boom in recruits, though some of these are former members of active orders whose rate of change they find too rapid, and the charismatic prayer movement has helped to make the personal prayer of many religious less private and more fruitful. Shared prayer groups have sometimes had a decisive effect upon communities where not all the members share this enthusiasm, but it has been immensely supportive to many religious, dissolving the isolation that the taboo against talking about one's private prayer life, like one's sex life, once used to generate.

Openness to the world is another characteristic of the local church and also, therefore, of the religious, according to the Council, a principle which affects relations of religious with the laity, non-Catholics, non-Christians and the irreligious. Relations with the laity in the past have been bedevilled by the tendency to state that the religious calling is somehow better than, rather than different from, the calling of the Christian lay person, an odious comparison which the laity have themselves helped to perpetuate. Secular institutes and mixed communities of lay people and religious have helped to blur the distinction, however, and manifestations of the religious life are so diverse that most commentators would prefer not to attempt to define it at all; if pressed, they would say that while both lay people and religious try, according to ability and the gifts of the Spirit, to live chaste and simple lives, the religious, by means of celibacy and non-ownership, do the same in an exaggerated and prophetic fashion.

Ecumenical relations have greatly helped the development of Catholic religious life. If, as Hans Küng said, Vatican II was the Protestant Reformation four hundred years too late, then, since both denominations are still developing, they are still learning from each other. While the numbers of Catholic religious had begun to decline before the Council, the smaller Anglican and Protestant bodies have shown steady growth, and, as a vibrant example of real ecumenism, simplicity, prayer, witness and outreach, few individual communities have had such an impact as the post-war Protestant monastic foundation of Taizé in Burgundy.

Plurality is now so much the keynote of the work of religious that it is impossible to generalize, except that one trend is apparent. Whether from lack of manpower or from conviction, religious are giving up the organization of their parishes, schools and other large operations, and are going, singly or in small groups, where they are needed and their abilities can be well used. In deciding priorities and in changing their apostolates, religious have been helped by the Pastoral Investigation into Social Trends, a research project undertaken by the Liverpool Institute of Socio-Religious Studies and sponsored by the Conference of Major Religious Superiors (in England and Wales). Following Ivan Illich's lead, many priests who are religious believe that they would be better ministers if they worked at secular jobs, a calculated risk that causes much dismay since it threatens the existing parochial structure.

Success in terms of numbers of religious is not the sole standard by which the religious life in 1980 should be judged, but the statistics, for all their limitations, are instructive. There is general agreement about a disastrous post-conciliar slump in vocations and an increased number of defections and that from about the mid-1970s there has been a small but steady stream of vocations and a drop in the defection rate; but a top-heavy age structure means that it will be a long time before numbers stop falling. Figures (from *The Catholic Directory*) for men religious in England and Wales show that between 1973 and 1980 numbers dropped by 12%, despite the addition of some new orders, and so on, to the list, compared with a drop of 10% between 1958 and 1968. It would be difficult to find any major order or congregation that has been exempt from this decline, though individual houses and new foundations have done relatively well. One of the big success stories has been the selection and training of recruits: there is usually a higher age requirement than hitherto, and training is much more open and suited to the individual's needs; the Conference of Major Religious Superiors has made vast strides in the pooling of resources for the training of sisters; and many older religious have the opportunity for in-service formation. The result is that there are fewer defections after vows, though many drop out before they have to make a lifetime's commitment.

The written word is an inadequate vehicle with which to convey the richly varied experience of the religious life of 1980, and looking back over the past 1500 years is easier than trying to predict what will happen in the next five years. Those who enter the religious life in 1980 may either not remember what happened fifteen years ago or realize what a revolution has happened since. Perhaps a religious version of Mao's Cultural Revolution is needed, to remind the new generation of the past and to spur it on to new efforts. Though some of the new recruits seem to be more conservative than their forefathers, the religious body as a whole does not appear to be a burnt-out case, and although some, especially those connected with the Catholic Renewal Movement, feel themselves pushed increasingly to the perimeter of the Church, the majority are aware of important tasks ahead and are taking active steps to fulfil them.

Selected bibliography
Marcelle Bernstein, *Nuns* (London, 1976, 1978)
Sister Edna Mary, *The Religious Life* (Harmondsworth, 1968)
D. Goergen, *The Sexual Celibate* (London, 1976)
Gerard Huyghe, ed., *Religious Orders in the Modern World* (London, 1965)
Geoffrey Moorhouse, *Against All Reason* (London, 1969)
Daniel Rees, ed., *Consider Your Call* (London, 1978)
Roger Schutz, *Living Today for God* (Baltimore, 1963)
Cardinal Suenens, *The Nun in the Modern World* (London, 1966)
Colin Urquhart, *When the Spirit Comes* (London, 1974)
René Voillaume, *Brothers of Men* (London, 1966)

Organization and renewal

RASHID MUFTI

THE ARCHBISHOP of Cardiff and the Libyan Head of State have at least one thing in common: each rejects that concept of democracy which gives authority to a numerical majority. Before the National Pastoral Congress of the Church in England and Wales, held in Liverpool in 1980, Archbishop John Murphy of Cardiff said that the Congress was not to be interpreted as an attempt to democratize the Church; it was not designed to establish the 'divine right of the 51%'. In part one of his 'Green Book' (*The Solution of the Problem of Democracy: The Authority of the People*, London, 1976), Colonel Muammar Al-Qadhafi writes: 'Political struggle that results in the victory of the candidate with 51% of the votes leads to a dictatorial governing body disguised as a false democracy, since 49% of the electorate is ruled by an instrument of governing they did not vote for, but had imposed upon them. This is dictatorship'. This comparison may appear inappropriate, but it provokes very pertinent questions about the rôle of the Church in the contemporary world.

Superficially, the Archbishop and the Colonel speak from totally different, if not opposed, positions: the one religious and the other secular. The former is concerned with asserting the magisterium of the Church in the face of forces which threaten to undermine it, whereas the latter is offering a secular theory of democracy which places ultimate authority in the hands of the people. But are they wholly different? Both statements are, in a sense, symbolic of a particular crisis relating to institutionalized religion in the modern world: the conflict between the sacred and the secular, between tradition and modernity, authority and democracy. It should be remembered that Colonel Qadhafi belongs to an Islamic tradition which has never made the same kind of distinction as Christianity between the spiritual and the temporal domains. For Islam the proposed *solution* to the conflict between the two is to incorporate secular political theory into an Islamic conception of life. Ultimately, there is no distinction between Church and State.

Elsewhere in his 'Green Book', Colonel Qadhafi writes: 'The genuine law of any society is either tradition or religion. Any other attempt to draft law for any society, outside these two sources, is invalid and illogical. Constitution is a basic man-made law... Freedom is threatened unless society has a sacred law based on stable rules which are not subject to change or substitution by any instrument of governing...

Religion embraces tradition, which is an expression of the natural life of the peoples. Thus, religion, embracing tradition, is an affirmation of natural law. Non-religious, non-traditional laws are invented by one man for use against another. Therefore they are invalid because they are not built upon the natural source of tradition and religion'. I should not be astonished to learn that Archbishop Murphy had some sympathy with these sentiments.

Unlike Islam, Christianity has traditionally made a sharp distinction between the sacred and the secular: 'Render unto Caesar the things that are Caesar's, and to God the things that are God's'. However, even for Islam the relationship between the temporal and the spiritual may not be so easily resolved in practice — as recent events in Iran and elsewhere have shown. Indeed, both Christianity and Islam today face the same basic problem: how to come to terms with a rapidly changing, increasingly complex and ideologically plural world.

In spite of the creative possibilities opened up by Vatican II, the relationship to the world of the Church in Britain and Ireland has been translated into an almost paranoid concern with its *institutional* survival in a secular age. This is hardly surprising. Any institution — secular or religious — must cope with changing circumstances. Today, the Church is simply one institution among many, attempting to assert one set of values in competition with rival value-systems and ideologies. Its members inhabit a world in which the secularization of human consciousness and objective political and economic realities increasingly push the Church into a marginal situation.

In *The Social Reality of Religion* (London, 1969), the sociologist Peter Berger suggests that institutionalized religion has two options in this situation. It can either accommodate to the world by redefining its dogmas to make them more congenial to modern men and women, or it can rigidly maintain its traditional doctrines and refuse to make any concessions to the secular order. Both options have their own peculiar problems. The attempt to present Christian theism in a form acceptable to contemporary man, for example, carries with it the danger that the Christian message may be emptied entirely of its theistic content. But to retire behind a rigid wall of orthodoxy is to place the Christian believer in the position of what Berger refers to as a 'cognitive minority', mediating a traditional universe of meaning to a shrinking Church.

Berger's argument depends upon a view of religion as organizationally distinct from the world and as responding in a particular way to the secular reality. However, there exists, I believe, another viewpoint which sees religion not in terms of its *organizational* separateness from the world, but as something which is part of the totality of human life and experience. In his book *Church and Colonialism* (London, 1969), Dom Helder Camara, Archbishop of Olinda and Recife in north-east Brazil,

quotes Pope Paul VI: 'The Church cannot remove herself from temporal affairs, because the temporal is the activity of men, and all that
concerns men concerns the Church. A disembodied Church, separated
from the world, would no longer be the Church of Jesus Christ, the
Church of the incarnate Word. The Church, on the contrary, interests
herself closely in every generous endeavour which helps to set humanity
on the road to heaven, but also in the search for well-being, for justice,
for peace, for happiness on earth'.

These words clearly echo Vatican II's recognition that the destiny of
the Church is inextricably linked with the destiny of all mankind, and
that a concern for justice in the social, economic and political spheres is
essential if Christian witness is to be a living reality in the modern world
(cf. *Gaudium et Spes*).

For Helder Camara, who is deeply committed to the struggle for
human rights in Latin America, the implications of this recognition are
quite clear: 'Our first duty as active Christians in the working-class
environment, is to speak the truth without fear and without exaggera-
tion. The second, common to all men of goodwill, is to face the whole
truth and to accept the demands which it makes. . . There is a heavy
responsibility on lay Christians from every stratum of society to involve
the Church and Christianity in life and in the problems of humanity.
The technician, the politician, the teacher, the student, the supervisor,
the scientist, the intellectual, in other words all those who accept the
truth of the Gospel in their lives and who are called to play their part in
the defence of man and of justice — the solutions to the problems of the
people depend on these laity. Our faith — faith in God and in man —
demands action. It does not dictate concrete solutions to our problems
but it does teach us the Christian approach to life and to involvement in
it'.

Camara realizes that faith is never a static element in the Church, but
a form of *praxis* aimed at transforming the world. As the 1971 Synod of
Bishops stated: 'Action on behalf of justice and participation in the
transformation of the world fully appear to us as a constitutive dimension of the preaching of the Gospel, or, in other words, of the Church's
mission for the redemption of the human race and its liberation from
every oppressive situation'.

Since the second Vatican Council, the Church in these islands has
made little attempt to involve itself directly in 'life and the problems of
humanity' or to participate in the 'transformation of the world'. Instead,
it has concentrated almost exclusively on its *organizational* viability in an
age when it is in institutional decline, and when it is apparent, as the
recent English Gallup Poll survey of *Roman Catholic Opinion* indicated,
that many of its members seriously question the Church's traditional
teaching.

Since Vatican II, the Church in England and Wales has taken two major initiatives in an attempt to re-assess its rôle in the modern world and to respond to the challenge of the Council. One has been the establishment of a number of official commissions, which act as advisory and consultative bodies to the hierarchy on a wide range of issues, including the liturgy, the rôle of the laity in the Church, ecumenism, justice and peace, social welfare and racial justice. The other was the decision, announced in 1978, to hold a National Pastoral Congress which finally took place in 1980 — fifteen years after the ending of the second Vatican Council.

Both initiatives were attempts by the hierarchy to involve the whole Church, especially the laity, in the process of renewal, consultation and the formation of pastoral policies. Unfortunately, both may fall seriously short of achieving these objectives because of the bureaucratic and authoritarian manner in which the hierarchy have handled the issue of consultation. It is, perhaps, too early to make any definite judgment on long-term effects of the National Pastoral Congress, but the commissions have largely failed to make any real impact on the life of the Church in England and Wales. No such initiative has been taken in Scotland or Ireland.

How many Catholics, for example, know anything of the work of the *Justice and Peace Commission* or the *Catholic Commission for Racial Justice?* How many clergy are willing to offer their active support to these organizations at the parish level? How frequently does one see the publications of the commissions among the CTS pamphlets at the back of a church?

The inability of such official bodies to penetrate the consciousness of individual Catholics or to affect parish life is due, in part at least, to the general conservatism of English and Welsh (and, of course, Scottish and Irish) Catholicism. This is manifested either as a definite lack of interest in areas of social concern or as overt hostility to the suggestion that the Church should be involved in anything of a political nature. Indeed, the concern for justice at the parish level is generally dominated by a 'mission mentality'. This product of western Christianity's historical association with the expansion of European imperialism perpetuates a patronizing attitude towards the people of the developing world, and prevents an adequate understanding of the political and economic dimensions of injustice. A more significant reason for the failure of the commissions is their very nature: that is, the way in which they were constituted and their relationship with the hierarchy.

The Anglo-Welsh commissions are directly responsible to the Bishops' Conference of England and Wales, and in principle their reports and recommendations are confidential to the Conference. Hence there is little opportunity for any meaningful involvement of the wider

Catholic community in discussion of, and consultation on, the many issues affecting the life of the Church. In addition, the advisory and con-sultative procedure of the commissions works in only one direction: they cannot share directly in the decision-making. The Bishops' Conference, in its 1971 review of the commissions, emphasized that they had no legislative or executive power; though they shared in the decision-making process of the Church, that 'should not be interpreted as part of a process of "participatory democratization" in the Church'. As if to ensure that the commissions do not become too independent and autonomous of the Conference, each has at least one episcopal member who acts as chairman or president.

The manner of appointment to membership of the commissions, and the nature of that membership, affect their probable rôles in the life of the Church. Some members are appointed for their technical expertise in a particular area. Others may be 'elected' or 'nominated' as represen-tatives of dioceses or approved Catholic organizations. The net result is that the membership of the commissions tends to consist largely of 'establishment-type' Catholics who are generally acceptable to the Bishops' Conference. The cycle of authoritarian and bureaucratic con-trol by the hierarchy is complete.

In an article on the commissions in *The Month* (March, 1975), Michael Hornsby-Smith and Penny Mansfield claimed that the lay membership of the commissions was overwhelmingly middle-aged and almost entire-ly middle-class. They did not find one instance of a lay member in a manual occupation at the time of their study, and there was thus no evidence of any strong working-class or trade union influence in the commissions. In the Laity Commission, for example, a discussion on 'working life' gave no consideration to the part played by trade unions; there was not a single manual worker in the relevant working party.

Whether the same pattern exists today is a matter for empirical in-vestigation. My own experience on one national commission (the Secretariat for Non-Believers) and on a diocesan Justice and Peace Commission suggests that it does. What is clear is that the commissions are potentially, if not actually, élitist organizations which, because of their structure, the nature of their membership and their prescribed relationship to the Bishops' Conference, are unlikely to have anything other than a minimal impact on everyday Catholicism and will fail to be truly representative of all shades of Catholic opinion. There is no evidence of anything better in Ireland and Scotland.

Similar doubts can be raised about the National Pastoral Congress, which took place in Liverpool in May 1980. At first glance, the Congress appeared to be a genuine exercise in shared responsibility, with the 'ordinary' lay Catholic participating, for the first time, in establishing the pastoral strategies which would guide the Church in England and

Wales through the next few decades. Over two thousand delegates, predominantly lay people, took part in the Congress. There were delegates from each diocese as well as official representatives from national Catholic organizations, including the commissions, Catholic colleges, the armed forces and the prison service. In addition, a number of 'experts' were appointed, either as delegates or specialist advisers. Clearly a wide range of opinion was represented at the Congress, but just as clearly certain important groups were omitted or under-represented. There was, for example, no official representative from the Trade Union Movement, and little evidence of any significant working-class influence in the Congress. Equally, and this was clearly evident in the topic group on racial justice, black and ethnic-minority Catholics were heavily under-represented. It is doubtful, therefore, that the majority of delegates had any real understanding of the more crucial issues in modern society — those which the Church must face if it is to formulate adequate pastoral strategies for the future.

Other reservations concerning the Congress (for example, its entire preparation was in the hands of an organizing committee whose decisions were not open to public discussion, and whose minutes were not available for inspection) suggest that it remained firmly under bureaucratic control from the beginning, and raise serious doubts as to the fate of some of the more enlightened proposals that were made there.

These two examples — that of the official commissions and the National Pastoral Congress — indicate at best that the Church in England and Wales (ostensibly more 'democratic' than the Church in Scotland or in Ireland) has allowed consultation and shared responsibility to take place only under conditions where they remain firmly under pre-ordained forms of control.

A pre-condition for authentic dialogue is the absence of power relationships which distort communication between the participants. Though we must remember that dialogue in the Church takes place within the context of a particular theological understanding of the Church's divine mission and of the differing rôles of the priesthood and the laity, we must never forget that forms of domination can hinder effective communication and dialogue in the Church just as easily as in other organizations. Neither the Anglo-Welsh commissions nor the National Pastoral Congress represent authentic dialogue in the Church, since the 'agenda' and the conditions of its articulation are pre-determined by those wielding bureaucratic power. This is a characteristic feature of all organizations concerned with their institutional survival, and the Church is no exception to this rule. Hence a false consensus is 'manufactured' in the interests of organizational stability, and there is no room for the emergence of a true consensus based on free and open dialogue. The fact that the most oppressed members of society are generally excluded from the consultative process only serves to reinforce the inauthentic nature of this form of 'dialogue'.

The contemporary Church in these islands is in an increasingly marginal situation. It operates within a particular terrain whose boundaries are set by political realities beyond the Church's direct influence. One consequence is that the Church is subject to outside pressures which affect both its institutional structures and its members' traditional beliefs. Then the Church may find itself facing the dilemma described by Berger: should it retire into orthodoxy or translate its message into a form which appeals to the modern world? The dilemma is not easily resolved, and the Church in England and Wales has, I believe, adopted an uncomfortably ambivalent position in relation to modern society. On the one hand, it has tried to take account of modern developments and changing attitudes — hence the Anglo-Welsh initiative of the National Pastoral Congress. On the other hand, it is reluctant to allow consultation and dialogue to become too open and democratic. Equally, while it has addressed itself to some of the major issues of the day — racism, unemployment and nuclear war, for example — on the whole it has been content to articulate general principles rather than to confront those issues forcefully and publicly. Perhaps any such confrontation would bring the Church into direct conflict with existing society and further endanger its institutional survival.

Islam may yet prove more successful than Christianity in arriving at an adequate understanding of its appropriate relationship to secular reality. The Church in England and Wales (the situation in Scotland and in Ireland is even worse) has opted for an uneasy compromise with the world in an attempt to retain its institutional credibility, and has made only tentative efforts to widen the basis of consultation and dialogue within the Church. While this may help to maintain its organizational viability, the result is a loss of vision — oblivion to the fact that today, perhaps more than in other times, the Church as the *whole* people of God must be a 'sign of contradiction' in the world.

The Church and religious education

V.A. McCLELLAND

Britain

ONE OF THE main criticisms urged against public sector non-denominational schools is that they have not developed an acceptable and coherent unifying principle within their curriculum and organization to fill the vacuum left by society's widespread abandonment of religious conviction. It is demonstrable that Christianity, rejected by the schools as dogma while preserved as sentiment, has lost its former synthesizing function in pupil-teacher relationships as well as in connexion with more routine processes of school life. It would be disingenuous, however, to maintain that denominational schools are themselves succeeding spectacularly in the task of forming 'the complete man'. The recent survey conducted by investigators from Surrey University into Roman Catholic opinions in England and Wales,[1] while not primarily interested in exploring the nature, ideals or internal procedures of Catholic schools, suggests the correlation between a Catholic education and subsequent religious understanding, commitment and life style is but marginally positive. The view is inescapable, in fact, that religious teaching in schools of all types remains located too narrowly within a separate curricular compartment, inadequately integrated with the intellectual interests, leisure activities and personal life stances of children, remote from parental aspirations and out of touch with changing values of home and community.

In all systems of sound educational pedagogy it is axiomatic that the educative process forms a partnership encompassing parents, children and teachers. Catholics, in particular, have strongly emphasized the Church's function in buttressing the rôle of the family as a social unit and that of the school as an extension and support of family life and teaching. By a strange *bouleversement*, however, the propagation of teachings germinating from the second Vatican Council has tended to erode the sense of partnership between home and school. The reason why reflective Catholics choose to send their children to a Catholic denominational school is that, holding a particular philosophy of life, they desire to have them taught within the full context of that faith cherished by the family, sharing ideals and beliefs in common with themselves and adhering to specific moral standards untainted by the contamination of modern situational ethics. They seek, in short, a cementing of the spiritual bond with their children in the common pursuit of a recognizable religious ideal. The belief which has recently gained exposure in the religious teaching of some Catholic schools, however, that the faith was dramatically reformulated by the teachings of Vatican II, has resulted in religious attitudes treasured within the confines of the Catholic family and religious practices matured over generations being spurned as outmoded. An increased emphasis upon the primacy of individual conscience often at the expense of devaluing the importance of formulated rules of conduct, the stress placed upon good neighbourliness as a manifestation of Catholic citizenship in the world coupled with inadequate consideration of the nature of personal worth and specific virtue or of well-tried avenues to sanctification, a dearth of instruction on the nature of sin and accountability for individual actions to a benign and all-loving Creator, have interposed a barrier between generations of Catholics and alienated or bewildered parents. Instead of using the strengths of the family in forging unity of intent and action in the spiritual formation of the young, the Catholic school in certain clearly defined areas seems to be fulfilling a divisive function, preparing the young for conflict with parental attitudes and with their more traditional approaches to religious practice. Time-honoured religious observances within the daily routine of school organization have been designated 'mawkish', and abandoned as conflicting with notions of 'religious freedom' and 'personal maturity'. Liturgical innovation and novelty have been introduced as a regular feature of school worship. These developments earn parental disapproval and constitute a source of disquiet. An older generation of Catholics who believe the faith to be one and indivisible, unchanged and unchangeable, find it difficult to accept that it is suddenly *unorthodox* to be somewhat lacking in enthusiasm for more advanced forms of ecumenical activity. While many parents wish their children to be understanding, fair and constructive in their study of other religions, loving and tolerant in their relationships with adherents of faiths other than their own, they wish these attitudes to be firmly grounded in a position of strength in their own faith, one based upon conviction and characterized by spiritual commitment. Their fear is that spiritual vigour is not being engendered by the main direction now followed in the religious teaching of the Catholic school. If this is so, the consummate challenge facing the Catholic school today is how to restore its credibility with the older generation of the faithful and how to repair the cleavage that has formed between the beliefs, attitudes and practices of the post-Vatican II generation and those of their parents. Above all, the view of the teacher as being *in loco parentis* should not be permitted to result in a synchysis of meaning leading to an usurpation of divinely-ordained parental responsibility. The lack of consultation with the laity over liturgical innovation is an undesirable precedent to follow where the religious education of children is involved.

In recent years, together with the widespread abandonment of traditional prayerful practices punctuating the various secular activities of the school day, there has emerged a distinct tension in the mode of presentation of dogmatic truth. Pedagogical developments stemming from some of the national and regional centres of catechetical study have emphasized the general principle that in the presentation of religious matter genuine commitment without full understanding is impossible and the attempt to inculcate it undesirable. Children are to be encouraged to evolve answers and arrive at ultimate formulations of truth by means of gradual processes. Such a task, it is anticipated, will occupy a lifetime in the honing and refining of belief. This approach does not imply, of course, that the teacher should attempt the impossible — 'neutrality' — in the presentation of religious belief, but it is a methodology which necessitates in religious matters the furnishing of an empty room rather than a readjustment of the contents of one already partly furnished. It must be recognized, however, that no Catholic teacher is presented with a child who has not already imbibed distinct religious attitudes, habits, beliefs and practices from parental teaching and example. The significance of this fact, however, is often ignored by pedagogical pundits and curriculum cursitors who imagine they have a *tabula rasa* fit for experimentation. Edward Hulmes of the Farmington Institute has recently argued that the teacher is not engaged in playing a sort of game based upon his experience, practice and training. On the contrary, he asserts, 'commitment is both the point of departure and the final goal of all religious education ... It is a dynamic quality, associated with growth, vulnerability, decision and change'.[2] The example of teachers and parents in living the faith, in behaving in accord with Christian principles in dealings with others, and in showing that their own lives are regulated by a richly personal devotion to the teachings of Jesus Christ will be the ultimate factor in enabling children to choose whether or not they wish to model their lives permanently upon the Christian belief and ethic. What this amounts to is that religious education, while striving to present Christian teaching within the framework of true dialogue, must not neglect to embody basic tenets within the context of a recognizable rule of life. Not the visible membership of the Church alone but the living of the Christian life is the final touchstone of Christian maturity, an involvement which for a Catholic must also imply an acceptance of truth as indivisible and of morality as universal.

If the denominational school is to continue to justify an unique place in a system of national educational provision it must revert to the task of inculcating within its religious programme a discernment of man alone with his God, a consciousness of man's destiny being to work out his salvation in time for eternity, together with an awareness that this cannot be achieved without exuding care and love for fellow men and realizing the nature of personal frailty and dependence. Since Vatican II the Catholic school has been refurbishing the importance of the concept of Christian community, a development underlined indeed by changes in the form of the Church's liturgical worship. It has achieved this to some extent at the expense of under-valuing the importance of developing individual relationship with God through personal prayer. For Catholicism to survive as anything more than the pious practice of general benevolence the young must be made aware there cannot be a substitute for a personalized relationship with God; that men while in the world are not meant to be of the world; that they must evolve a way of life for themselves which will ensure they survive their sojourn in it with integrity and that the world becomes a better place for their living and people happier for their presence. This calls for a renewed — perhaps 'old-fashioned' — spirituality, individual but outward-looking. It seeks a new *sensus fidelium* within the Church community, uniting once again educative agencies with family life and traditions. It is a task which the Catholic school, reeling from the excitement and turmoil consequent upon the Council, is at present ill-equipped to fulfil. A religious education which concentrates its teaching upon notions of community is as warped as one which treats the spiritual dimension of personhood as the only matter worthy of attention. The intent of inculcating a spirit of community in children by urging them to collect funds for *Cafod*, the desire to instil an ecumenical spirit by taking children on a tour of the local synagogue, the wish to interest the young in liturgical renewal by organizing 'pop' masses preceded by a ceremony of collective absolution, the intention to develop a social conscience by organizing errand-running for pensioners can never be a *substitute* for the educating of children into a realization of the spiritual dimension of their personal lives. In this latter task must lie the true *raison d'être* of any Catholic school.

If we are to revitalize the approach to religious education by bringing about a realization of the importance of individual worth to the process of making society more conscious of the things of the spirit, to the constructing of a society which has Christ-like attitudes towards those in need as well as to the right use of possessions, wealth and power, it is important that the school should be a microcosm of a community in which Christian values are in operation. It is in this fact that the Catholic school does not convey conviction. Let us take an obvious example. It is a scandal to witness the energy devoted by priests and religious to providing an exclusive education for the children of the rich, thus blessing and perpetuating within the body of the Church itself the social disunion of secular society which militates against the fulness of Christian living. There are some religious orders in Britain — the English and Scottish Benedictines being perhaps noteworthy examples — whose entire school-teaching skills and energies are placed exclusively at the disposal of a materially privileged clientèle. A religious community holding dear a Christian view of man ought not to promote, by means of its own resources of men and ability and from its own volition, the education of either the rich or the intelligent in a way which deprives the poorer or less privileged sections of society of its services. If it does then it bears witness to using a double standard in its corporate fulfilment of Christ's teaching and example. In his little book *The Catholic Schools of England and Wales* the late Outram Evennett argued over thirty years ago that 'behind every system of education there must be, either consciously formulated or unconsciously assumed, some body of beliefs or traditions regarding the nature of Man and Society'.[3] Religious orders and congregations which devote the major part of their energies to the education of the rich and privileged sections of society are expressing very eloquently their view as to the nature of that secular society of which they become, in a real sense, pensioners. This matter cannot be any longer ignored by the Church if it is to retain ecclesial credibility in Britain and the time is opportune for a frank and courageous reappraisal of the use of priests and nuns in work which is both socially and ecclesiastically divisive.

If the energy and resources devoted to the perpetuation of a system of Catholic Public Schools constitutes an upas tree flourishing within the Church, there is also need to be concerned about certain attitudes and practices in operation in less exclusive establishments. The thoughtless employment of elaborate systems of rewards and punishments, the adoption of a rigid organization of ability streaming, the inequitable distribution of the best qualified professional staff in such a way that children with a low IQ often receive the least inspiring teaching, the overriding competitive ethos within many Catholic schools permeating work and play, the undue stress often placed upon examination achievements, personal successes and doing better than one's neighbour, all conflict with the Christian message. By adhering to such practices Catholic schools are placing a wordly message before their pupils and doing it as effectively as if they had planned to proclaim the total irrelevancy of the Christian message for daily living. The Church ought not to countenance attitudes of this nature in the organization of secular teaching within a métier ostensibly Christian. Mrs Mary Warnock has written cogently on this particular problem, pointing out that patterns of behaviour emerge from *real* contexts, not merely from exemplary ones.[4] The first rule of teaching must always be sincerity and children are hurt by hypocrisy even when it is most subtly veiled.

Is there a fundamental step which ought now to be taken to attempt to heal the dichotomy between the teaching conveyed in the family and that in the school? Of prime importance is that the Church should embark upon a major programme of adult education in an attempt to offset the conflict which has arisen between generations. This procedure must entail machinery for listening and consultation as well as for teaching and the institutional Church must not be surprised if what it hears seems out of joint with some of the postulates and innovations which have emerged in theological thinking in recent years. If the views of the people of God are to be sought the process must be undertaken in an open-ended fashion. The temptation for energetic priests or parish activists to embark upon a policy of brainwashing the faithful must be firmly resisted. If it is not, then any systematic programme of genuine adult education is doomed to disaster. Torsten Husén has maintained that recurrent education is vital for all men living in a continuously changing society and his argument is even more cogent for a body of Catholics subjected to traumatic internal readjustments and external pressures. Every reasonably-sized parish ought to make formal provision for a programme of adult education on urgent problems concerning the religious attitudes of the day, such as the relationship of parents with schools, changing approaches to moral and social problems, family and marriage difficulties, the nature and types of social involvement, and ecumenical activities that parishioners can reasonably be expected to undertake. The bishops should ensure that every seminarian is given pedagogical training as a compulsory part of sacerdotal formation and that this includes a knowledge of the scientific processes involved in the recurrent education of adults. Every priest should consider it to be a major part of his work to interest the pastoral council in the inception of adult education schemes for the parish. Such a development would also have clear implications for Catholic schools, the religious teaching of which would need to be of the kind that prepares the groundwork for continued development in later life. Only in this way will the Church be able to secure the true measure of the developing nature of society and the moral, intellectual and spiritual challenges consequent upon societal change. Some of the manpower resources of Orders and Congregations, released from superfluous education ventures at a time when there is unlikely to be for the forseeable future a shortage of good Catholic lay-teachers, could with profit be redeployed into this new kind of parish apostolate.

As we approach the year 2000 the pace of technological development will increase rapidly and lead to questions being asked as to the right use of increased leisure time, some of it engendered by schemes of early retirement. Inertia, boredom, the mindless pursuit of entertainment and the search for pleasure are the traditional enemies of religion. In its system of adult education, the Church will have to help with the more general instruction of the faithful by the initiation of discussion groups, socially-worthy activities, religious study classes and similar educative programmes if it is not to put at risk the effectiveness of its apostolate. Courses in child development and upbringing, moral and sex education, the causes of tension in family life, career choices, and patterns of aberrant youth behaviour are examples of possible worthwhile attention. The future progress of the faith will depend upon the structuring of programmes such as these and there is little time to be lost in initiating them. Relevant expertise already exists in university departments of adult education and extra-mural studies and this source of advice could be tapped at diocesan level in the immediate task of setting up experimental learning cells in selected parishes. If the Church begins to educate parents through the parishes in a *systematic* and *organized* way there is likelihood that the quality of home-school relationships will also improve and the generation gap begin to close. If these developments can also be coupled with a fundamental re-examination of the nature of the Church's participation in second-level education, and of the ways in which Catholic schools can become more effective Christian witnesses in an increasingly secular world, then the current *malaise* at the heart of religious education will begin to disappear.

The Republic of Ireland

Two major criticisms may be directed at the Catholic Church's participation in denominational education in Irish schools. One of these refers to an instinctive reluctance to involve enthusiastic laymen and women in the assumption of an important teaching rôle in the religious education and formation of youth in the Church's independently-run secondary schools, and this in spite of the evidence that there appears to be a pronounced unwillingness among religious to teach religion.[5] The other criticism relates to the Church's non-involvement in senior teaching responsibilities within the public sector of vocational schools, a sector which in practice seeks to give a general but limited second-level education to the poorest and most deprived of Irish children. The position is compounded by the curious attitude of the university institutions in the Republic, some of which do not include religious and moral education as constituent elements of the programmme of courses leading to the award of the obligatory professional passport for teaching in Irish secondary schools, the Higher Diploma in Education. Furthermore, the National University of Ireland does not posses a theology faculty and the one or two in-service courses it provides leading to the award of a Diploma in Catechetics rely heavily upon the attendance of women religious to ensure their viability, and are frequently taught by clerics whose sole claim to specialized training for the undertaking is what they have managed to put together from their priestly or religious formation and work experience, although a few of these teachers have managed to acquire diplomas from colleges in the United States or catechetical centres in the United Kingdom. The situation, however, is by and large one of the blind leading the blind. Indeed, unlike the provision made at the universities of Belfast and Coleraine, there is no procedure by means of which a young man or woman can enter a university in the Republic with a view to becoming a specialized teacher of religion. In Irish secondary schools the religious programme is taught either by a non-specialist whose initial degree has been taken in another discipline or by a cleric or religious who may or may not have shown a professional interest in teaching the subject. What specialized training of lay teachers does exist is confined to the instruction given to would-be primary teachers in the country's colleges of education and to courses of varying worth run by private educational ventures such as the inadequately financed Mater Dei Institute or that at Mount Oliver, Dundalk. The dearth of trained specialist lay teachers of religion encourages the young to consider religious teaching and everyday living as discrete matters each bearing little relevance for the other.

The State's reluctance to encroach upon ecclesiastical preserves is evidenced not only by its ambivalence to such issues as contraception and civil divorce but by the fact that religious education does not even appear upon the Minister of Education's schedule of recognized subjects for the curriculum of the secondary school; a lack of recognition, one might add, that is not entirely unconnected with the State's long-standing weakness in failing to develop the vocational school sector to the level at which it might constitute an attractive alternative to the Church's secondary schools with their arts-dominated curriculum. If further proof of this ambivalence is needed evidence is provided by the State's refusal to make mandatory the possession of the Higher Diploma in Education for university graduates who decide to teach in vocational schools, a policy which since its inception fifty years ago has ensured the retention in many schools of outdated and unenlightened pedagogical practices giving rise to a sharp divide in Irish post-primary education. When the new State comprehensive and community schools were projected for specific locations, the pattern of the vocational sector was followed rather than that of the prestigious private sector. The difficulty of providing adequate teaching of religion in these schools was more pronounced, in fact, than in the religious-order-dominated secondary system. The Church of Ireland has shown greater awareness of the nature of the whole problem than has the Catholic Church. The first proposal of the Advisory Committee on Religious Education of the

General Synod of the Church of Ireland, which reported in 1972, declared: 'We place first among our recommendations that the General Synod should treat as a matter of urgency the need to provide and support the pre-service and in-service training of teachers (of religion).[6] In that Report it was urged there was a great need for syllabus development for religious education at all levels, for a re-examination of teaching methods in the subject, and for attention to be given to the requirements of special education and to continuity of development between the teaching of religion at various age levels. That this renewal was necessary for Catholic schools too was to be evidenced by the FIRE Report which was written a year after that produced for the Synod of the Church of Ireland and admitted that there was serious confusion in Catholic schools throughout the Republic as to what to believe and what to teach. It was pointed out as a matter of some incredulity that 'a great many teachers — and priests — do not seem aware of the existence of the *General Catechetical Directory* ... issued from Rome (Sacred Congregation of the Clergy) in 1971'.[7]

There is little doubt that theological developments initiated by the second Vatican Council have given rise to a more pronounced degree of confusion in Irish Catholic schools than is the case with Catholic schools in the United Kingdom, and especially in regard to the form in which religious education programmes are to be devised and presented. The confusion has been made grievous by an initial lack of leadership from a theologically jejune episcopacy and from the lack of adequate guidance or direction at diocesan level. Some male and female religious have evinced reluctance to shoulder responsibility for an antiquated religious education programme which is no longer based upon a secure foundation of religious conviction. If this is their predicament how much more intolerable is the position of lay teachers of religion in public sector schools, bereft of both appropriate initial training and adequate academic in-service support, and denied up-to-date spiritual leadership. A serious credibility gap has rapidly arisen involving the nature of religious education in schools, the conservative attitudes of large numbers of Irish parents and youth culture responding instinctively to what it considers to be, rightly or wrongly, the need for ecclesiastical emancipation and moral liberation. Indeed, it was with a view to supplying some commendable semblance of form and structure to the religious teaching in his diocese that the Catholic Bishop of Cork produced a new catechism of religious doctrine for use in schools, although he did it as though giving credence to the view that the days of the pat answer to the pert question were numbered even in Irish primary schools. His example was not followed by other episcopal colleagues elsewhere nor was his catechism (a good example of its *genre*) widely adopted outside the confines of his diocese. Recently, however, remedial action in the

area of syllabus design on a national level has been initiated with promise of success. An interesting example of this can be found in the new
series of work books with accompanying teacher guides for use in
second-level schools, entitled *God and Man*, planned for publication by
Veritas of Dublin. Three of the eight books designed for the senior cycle
of the secondary school have been issued — *Jesus of Nazareth, The Moral
Life* and *The Christian Heritage*. A fourth, *The Mystery of God*, is in preparation. Others expected to follow shortly are *Church and Worship, The Christian Society, Approach to Scripture* and *Makers of Modern Thought*. The three
books which have been produced at the time of writing are attractively
presented and pedagogically sound, although the volume on *Moral Life*
treats problems relating to sex and marriage in such a cut-and-dried
fashion that they are hardly likely to lead to the kind of open class discussion desirable when dealing with human topics. The detailed description
of the processes involved in aborting a foetus (p. 101) is obscenely
clinical and quite unsuitable for use with children of the age intended.
The series as a whole, however, shows concern and is a positive step in
the process of redesigning a religious curriculum which avoids the worst
excesses of that artificial searching for novelty associated in England
with the work of Frs Anthony Bullen and Derek Lance. Similarly, the
Children of God series for Irish primary schools (also published by Veritas)
is presenting a healthy alternative approach to the drearily entrenched
processes of religious dogmatizing characteristic of many Irish primary
schools. The team of contributors brought together for the series —
Fr Seán McEntee of Raphoe diocese, Sr Kathleen Glennon of Elphin
diocese and Fr William Murphy of Kerry diocese — have produced a
spiritual methodology emphazing the positive themes of love, praise,
gratitude, mystery and personal response and they have succeeded in
blending into the scheme the teaching of doctrinal, moral and sacramental life in a reverently gentle manner. These are wholesome
developments and an indication that the Irish Church is at last beginning to overcome the paralysis which seized it in the aftermath of the
Council. Perhaps the time is now also approaching in the Republic when
the example of what took place recently in northern Ireland will form a
basis for similar action in the south. In the mid-seventies in Ulster a
GCE 'O'-level course in religious education was planned for the
Northern Ireland Board by a joint panel consisting of Roman Catholic,
Church of Ireland, Presbyterian and Methodist membership. If programmes of religious education leading to examinations at Intermediate
and Leaving Certificate levels were to be introduced in the Republic
they would not only provide opportunity for ecumenical approaches
with other religious bodies but give that measure of academic respectability to the teaching of religion that is vital if its status is to be
reviewed in schemes of initial and in-service teacher training.

Encouraging as this activity in curriculum planning is, the task facing the Church in the area of adult education is more formidable than it is in the United Kingdom. Agencies for adult education in the Republic from which encouragment, advice and assistance could be sought in the early stages of development are woefully inadequate. The universities in the State have never entered into the field of extension studies of in-service training with anything approaching the commitment and expertise shown by the British universities, including those in Northern Ireland. The Irish national body for the development of adult education, *Aontas*, has struggled for years to survive on an inadequately-financed budget and a parsimonious allocation of staff. The creation of a national system of adult education in regard to religious teaching, however, is a *sine qua non* for the Church if it is to educate its followers into the twenty-first century and attempt to heal the theological and spiritual ravages which are there for all to see. The authors of the FIRE Report pinpointed the dangers five years ago when they noted that young Irish people 'readily engage in the corporal works of mercy but haven't time for the spiritual. Often eager to be involved in doing something about the social problems they see about them, they are impatient with "theory" which they treat either as of far less importance or as something to be taken as read. There is a noticeable lack of doctrinal knowledge'. The task facing the Church is a gigantic one involving a major exercise in parish renewal, initiatives in teacher training, attempts to persuade university institutions to assume a rôle in the teaching of religious studies, and pressures on the State to give added status to the study of religion in schools of all types. Above all, there needs to be a revitalization of seminary training and formation schemes for religious to enable them to harness lay co-operation in joint enterprise. The institutional hierarchy must be persuaded to give a firm lead in these developments, perhaps initially through the agency of the new Irish Episcopal Commission on Catechetics. That the bishops are becoming alive to their responsibilities is indicated in their Lenten pastoral letter of this year in which they emphasize the function of the family in religious renewal and forecast the establishment of parish and diocesan programmes to that end.

A change of direction along the lines indicated, however, is only a part of the problem confronting the Church in a society becoming increasingly consumer-conscious and stridently critical of its institutions. In the last fifteen years the ratio of religious to lay teachers employed in Catholic secondary schools in the Republic has declined by a third, but congregations of brothers and sisters appear reluctant to hand over to lay direction schools they can no longer adequately service. In 1973, the last year in which a major national analysis of the problem was undertaken, somewhat less than one-fourteenth of the Catholic secondary schools in the Republic were managed by lay people, and it was forecast then that

within a period of three years there would be at least fifty secondary
schools possessing only one or two religious teachers, one of them the
principal. The proportion of religious to lay students taking the one-year
course of professional training for secondary teaching in University College Dublin declined in the ten-year period prior to 1973 from 34% to
6.5% of the whole. Almost a third of religious sisters in the Republic are
today over sixty-five years of age. The conclusion to be drawn from
these trends is clear. Religious must relax their control, concentrate their
efforts in fewer educational enterprises and hand over gracefully to lay
management a large number of the country's secondary schools. If they
are reluctant to do this they will not only lose credibility in the eyes of lay
teachers but will be accused of being unduly influenced by those very
qualities it is claimed their example in the schools is intended to offset —
the undue desire for money, property, power, prestige and a comfortable life. Their withdrawal could certainly be effected without detri-
ment to the academic quality of Irish secondary schooling as a whole.

As is the case in Britain, the values and internal practices of the Irish
Catholic secondary school need a thorough re-examination if the institutions are to retain maximum credibility. The secondary schools of the
Republic are examination-orientated to a higher degree than those of the
United Kingdom and there exists much less opportunity in them for experimentation in curricula or methodology. A school staffed by priests,
brothers or sisters which adheres to a tight curriculum emphasizing the
needs of competitive examinations to the exclusion of more general
educational programmes is one contaminated by the values of the world
and the struggle for 'place' and 'honours'. If a Catholic school has a
function it must surely be to counter the spirit of the world not to pander
to it. It is desirable that individual achievements should grow naturally
out of a balanced and broadly-based curriculum and from humane
teaching, unalloyed by the smell of the chase or anticipation of the spoils.

Notes

1 M. Hornsby-Smith & R. Lee, *Roman Catholic Opinion: A Study of Catholics in England and
Wales in the 1970s* (London, 1980).
2 E. Hulmes, *Commitment and Neutrality in Religious Education* (London, 1979), p.87.
3 p.1.
4 Mary Warnock, *Schools of Thought* (London, 1977) p.132.
5 *FIRE Report* by the Working Party on the Future Involvement of Religious in Education, February 1973, p.42. The Report, which was not published, was presented to the
Chairman of the Education Commissions of the Major Religious Superiors and the
Hierarchy in Ireland.
6 p.5. It is indicative of the attitude of the two Churches that the Church of Ireland
Report was pulished with a recommedation that it should be made generally available to
parents, teachers, clergy and 'such other persons as may be interested to read it' (p.7),
whereas the Catholic FIRE Report was not intended for publication or wide circulation
because, it was felt, 'this would have inhibited the manner of expression of certain views
and recommendations' (p.6).
7 *FIRE Report*, p.42.

Marriage and the family

JACK DOMINIAN

1. INTRODUCTION

Any examination of marriage and the family in the Church in Britain and Ireland must consider the topic within the wider perspective of what is happening to those institutions in society at large. It is important to decide how far the Church has grasped the major transformations that are in process and has responded effectively to them. The Church has the responsibility of affirming what is good in secular development and of making a constructive criticism of whatever appears to be a major deviation from accepted norms. It will be argued in this article that, whereas there is major progress in understanding human aspirations in this field, in general the Church has so far failed to integrate the secular advances with its own thought, and has persistently given a much clearer impression of what it condemns than of what it approves. Furthermore, there is as yet no convincing picture of Christian marriage in the light of the teaching of Vatican II. Certainly very little has been done to inform Roman Catholics of the innovating teaching of the Council, so that even the breakthrough made there has yet to be grasped by the majority of Catholics. There has been a singular absence of teaching on this topic in the last fifteen years and it is only recently that marital breakdown has forced attention on the subject. The sad truth is that contraception has overshadowed, and even paralyzed, thinking on marriage and the family. Since secular society has come to terms with birth control and has moved on to other matters, the Church is inevitably preoccupied with ideological issues that no longer impinge on the world.

2. SECULAR DIMENSIONS

In western society the current major social issues are the emancipation of women and the implications of the man-woman relationship. There is a major sociological transformation towards an equality of worth of the sexes, who are now treated with the dignity applicable to persons independent of gender. The Church in our islands as elsewhere is faced with considerable difficulties in this matter. Traditionally women have been allocated a rôle secondary to that of men and in marriage the glory of woman has been identified with motherhood. Clearly this gives rise to a clash of ideologies. Women see themselves as persons in their own right and not merely as instruments of childbearing. The increasing reduction of family size is an active expression of the fact that, whilst having children is still acknowledged to be an important part of marriage, it is no longer seen as its supreme value. This conflict of viewpoints will be considered later.

Another aspect of the emancipation of women is their desire to work, either for the sake of money and companionship, or to advance their academic or professional life. The exclusive distribution of responsibility whereby the family depended solely on the earnings of the husband is giving way to a mutual sharing of work, of the economics of the home and of responsibility for running it. The husband is expected to play a far more active part in looking after the home and young children.

At a deeper level there is an increasingly conspicuous need to realize one's human potential. This potential is no longer seen in terms of the fixed rôles of the sexes but as a progressive deepening of awareness of feelings, emotions and sexual fulfilment. This revolution in the inner world of the couple is just beginning to be grasped and so far there has been only the most elementary response towards recognizing and nurturing it.

In addition to these subtle changes there have been more overt ones in the areas of abortion and divorce. I shall return to these topics but it is sufficient to say at this point that, in these areas, the Church has been on the defensive and condemnatory. In the area of marital breakdown, the radical thinking needed has only recently begun to receive ecclesiastical attention.

In summary, therefore, there are major changes affecting the man-woman relationship in society which the Church has yet to consider in depth. Condemnation of abortion, divorce and birth control is insufficient. A positive approach is needed to specify the Church's care for those who reluctantly break the rules, and also the preparation it can offer for an alternative, specifically Christian style of activity. But the Church is seen constantly to be reacting to events instead of leading and initiating thought.

This is well exemplified in the matter of sexual intercourse. For hundreds of years the Church has concentrated on the negative and dangerous aspects of sexual pleasure. There has been no profound evaluation of the meaning of sexual pleasure unless it is connected with procreation. The widespread availability of birth regulation methods has succeeded in detaching coitus from procreation. The Church has condemned this separation but, even when 'natural' family-planning methods are used, coitus occurs without the intent of procreation. What is the meaning of sexual intercourse under these circumstances? The world has seen the dissociation between sex and procreation as an opportunity to indulge in sexual pleasure; the Church, however, with its negative attitude to pleasure, has not been able to endorse this trend.

The Church rather has the responsibility of finding the meaning of sex in personal relationships which facilitate the deepening of love. The traditional answer has been that coitus is only permissible within marriage when linked with procreation. This is no longer a sufficient interpretation of the meaning of intercourse, even if we grant that it should remain exclusively within marriage.

3. VATICAN II

For the most part, the conciliar decrees of Vatican II have remained the basis of the teaching and aid afforded by the British and Irish Churches in regard to marriage. The second Vatican Council offered some promising insights into these issues. The few pages on marriage and the family in the Pastoral Constitution on the Church in the Modern World were of the greatest importance. It is a great pity, therefore, to have to acknowledge that the major changes contained within them have hardly impinged on the consciousness of the Catholic laity. There has been a comprehensive silence on the teaching of Vatican II on marriage which contrasts with the increasingly reverberative noise about birth control.

(a) Community of love

In the conciliar document on marriage and the family, the opening paragraph speaks of fostering this 'community of love'. Marriage is described in terms of love. Although love has been slowly entering the theology of marriage, until the Council it was understood more in terms of its ends. The traditional ends were the primary ends of the procreation and education of children, and the secondary ends of the 'mutual help' of the spouses and the 'remedy of concupiscence'. This language of ends was clear enough in the mind of theologians so that notionally both primary and secondary ends were of importance. In practice, however, marriage was very often understood almost exclusively in terms of having children. This confusion is no longer possible. Whilst the Council still stresses the importance of children, the personal aspects of marriage are highlighted: 'Marriage to be sure is not instituted solely for procreation'. Here is a sentence that dispels once and for all the erroneous idea that all the Church cares about is numerous children. Instead, the concept of community of love refers to the quality of personal relationships within the family. This is a concept that needs further clarification.

Since children are dependent on the love and stability of their parents, the community of love is first of all concerned with the happinesss and fulfilment of the spouses. This emphasis on the spouses had been implicit in the tradition of the Church but it now becomes overt in the official statement. After declaring that marriage is not solely for procreation, it goes on to say: 'Rather, its very nature as an unbreakable compact between persons and the welfare of the children demand that the mutual love of the spouses, too, be embodied in a rightly ordered manner, so that it may grow and ripen'.

(b) Conjugal covenant

This community of love is 'rooted in the conjugal covenant of irrevocable personal consent. Hence, by that human act whereby spouses mutually bestow and accept each other, a relationship arises which by divine will and in the eyes of society is a lasting one'. This is a passage of singular importance. It confirms indissolubility and the fact that it is the partners who confer the sacrament by the mutual commitment of their whole person to each other. But thereby the nature of marriage is returned to a scriptural notion of covenant which is to be found in the Old and New Testaments. Hence the couple's everyday experience of love is enriched by becoming connected with, indeed taken into, the covenant of the love of God with his people and with Christ within the Church. The covenantal love of spouses brings them into direct relationship with God's relationship with man. Just as God commits himself unconditionally to love his people, and sent his only Son to express this fully, so the love of the spouses for each other participates and is taken up in the covenantal relationship between God and man.

This richer vein of theology has hardly been exploited as yet, and in many ways the sacrament of matrimony remains the poor cousin of the others. Yet Vatican II spells out the link between divine and human love: 'Authentic married love is caught up into divine love and is governed and enriched by Christ's redeeming power and the saving activity of the Church ... By virtue of this sacrament, as spouses fulfil their conjugal and family obligations, they are penetrated with the spirit of Christ. This spirit suffuses their whole lives with faith, hope and charity'. Here is a theology which converts the community of love into the domestic Church whose members encounter and embrace Christ in the course of the daily activity, however trivial.

(c) Healing and perfecting

The community of love, infused with the presence of Christ, is living a life of love which the Council sees in terms of healing and perfecting. In an earlier encyclical, *Casti Connubii*, Pius XI said: 'Charity is not an attachment founded on a mere carnal and transitory desire or limited to words of affection; it is a deep-seated devotion of the heart which, since true love shows itself in works, is manifested in action. This action in the home is not confined to mutual help; it must have as its higher and indeed chief objective that of shaping and perfecting the interior life of husband and wife'.

There is a movement of thought of some fifty years duration which points towards an internal experience of healing and growth. This period has coincided with an unprecedented expansion of dynamic psychology and therapy which has given us profound insights into human development. Nevertheless, with few exceptions, there has been no systematic development of this theme of conjugal love translated into personal perfection. When one considers that for 95% of people marriage is the vocation through which they will attain wholeness and holiness, the absence of a synthesis betweem everyday conjugal experience and salvation is a massive lacuna.

Not that Vatican II missed this point. Apart from showing that healing and perfecting are the special gifts of marriage, it made clear that the love of the spouse is an eminently human one involving the good of the whole person.

Here is an area of great significance. For, if Christianity can lead the way in showing the positive features of marriage, then a hungry world will listen. The world is longing to understand the meaning of depth in marriage and the Roman Catholic Church here as elsewhere has the resources to do just that. Indeed, the Council asks the laity 'to do their part in bringing about the needed cultural, psychological and social renewal on behalf of marriage and the family'. This, however, can only be done if the average Catholic knows and understands what the Church is teaching. The singular absence of teaching in Britain and Ireland on the Vatican II declaration means that the married laity have to try to do their best without the help of up-to-date thinking.

(d) Sexual intercourse

Mention has already been made of the crisis of meaning of sexual intercourse now it is no longer related exclusively to procreation. The Council made a tentative start to answering this question: 'The love (of the spouses) is uniquely expressed and perfected through the marital act. The actions within marriage by which the couple are united intimately and chastely are noble and worthy ones. Expressed in a manner that is truly human, these actions signify and promote that mutual self-giving by which spouses enrich each other with a joyful and thankful will'. These sentences speak positively about sexual intercourse and sweep away generations of doubt, uncertainty and even hostility towards coitus. The paragraph refers to mutual self-giving which enriches the couple.

How are the couple enriched? The world is busy elaborating the pleasurable aspects of intercourse, and there is an extensive literature on the physical aspects of coitus. Clearly this is a body language with its own meaning conveyed through pleasure. Yet once again, with few exceptions the meaning of intercourse has not been explored or elaborated. But sexual intercourse is the central recurrent act of worship between spouses. Intercourse is the sustaining activity which bridges body, mind and feelings and fuses the genital with the affective aspects so that the integral whole plays a prominent part in the understanding of love between the spouses.

The published and spoken understanding of the subject is limited because the furtherance of meaning here is something that has to be studied by the married themselves. If they continue to await and expect hierarchical directions on sex from their Church, little progress is made, for the subject is outside the experience of a single, celibate person. Of course the laity have to make their own contribution to the discussion of married love and must bear some responsibility for the inadequacy of thought on the subject, but the British and Irish hierarchies must also acknowledge their heavy responsibility for their failure to encourage the laity in this regard.

(e) Children

The teaching of Vatican II on children is an amalgam of past and present ideas. On the one hand, children are seen as the focus of marriage and a large family is praised; on the other hand, parents are reminded of their responsibility of limiting the size of their family within their total resources.

The Vatican document makes it unequivocably clear that marriage and children are intimately related and, indeed, there are few who would disagree with this view: 'By their very nature, the institution of matrimony itself and conjugal love are ordained for procreation and education of children, and find in them their ultimate crown'. Then the document praises the large family: 'Among the couples who fulfil their God-given task in this way, those merit special mention who with wise and common deliberation and with a gallant heart undertake to bring up suitably even a relatively large family'.

The emphasis is on the wise deliberation of the spouses, who are expected to make a decision on the size of their family in the light of the material and spiritual conditions of the times as well as of their state in life. It is absolutely clear that the Church in no way imposes irresponsible procreation. It asks a couple to make a responsible decision about the size of their family when all circumstances have been taken into consideration. This responsible decision does not extend, however, to methods of birth control. Sex during the infertile period is the only method permitted by the Catholic Church here as elsewhere.

Since the subject of contraception was so controversial, the Pope set up a commission to advise him on the subject and Vatican II closed without a conclusive answer on the controversial subject other than a continuation of the ban on artificial methods.

(f) Abortion

For the Church, opposition to contraception and abortion is one front, but many Catholics and Christians see these two topics as distinct issues. The Council considered abortion and infanticide to be unspeakable crimes. Whereas the Church continues to adopt this attitude, societies all over the world have brought in laws to make abortion easier. These laws have met with the most articulate opposition from the Church, a position which has received a lot of sympathy from other denominations and from non-Christians. Perhaps the most prominent commonly-recognized feature of the attitudes of the post-Vatican Church in Britain and Ireland is its determined opposition to abortion. This stand undoubtedly reflects accurately the majority Christian view. Unfortunately the relative silence of the Church on all other topics has given the impression that British and Irish Roman Catholics are really concerned only about abortion.

Furthermore, the official concern with abortion has seemingly been expressed solely in terms of opposition. The hard work that goes on behind the scenes to support pregnancy hardly ever hits the headlines in the national press of our nations. Indeed, here is one area where the Church must not only oppose but show with absolute clarity what steps it is taking to prevent the necessity of abortion. But in this it is handicapped in the eyes of the public by its stand on contraception. Any ability of the Church to convince society that it has a more positive approach to sex, marriage and problematical pregnancies beyond its condemnation of abortion and birth control has yet to emerge clearly.

(g) Conclusion

One has to conclude reluctantly that the Council's hope that duly trained priests would nurture the vocation of spouses with a variety of pastoral means — by God's word, by liturgical worship and by other spiritual aids — has been realized only partially, and then in a patchy way. The overwhelming majority of priests and bishops in Britain and Ireland have ignored or played down the topic of a positive and creative approach to marriage.

4. HUMANAE VITAE

As already indicated, one of the main reasons for the Church's neglect of marriage and the family has been its preoccupation with contraception. The encyclical *Humanae vitae* appeared in 1968 and reiterated that: 'Any use whatever of marriage must retain its natural potential to procreate human life'. The encyclical went on to say that it was certain that others would be convinced that this teaching was in harmony with human reason. Unfortunately for the official Church, the overwhelming majority of people and of Roman Catholics in these islands remain totally unconvinced that the case put forward by the Church has any validity. Indeed, in the recent Gallup poll survey for England and Wales of Roman Catholic opinion carried out by a team from Surrey, only 13% disagreed with the statement, 'A married couple who feel they have as many children as they want are not doing anything wrong when they use artificial means of birth control'. Furthermore, some 60% of regular Mass attenders agreed with the statement. There is an enormous gap between the teaching Church and the married on this matter. Of all the topics regarding the family, the ban on contraception has been the only one rarely out of the news. It would appear that the Catholic married laity know quite well where the Church stands on this matter but that large numbers of them ignore its teaching. This is a matter of considerable concern for the official Church, and for its impact and reputation in this and other respects.

It is difficult to see how this issue will be resolved, for in Britain — and to a certain extent in Ireland — Catholics are increasingly dependent on the use of 'artificial' contraceptives. It is of course always possible that methods of birth control relying on the infertile period will improve so substantially that they will merit use in their own right. The disadvantages of 'artificial' contraceptives are such that there could always be a movement towards 'natural' means of birth regulation. But such a trend will be based on the practical benefits of the means, and not on the grounds of a conviction that only 'natural' methods are morally justifiable.

Another possibility is that the laity will appreciate that some artificial methods of birth control prohibit a full and intact exchange of bodily contact. For instance, coitus interruptus and the condom impair the full physical exchange required in sexual intercourse. The Church would present a much more convincing case for its recommendations if it discussed each contraceptive means from the viewpoint of how much it enhances or limits human intactness.

Finally, is it not possible that the persistent and widespread opposition of Catholics to the official rejection of contraception may express a genuine demand of the Spirit for the Church to develop further its theological understanding of this matter? The very thought of such an idea inspires fear and hostility amongst traditional Catholics who feel any radical change is unthinkable. But such opposition to change springs from a very limited view of the Church. 'How could we have been wrong?' is an attitude of genuine anxiety. The idea that the Church could be in any way wrong is beyond the comprehension of such minds. But it is not a question of the Church being wrong. The Church has changed its attitude to innumerable topics once a new understanding of the truth has permeated its life. There is so much change in human life and in our notions of human behaviour that we must constantly modify our understanding of what is appropriate. And what is appropriate in sexual intercourse now is exploration of its meaning in depth; the biology of sex is the least important aspect of its complexity.

5. MARITAL BREAKDOWN AND DIVORCE

Vatican II — and, indeed, the whole Roman Catholic tradition — has condemned divorce. The conciliar statement refers to the 'plague' of divorce; later on an ardent hope is expressed that marital love will not be profaned by divorce. Unfortunately the Catholic community in England has not been spared the immense increase in marital breakdown and divorce. Once again the study from the University of Surrey shows that the number of divorced Catholics is of the same order as that for the rest of the community. How is the Church responding to this fact? There are three answers. First, there is the work of the Church's tribunals which consider matters of nullity; second, there is pastoral care; and third, there is the task of prevention.

(a) Matrimonal jurisprudence

The Church's matrimonial tribunals continued to operate during the Reformation and up to now. Their decisions have contributed to a deepening of the theology of marriage. The tribunals start from the basis that once a marriage is truly constituted it may not be dissolved by any human authority so that the partners are free to enter into another marriage. But the question remains: when is a marriage truly constituted? When, in practice, is a marriage a marriage? Taking as their basis the teaching of Vatican II, the tribunals emphasize marriage as a mutual self-giving of two persons with a view to a permanent, exclusive and procreative partnership, brought about by their irrevocable personal consent. When a person, by virtue of grave disturbance of the mind or of the personality at the time of the marriage, cannot fulfil what is promised he or she is consequently incapable of marriage. The number of annulments given on this basis has increased in the last decade, for the tribunals have appreciated far more clearly the psychological and psychiatric impediments which interfere with the realization of the promises made at the wedding ceremony.

This increase in acknowlegments of nullity on the grounds of lack of due discretion has not gone without criticism. A number of people within and without the Church see this type of nullity as another way of sanctioning divorce. This misapprehension is largely due to failure to appreciate the exact nature of the Church's thinking in this matter. In practice such nullity decisions are constantly refining the criteria for a fully human marrige; this is one area where true advances in depth have been made in comprehending the nature of marriage.

(b) Pastoral care

The number of nullity cases is few compared to that of total breakdowns
of Catholic marriages. A large number of marriages of Catholics include
a divorced partner. If we add the divorced who remarry to those whose
marriages are invalid for other reasons, some 22% of currently married
couples (according to the Surrey survey) are in canonically invalid marriages. This represents a large number of Catholics whose spiritual life
needs care and nurture. The need to keep this group of men, women
and children near the life of the Church is paramount. One constantly
hears the view that, since they are divorced and remarried, there is no
place for them in the Church. And yet a place must be found for them,
for these families need the support of the Catholic community more than
ever. A sensitive and compassionate approach is an urgent matter for the
Church which has been reconsidering its attitude in this regard but has
as yet failed to formulate an agreed policy. Any policy must be flexible,
both for the parents and the children, so that they remain close to Christ,
the source of all love.

(c) Prevention

Whereas care for the one-parent family, the divorced and the remarried
must become a feature of the pastoral service of the Church, there is little
doubt that the primary concern must remain one of prevention of
marital breakdown.

The work of preparation for marriage has been largely initiated by the
Catholic Marriage Advisory Council with its courses for engaged
couples. This work is more integrated in the cohesive Catholic community of Ireland. In England and Wales the courses attract different
proportions, depending on the locality in which they are situated.
Despite the large numbers that attend these courses, many more do not
do so either because they do not know about them or because the nearest
CMAC centre is too far away.

Courses for the engaged to be married are helpful, but there is also a
need to support couples during various critical periods in the course of
their married life cycle. This work of supporting married couples after
they have been married is of vital importance. Traditionally the Church
had been concerned with all the details leading up to the wedding. Indeed, if the wedding is validly carried out and the couple consummate
their marriage, then a full sacramental marriage has taken place. This
concern with the initial moment of marriage has obscured the fact that
the marriage begins on the wedding day and unfolds into a loving relationship in which the couples have to love each other with their bodies,
minds and feelings. The expression of this love is conveyed in a number
of ways as the relationship unfolds. It is during these phases of the marriage, particularly in the early years, that the marriage encounters

critical crises. The cessation of work by the wife, the first pregnancy, the first baby, the advent of other children, their departure to school, the return of mother to work — these and other features which involve the sexual and emotional life of the couple require effort and perseverance if they are to be negotiated. At these times, when they encounter specific problems in their life, the couple can make good use of help and support. Their ability to be helped is enhanced when aid is directly related to a current crisis.

Prevention of breakdown is a matter of education and support before and after marriage. Before marriage there are a number of years when the school can participate in education for marriage and the family. Traditionally the school is concerned with the three Rs. There is room for a fourth R, which stands for relationship. Relationships of love between persons and between the sexes need to stress the fusion of love and the affective life. The abilities to give and to receive love, to resolve conflict with forgiveness and reparation, to communicate effectively, to sustain and promote healing and growth, to accept others unconditionally, to realize that love requires commitment and effort, and to learn to feel loveable, worthy of receiving and giving love and to appreciate the world of feelings, emotions and instincts, are all aspects of love that need development.

Thus a framework of love at home can be enlarged at school, in courses for the engaged, and in support for the married afterwards. This is a pattern of care which, when combined with the use of findings from contemporary research, can help the work of prevention considerably. At present this continuity of training and support is patchy in Britain and Ireland. Engaged couples' courses are the most successful enterprise but there is need for increased pastoral work after marriage and for the animation of schools as communities where loving relationships are promoted.

6. The rôle of the CMAC

In the field of preventive work, one organization stands out: the Catholic Marriage Advisory Council which, in its thirty-three years, has spread throughout Britain and Ireland. In many ways it has been a success story. It has promoted remedial and educational counselling and medical work. Within it there has flourished a rich theology of marriage which has animated and inspired its members. It can be truly said that the single most important contribution of thought to the subject of marriage and sexuality has come from the membership of the CMAC. Unfortunately the organization has not managed to carry with it the majority of parish priests, who never felt an intimate connection with it. Referrals to the CMAC have been sporadic and have varied from place to place. Furthermore, the theology which emerged from the organization

— which was very close to Vatican II — was not always comprehended or appreciated, and the CMAC remained somewhat distant and isolated from grass-roots Catholicism. Apart from these limitations, a good deal of positive work needs to be done by the parishes themselves; it has never got off the ground because most work on marriage was left to be done by the CMAC. These problems do not necessarily affect the Irish CMAC which, as a later arrival, has learned how to avoid some of these mistakes.

7. MIXED MARRIAGES

Catholics of a previous generation were clear in their minds that they should marry a fellow Catholic if it was at all possible. The Church firmly stressed the importance of intra-faith marriages; this was done for the very good reason that marriage between fellow Catholics was likely to be more sustaining, and that the children had a better chance to be brought up at least as convinced Christians if not as Roman Catholics.

The Surrey survey has some interesting figures on this subject for England and Wales. Valid non-mixed marriages were nearly 70% of marriages up to 1939 and were down to 30% in the 1970-77 era. Valid mixed marriages increased from 22% to 33% over the same period and invalid mixed mariages (often involving a divorced person) rose from 5% to 33% over the same period. Quite clearly a major sociological change is occurring. The pattern of non-mixed marriages is disappearing. The number of valid and invalid mixed marriages is increasing. The valid non-mixed, mixed and invalid mixed constitute about a third each of the total number of marriages.

The pastoral consequences for children in England and Wales are enormous. The cohesion of the Roman Catholic community, which relied on intra-faith marriages, is threatened by mixed marriages. These mixed unions demand a new ecumenical concept of pastoral service, particularly in regard to the education of children. But, beyond the education of children, the whole structure of marriage and the family has now to be built on a truly ecumenical Christian basis. This pastoral work will demand considerable sensitivity and innovation to ensure that justice is done to the sacrament of marriage and to individual denominational requirements for all members of the family.

8. CONCLUSION

Marriage and the family are in a state of marked transition. The expectations of equality of the sexes and personal fulfilment remain well ahead of preparation, education and support for these needs. The result is an unprecedented level of marital breakdown with its own trail of misery and suffering. Society may be blinded by divorce and may despair of ever delaying let alone stopping its progress. The Church in Britain and

Ireland has the clear teaching of revelation that marriage is a covenant of indissoluble love. Its task, therefore, is to promote and support — as far as possible — new expectations and at the same time actively to remind couples that indissolubility remains the ideal. It has to insist on commitment to fidelity and indissolubility and at the same time actively to support couples in the various phases of their marriages. It has to affirm what is good in modern change and to educate its members to realize it. This realization, however, will need both support and commitment. Ultimately the Church must help the married to perceive that their domestic community of love is their nearest and daily experience of God, and that everything that happens in their marriage is a journey of salvation in which their love for each other and the children shares in God's love for man and that of Christ for his Church.

Women and the Church

IANTHE PRATT

IN RECENT DECADES there have been great changes in society, not least in the position of women in Britain, and to some extent in Ireland. Better means of controlling human fertility have made it possible for people to choose to have smaller families; women have a better chance of a good education; there is greater degree of economic independence; and the drive towards sexual equality has gone some way to improving the opportunities and standing of women in society. Even in Ireland there have been moves towards greater equality before the law, but the Church there is so influential that it has very considerably hindered the widespread use of effective birth control.

In Britain Roman Catholic women as much as non-Catholic women have been affected by change in their family life and jobs, but in the Church appropriate attitudes to women have tended to lag behind those expressed in secular society. Traditionally, the Church regards change with mistrust and suspicion and is slow to recognize that it can produce good as well as bad.

Although Catholic married women go out to work as much as their neighbours once their children are at school, most Catholics still retain somewhere in their minds an idealized picture of the 'mum' concentrating all her attention on home and family. In particular, the clergy tend to think of women solely as wives and mothers, although they rarely think of men as husbands and fathers; this leads to an incorrect idea of marriage and the family, as well as a tendency to ignore the existence of the single or childless woman.

The Church in general and the Church in Britain and Ireland have not yet properly digested the lessons of Vatican II. The Pastoral Constitution on *The Church in the Modern World* rejected all forms of social and cultural discrimination in respect of personal rights on such grounds as sex, race or colour. Such rights were discussed to some extent by the 1971 Synod of Bishops, which was concerned with justice. The Curia fought hard to keep the subject of the rôle of women off the agenda, but the Canadian bishops insisted on its inclusion. This led to the establishment of a commission to study the position of women in the Church. It had little outcome save the production of a study-kit (which was badly publicized), and some of its conclusions being incorporated in the document *Women and the Priesthood* issued in 1976 by the Sacred Congregation for Doctrine.

That document is not very persuasive and the arguments used have much the same level of credibility as those used in *Humanae vitae* against birth control: for instance, much weight is put upon Christ not choosing a woman as one of the apostles, and in regard to the Incarnation the emphasis is misguidedly put on Christ's assumption of maleness rather than on his humanity.

The document does, however, make some valid points: for example, the importance of the rôle of women for 'the renewal and humanization of society and for the rediscovery by believers of the true face of the Church'. We need to explore what this true face of the Church might be, for an increasing number of women (and men too — they also are affected) feel that the Church is distorted by its male-orientated power structures.

It is now being argued that the domination of Church structures by men ought to be ended, not just out of sheer justice but above all as a way of finding a true balance in a Church which needs both women and men priests. On the other hand the view is put by others that the ordination of women can follow naturally only when we have developed a ministry of service rather than of domination. If that is so, the immediate need is to press for a form of ministry which is caring, outward-looking, open, and prepared to make mistakes in trying to serve; one that is concerned to build up community and to express that community in a form of worship that is a true celebration of joy.

The surprising thing in the recent Gallup survey of Roman Catholic opinion in England and Wales is not that the idea of women priests failed to win majority support but rather that as many as 25% were in favour of a change that would represent so radical a departure from established practice. Of people under twenty-five years of age, nearly half would accept women priests. This finding suggests that the Catholic Church in England and Wales is much closer to accepting the ordination of women than most people expected.

Opinion has already developed further among more educated Roman Catholics. A small-scale survey carried out in 1973 by the Newman Association (a UK body of university-trained and professional Catholics) showed that 81% of individuals responding were in favour of nuns being ordained in the mission situation of South America, where they are already running vast parishes, teaching, preaching, holding services, marrying and burying; doing, in fact, everything priestly save consecrating and absolving. Seventy-one per cent would have welcomed or accepted women priests in religious houses or in their own parishes.

The canon law of the Church discriminates against women and, although that law is in process of revision, regrettably there is not a single woman among the members of the commission for the revision or its consultators, although qualified women canon lawyers are available.

Some canon laws are widely disregarded, such as that requiring men and women to be segregated in church; whereas others, such as that prohibiting women and girls serving at Mass, is observed in Britain and Ireland but not in continental Europe or in North America.

The historical reason behind these canons forbidding women serving Mass or being ordained is the ancient taboo of menstruation, for in many cultures women were regarded as unclean at this time. During part of the Middle Ages women were not allowed even to enter a church, let alone to receive communion, when menstruating. Another lasting myth from the Middle Ages was the mistaken biological and genetic view of a woman as a deficient man (Aquinas, who has so heavily influenced Catholic thought, would seem to have believed that a female child was conceived if the seed was defective or there was a damp wind blowing). Although the official Church has now repudiated such ideas in the curial document *Women and the Priesthood*, there are many who feel very threatened emotionally at the idea of giving women the power to consecrate; ideas of uncleanness lurk beneath the surface. As recently as 1970 the readings laid down for the Easter Vigil included a reference to the misdeeds of the Israelites: '... to me their conduct is as unclean as a woman's menstruation'; protests led only to its optional omission.

It is interesting to note that whereas there are no theologians of any standing in the Roman Catholic Church who would subscribe to the arguments used against women priests in the curial document of 1976, a number of leading theologians in the Church of England are vehemently opposed to ordaining women, and not just for fear of ecumenical repercussions. Recent theological opinion in the British Isles from the Roman Catholic Church has in fact favoured the ordination of women. Fr Wijngaard, Vicar General of the Mill Hill Fathers (a large and well-known missionary order), has written a mainly scriptural study in his *Did Christ rule out Women Priests?* Paul Lakeland, SJ, in his *Can women be priests?* brings together insights drawn from theology, scripture, psychology and sociology. Both these authors believe there is no intrinsic bar to women becoming priests, and that this is likely to happen in the future.

To some, of course, the question of ordaining women would seem to have been closed with the publication of *Women and the Priesthood* which was backed by Pope Paul VI, and with Pope John Paul II's remarks on the subject during his Irish and American tours, but even the magisterium has been known to alter its teaching when its position becomes evidently untenable — as has happened on questions like slavery, biblical criticism and ecumenism.

Some women who feel strongly about discrimination feel that the question of women priests is a side-issue and that what matters is how far women play a part in the everyday life of the Church. Why is it forbidden to have girl altar servers in Britain and in Ireland but not in Germany, France and Austria or in North America? Although there is an increasing number of women who read at Mass many parishes still discourage such participation by women, even when there are women used to speaking in public, such as teachers, available. A handful of parishes encourage the laity, women and men, to give the occasional sermon, but such parishes are few and far between.

If one looks at really dynamic parishes where the clergy welcome lay participation, one is likely to find women fully involved: for example, as extraordinary ministers of communion or helping to run groups concerned with the parish liturgy, third-world projects, justice and peace groups, youth organizations; they are as likely to be involved in catechetics or good-neighbour schemes, as well as the more traditional tasks of church cleaning and money raising. So much, however, depends on what is encouraged by the clergy. If they really believe that the laity should play a full part in the life of the parish, much can be done. On the other hand, individual women must have enough confidence in themselves to put themselves forward for this sort of work.

In Ireland, as in Britain, conditions vary from parish to parish, and from diocese to diocese but there is no widespread use of lay talent, either male or female. Where parish councils do exist, their critics suggest that they are not infrequently composed of yes-men chosen by the parish priest. The Church in Ireland has not been noted for taking a lead in seeking to alter the inferior status of women either in secular society or in religious milieux, and the disadvantages under which Irish women suffer, despite recent improvements, are held to be among the worst in Europe.

In Britain the Gallup poll on RC Opinion showed that in 1978 about 50% would agree with the suggestion that women should play a greater part in the life of the Church, the proportion in favour reaching nearly 70% among the AB social classes (professional and managerial). The 1980 National Pastoral Congress for England and Wales made a definite effort to bring women into its organization, and there was a high proportion of women on the organizing committee and among the people chairing the different sectors of the agenda, although considerable effort was needed to find a woman acceptable to the authorities who could chair the most sensitive areas of discussion. The diocesan proportions of women varied in the delegations, but on the whole efforts were made to balance age, sex, and so on. One study suggested that it was not women but the working classes who were under-represented: one more example of the problem of encouraging the less articulate to offer their views.

The Pastoral Congress was a step forward from the usual situation of national and diocesan commissions, which generally have few women members. In specifically lay bodies there has been a greater tendency towards equality, and several women have chaired organizations like the Laity Commission. At parish level much depends on the attitude of the clergy to lay participation. If the parish priest believes in it, women who are willing and competent will often be found in responsible positions.

Being willing and competent, however, is part of the problem of discrimination. Because of the way women are brought up and treated they often lack confidence in their abilities. Women can, however, often gain enough confidence and experience to take a full part in the work of the parish or wider community through working in groups and organizations. Family groups, such as those under the auspices of Family and Social Action or The Grail, are a particularly good training ground because they set out to help people to try and understand more about what it means to be a Christian in the world today, and to work together, not only to support each other but to meet the needs of others. For example, some family groups welcome newcomers to the parish, organize special days in the parish for parents to get together to discuss matters of concern to them (the children being cared for meanwhile), or organize special services for children during Advent or Lent.

Because of the circumstances of many women's lives much of their apostolate lies within the home. This does not just mean trying to hand on the faith to the children; the home needs to be open to others and the family to be concerned with people outside it. The inward-looking family is a corporately selfish one. People vary in how much they can cope psychologically and physically with keeping a really open house, but there is opportunity for Christian witness when a home becomes a focus of caring and understanding. Many women are particularly good at providing a 'listening ear' which can do much to heal and help those in distress — perhaps the bereaved, the bore who has alienated everyone else, or someone else's teenager.

More and more women are finding that their needs and those of their families are not being met by the rather joyless and formal worship in the parish church, and this leads them to see the value of worship in their own homes. This worship may take the form not just of house masses but of a variety of creative acts of worship which are developed to meet the needs of the participants. These may include penitential services for family groups; special family services celebrating Holy Week or Advent in a way that is meaningful to children; and Christian passover meals or 'eucharistic picnics'. Generally other families and single people join in such celebrations which combine elements of rejoicing, praying, discussing, and singing together with social festivities. Often those taking part in a Christian passover meal are so enthusiastic about the experience that the following year they organize a similar celebration, so that the practice spreads. Creative worship is a growing aspect of Christian life and one in which women play a leading part (such forms of worship I have described with my husband in our books *Let Liturgy Live* and *Christmas and Easter Ideas Book*).

One advantage of worship in the home or group is that one can use language which is appropriate and forms of service which are specially adapted to the needs of the group for which they are intended. Only in recent years have Christians begun to realize how important language is in helping shape attitudes and ideas. Public prayer generally ignores the existence of women and any protest about this is often dismissed on the grounds that the matter of language is trivial. As late as 1980 a feature writer in the *Tablet* maintained that it was pedantic to object to the congregation (which probably held more women than men) being addressed as 'brothers'. It has been suggested by the RC International Commission responsible for worship that the congregation should be addressed as sisters as well as brothers, and that where men are referred to 'and women' should be added. The adverse reactions which these modest proposals aroused show how little understanding both men and women have of the insidiously depressing effect on women of not being explicitly included. Even those in the forefront of renewal in the Church have only recently begun to realize how sexist some of the language used in experimental liturgy has been. Apathy makes it difficult to get changes in the field of public liturgy; many women do not notice the injustice; others do, but are not sufficiently aroused to press for change; and many women are irritated if any objections are raised. Yet a not inconsiderable number of women have been alienated from the Church because of what they see as its male-orientated structure and life. The language issue has often been the final breaking point. Furthermore, we should not underestimate the psychological effect of always presenting the masculine as the norm.

In recent years the long-established RC womens' organizations have often branched out from traditional activities to meet new needs, but they have not undertaken a critical reappraisal of women's rôle in Church and society. The Union of Catholic Mothers encourages a traditional good-neighbour rôle which can be very valuable where there is a lively branch, and they have been running useful Vatican II-orientated training days, but often they are used by the parish only as a sort of communal housekeeper, for cleaning the church, providing first-communion breakfasts and the like. Catholic Womens' League activities likewise vary from branch to branch, but they have an established tradition of catechetical work and aid for refugees. As with other church organizations womens' organizations have difficulties in attracting younger Catholics. Even the National Board of Catholic Women, which is intended to represent women's voice to the hierarchy, finds it difficult to get representatives under retirement age; four of the last six presidents have been single women or childless married women, who are not really representative of the majority of Catholic women.

Two organizations exist specifically to try to achieve equality of the sexes within the Church: St Joan's Alliance and the Roman Catholic Feminists. St Joan's is part of an international alliance which has United Nations status, as it concerns itself generally with the status of women. This organization has for many years been the lone voice calling for the ordination of women, the revision of discriminatory canon laws, and so on. The Roman Catholic Feminists was set up in 1977 as it was felt that feminists who were Catholics had specific denominational problems which could not be tackled adequately within secular women's liberation movements or even by interdenominational Christian feminist organizations. The Catholic Renewal Movement has the broader interest of working to end any form of injustice in the Church; a number of its conferences and reports have dealt with the issue of sexism in the Church. The Pastoral Development Group sees the treatment of women in the Church as a key issue in pastoral renewal and has published useful discussion material (*Women — Second Class Citizens?*) geared to parish use.

Many younger women who feel strongly about the place of women in the Church seem to gravitate to the ecumenically-based Christian feminist groups that have been formed up and down the country in the last few years. These meet together regularly for study, prayer and mutual support; some organize high-powered conferences on feminist theology, politics, education, human relations and so on.

There is a need for these Christian feminists to come together because many of them are out of sympathy with the Woman's Liberation Movement as it is developing in society, with its tendency to overreact, to hate men, and to wish to exalt the rights of one section of society (women) against the others — which is just what they have been complaining of in the treatment of women. The secular movement also has an almost fanatical belief in the desirability of abortion with which a Christian feminist would be unlikely to agree, although she might well believe abortion to be morally permissible under certain circumstances; in general, a Christian feminist is more 'pro-life' and 'pro-family' than her secular sister.

Christian feminists are seeking a just balance in society and the liberation of women *and* men from attitudes and ways of behaving that diminish the dignity of both sexes. The male too is damaged by a society that exalts masculine characteristics. Both sexes need to be able to develop the other side of their personalities which have previously been inhibited. Society would benefit if men were allowed to be more compasssionate and concerned with personal values, and if women were able to develop their organizational skills and potential for leadership.

Most members of the Catholic laity, women no less than men, are not much concerned with questions of equality. The committed laywoman, often finding little scope in her own parish, may well direct her energies into Christian witness in other fields, such as helping to run multi-racial playgroups or set up battered wives' hostels. Others are involved with Shelter, Oxfam or other groups that try to raise funds for or to improve our understanding of the needs of the Third World.

A movement of great potential brought to this country by a Catholic woman nurse is the Faith and Light Movement; it is inspired by the work of Jean Vanier who believes in integrating the mentally handicapped into ordinary society. Faith and Light organize festivals and pilgrimages which bring together the handicapped and their families in joyful events. They set up support groups in various areas and run residential centres where the handicapped and the 'normal' live side-by-side. Members of this movement work within their parishes, often with great difficulty, to allow the handicapped to be accepted as full members of the parish and, for example, not to be denied communion. Where possible, regular local masses for the handicapped and their families are organized. Although fathers are involved, much of the work with mentally handicapped children falls upon the mothers.

Another organization that is trying to breathe life into the Church and bring the faithful to full commitment is the charismatic prayer movement. Many women are involved in prayer groups and it is not without significance that in ancient times the Spirit was seen as a feminine principle. Furthermore, the movement holds that a Church truly responsive to the Spirit would be more open and less rigid than one run on patriarchal and authoritarian lines. Women are included among the leaders of the movement, and in general women are accepted as equal.

Most church organizations today have both men and women working in them. This raises the issue whether there should still be any single-sex organizations at all. Perhaps the main point in favour of such bodies is that they can give women who lack confidence a place to gain experience and training.

Some single-sex organizations, like the St Vincent de Paul movement, have opened their doors to women, save for a few branches which reject women, even those previously members of mixed branches, if they move into a single-sex area. Women have long played a full part in bodies such as the Newman Association, and many have been officers of the Association. This body has a Family Committee which concerns itself with matters affecting the respective rôles of men and women in the Church and society, and in the early 1970s they conducted the above-mentioned survey on women's views and experiences concerning their rôle in the Church. It showed that at that time a woman living in the South of England was much more likely to take part in a parish council or read at

Mass than one living in the North of England, but that there were great variations between parishes in the same area.

The Hierarchy of England and Wales issued a consultative document *Marriage and the Family* in 1980 before the world Synod of Bishops, and the Newman Association, in its response to the bishops, called for the Church to act upon Vatican II's teaching on discrimination, and emphasized that human dignity required that each person should be treated as a unique human being whose potentialities should be developed. The consultative document had spoken of the profound change in the way we live likely to come from new technology, and the Newman Report emphasized that it was important that this should be seen as a challenge to share out work (paid employment, the work of raising a family, and voluntary work in the community) rather than allow an increase in pressure to force women back to domesticity against their wishes. Equally to be resisted were those pressures which forced women out to work against their will. The report also called for the need to rethink the rôle of the father, whose essential function in family life has been badly underestimated in the past where the family was considered the concern of the mother rather than a shared responsibility.

Such views come from the more educated end of the spectrum of Catholic views. Indeed, the majority of Catholics do not go to meetings or work in parish organizations, and there seems to be an increased tendency towards a less communal, more private form of religion despite the current emphasis upon the communal aspect of being a Christian. Light is thrown upon this by the 1978 Gallup poll (published in 1980) on RC opinion which showed that practically all Catholics believed the doctrines about God (which do not much affect how they live their everyday lives), whereas there was a strong current of disagreement in attitude and behaviour on moral questions such as birth control and divorce. Women are more directly threatened than men by the ban on artificial birth control, and there seems to be a strong conviction that celibate clergy are not really fitted to pronounce on such matters. The Gallup figures have not yet been broken down into answers from men and women on this subject but, taken together, only 13% agree with the official line on birth control and 54% would accept or welcome married priests. One should bear in mind that, at the time of the publication of the encyclical on birth control, research showed that there was only marginally less use of 'forbidden' methods among practising RCs than in the population as a whole.

One section of the Church in Britain, and to some extent in Ireland, which has really taken seriously the renewal called for by the Vatican Council is women religious. In the last fifteen years the work of many orders has moved away from traditional areas of teaching and nursing into all kinds of spiritual, pastoral and social fields. This sector has expanded in spite of the fall in the numbers of women religious; nevertheless, there are communities which have remained virtually untouched by renewal.

Nuns are now working alongside priests as university chaplains, and one of them co-ordinates the work of all the university chaplaincies. Nuns are also active in hospitals in teams of chaplains, visiting and taking communion to the sick. They are, however, particularly handicapped in their work among students as they are not allowed , solely on the grounds of their sex, to hear confessions from those they counsel, or to celebrate the Eucharist with the groups they work with. Here there is no psychological barrier to surmount as both men and women students with very few exceptions would find women priests acceptable. Pastoral needs suggest that women should be ordained for specialized ministries such as this, or in the mission field and religious houses.

More religious are now found working in the deprived inner-city areas, sometimes in ecumenical teams trying to build up the community and provide services in a centre. At other times a small number of religious live together in a small house kept as an 'open house' for neighbours round about, helping them with their problems, running prayer groups for those who want them, and being one with the people of the locality rather than set apart. An increasing number of parishes now have a 'parish sister' who is often the focus of activity: liturgical, catechetical, community building, counselling and so on.

The Church is becoming increasingly conscious of the need for the religious formation of adults, and nuns are in the forefront of this movement. They not only help to train suitable people in catechetics but run retreats, teach in seminaries and so on. Women religious have seriously and professionally addressed themselves to meeting the challenges of contemporary society. Various associations of nuns, such as the Association of Parish Sisters or the Association of Teaching Religious, offer a wide variety of training courses, as does Signum, the Sisters' Information service run under the auspices of the Catholic Information Service; Signum offers not only training but a very useful service of information and discussion about the issues arising in pastoral service. If only in-service training were taken as seriously by the parish clergy, the Church in these islands could make enormous progress in realizing the vision of Vatican II.

What of the future? The position of women is tied up with the whole question of how far lay participation is taken seriously. If the structures of the Church and its ministers can be helped to develop away from authoritarian over-masculine ways of functioning towards a more participative and caring way of life, it will be natural for women to play a greater part in the Church. There is, however, a great need for adult religious formation at all levels before this can come about. The clergy need to learn not to feel threatened by sharing their work with lay men and women and to be trained in the skills of building community. Laywomen need to be aided to grow out of the conditioning which makes them regard themselves as subservient and able to contribute little except the domestic arts. The layman or laywoman needs to see that the Church is more than a building and that his or her rôle is not just to provide the money needed to keep it and its attendant activities going — many parish councils tend to reinforce the idea that the Church is a building and not the people. A significant proportion of women religious have been giving a magnificent lead in retraining, rethinking and venturing out as a pilgrim people into today's world. It is to be hoped that the rest of the Church will follow.

The Church and social class

ANTONY ARCHER, OP

THE CHURCH in Britain and Ireland has projected itself as above the toils of class conflict. Was this ever really the case? It is an urgent question for the Catholic Church. In recent times the only Church with a substantial working-class membership, it now appears to be in danger of losing that support.

No doubt to Europe as a whole it was always evident that the Church was deeply embroiled in the class-based politics of the nineteenth century. In the new order of Europe the bourgeoisie who had supplanted the *ancien régime* were engaged in constructing a utilitarian society based on the rights of man, more particularly understood as the rights of the bourgeoisie. Religion was no longer a public but a private matter; a concern of the spiritual rather than the material world. Whether it was useful or pernicious or indeed true was irrelevant to the new power of the bourgeoisie. But the Church had come to regard its essential interests as embodied in a former (i.e., Christian) civilization, and accordingly set about recapturing its lost power.

Its aim was the establishment of a new society based on the old principles, in the first place by intellectual means. The model of a territorial sanctuary, based on the papal states, was neatly transformed into the model of the intellectual fortress.

The truth in all its completeness had been revealed to the Church which, as Leo XIII implausibly pointed out in his encyclical *Inscrutabili* (1878), 'in God's name rules mankind, upholding and defending all lawful authority'. In this phrase, the new political theory was at work. The state had its sphere, recognized by God. But in a question of faith or morals this gave way before the higher spiritual sphere in which the Church spoke for God. 'Pontifical Thomism', as a philosophy incorporating an organic theory of society in which everyone had his place, provided material for a vision of a corporate society in which the Church would again have its place.

The pope, as the all-powerful Vicar of Christ, was the cornerstone of this development, for he was to combine 'the whole legislative as well as judiciary and cohesive power in his own person' (Augustine, 1919, vol. 2:7; he adds that the pope would remain as it were a complete Church, 'even if the entire body of the faithful would cease to exist'). Henceforth to be a Catholic would be defined by law, and obedience the proper virtue. The new construction was completed by the declaration of papal infallibility. The organization and the faith were now identified. To challenge the organization was to challenge the truth, even God. The laity's attachment to the sacraments, in particular the Mass, was the Church's wedge into society. The plan now was to marshal them in separate organizations, policed by the clergy and directed to restoring Christian civilization.

In *Rerum Novarum* (1891) Leo XIII provided the blueprint. As protector of the poor, the Church wanted a society that was more (but not too) collective, in which wealthy and working people would dwell in harmony, as nature and God intended.

But if the latter were to seek this themselves they would find some difficulties in the way. They were not to injure property, resort to violence or engage in disorder. While the right to property was defined as a matter of justice enforceable at law, its proper use was only a matter of charity: there was no right to claim it. However great the papal anguish at the condition of the working class, it was clear to all that the Church was right behind the ruling bourgeoisie.

Perhaps this was the only thing that was clear about the Church, for on other points it is difficult to see how the papal teaching connected with society at all. Nineteenth-century capitalism was not a world in which medieval guilds could be replanted; it was not organized around church and family; and it could not sustain the single unified vision of reality characteristic of the Middle Ages.

There was an air of unreality about the Church's pronouncements. It had announced itself to be an ideal entity, whose constitution had not changed since Jesus first drew it up. It was obliged to reject all modern trends, everything that had been released by the collapse of the medieval system, although to some this rejection was part of the attraction of Catholicism: 'If the Catholic Church lost some writers and some books, it has been a small price to pay for the preservation of traditional orthodoxy' (Woodruff, 1969). The Church was set up far above its members: neutral, uninvolved, perfect. This kind of neutrality effectively accepts the social world in which it is embedded. Besides, at any threat of social disorder, it was clear that the Church was not neutral. There was nothing there for the new working class. Attached to a parish system that could not be swiftly reproduced in the new industrial towns, the Church could not provide the welcome for the uprooted that might have held their loyalty. Attached to the bourgeoisie, it could offer them nothing that might attract them afresh. The European Church did not lose the working class; it never had them in the first place. This is exactly what happened in England to the Anglican Church.

In England, the Catholic Church had long since lost any power, and its recapture could hardly be imagined. The old Catholics who had survived in pockets of England — gentry and their dependants, tradesmen in some towns and poorer people joining the nineteenth-century movement from the land — had evolved an unemotional and unobtrusive religion, backed by an often itinerant clergy. They now wanted, quietly enough, to build up their communities.

Nevertheless, the new, belligerent religion from Rome was imposed at the restoration of the hierarchy in 1850. The ultramontane strategy was deployed through the model of restoring the ancient glories of Catholicism. Invoking not particularly well-informed notions of medieval Christianity, the ultramontanes now set about introducing the rococo Italian devotions, elaborate vestments and rather camp clothing of higher ecclesiastics which would become a familiar part of the English Church. Instead of the congregational control that some of the laity wanted, or the clerical oligarchy that most priests looked for, the Church was to be ruled by episcopal monarchy. It was an authoritarian organization, albeit clothed in the language of the family: the pope was the Holy Father, the priest a father, and the good sisters would teach in the school.

The new bishops faced a situation in which, as well as the shifting English population, large numbers of Irish immigrants were being driven by poverty to the rapidly-expanding industrial towns where work could be found. Manning said that he had 'given up working for the people of England to work for the Irish occupation of England', for people who 'by the sin and persecution of England' were here and 'alienated from our laws and legislature'. The exodus from country to town had begun the movement away from the gentry, the arrival of the immigrants completed it. The gentry were eased out of the counsels of the hierarchy. They could however have confidence in the fact that even when (as in Manning) the Church saw itself as protector of the poor, it was not going to disturb the established order. The Church would always be happy to mirror society. As Bishop Mullins said of schooling, for instance, at a meeting in 1979: 'The independent sector is part of the educational provision in the country and it is right that the Church should be making a contribution to it.'

Liberalism was the threat to the established order of Europe. It was hardly likely that the Church would allow outside intellectual influence or internal experiment (such as the rather evangelical scheme of mission huts and saying mass in the courts and tenements where people lived) to flourish in the Church.

This Church, spectacularly indifferent to local conditions, was too alien to have much effect on the indigenous population. Setting up separate Catholic organizations in accordance with the ideology of the Church as a counter-society emphasized this strangeness. Few outsiders had the opportunity of identifying with the Church's concerns. For this reason marriage, one of the few ways available of coming to identify with the Catholic community, has always been the principal source of converts to the Church. In addition, faced with the almost overwhelming numbers of new immigrants (among whom the poorer old Catholics were quickly absorbed) the clergy largely abandoned their efforts at evangelization among the English working class. They were not looking for new members, but to keep the ones they had got.

The policy of the Church contributed to the reputation of Catholics. They became (and still are) regarded as periodically disappearing into a curious Catholic world: going excessively to church, lighting candles, praying to statues, confessing their sins to a priest in order to repeat them with a clear mind, being bullied by their clergy and spending Sundays in the Catholic drinking club.

If the new Catholic Church was uncongenial to the native population, it suited the immigrants well enough. Ruled from abroad, with its foreign liturgy and indifference to particular nations and cultures, the Church was an ideal symbol of protest for people who did not wish to be absorbed in the local culture. The Church formed part of the buffer between the Irish and the English society by which they found themselves surrounded. The massive churches rising in the industrial slums were a very evident gesture of defiance.

The bishops understood themselves as restoring the ancient glories associated with Westminster Abbey and the like, and the faith of our 'British, Anglo-Saxon, Norman and Plantagenet ancestors' (the Bishop of Hexham and Newcastle, 1886). But to the Irish the 'faith of our fathers' was not that. It did not represent the English past but the Irish present which, despite the most strenuous efforts, the English had failed to crush. The two interests merely coincided in the fact that the Irish were perforce the bearers of the restored Christianity.

Separate Catholic organizations were set up in accordance with an official (though rather remote) ideology of initiating a counter-society; this too was what the Irish wanted. The system of territorial parishes, coinciding with the natural communities formed by the immigrants, fostered this development.

The Church laid great emphasis on the sacred — on the church building and its accoutrements, on going to church, on the institution itself as sacred. To be a better Catholic came (officially) to mean going to church more: daily Mass, visiting the church during the day, the special services and missions. The clergy and their activities became the major source of grace. 'When parents bless their children', according to a parish magazine of 1933, 'they express a wish that God may bestow on them this or that spiritual advantage. When a priest blesses a person he expresses a similar wish, but by reason of his priestly office as Christ's representative there is a greater likelihood of his wish being fulfilled.' In the 1930s religion wasn't carried into one's life. Religion consisted of going *into* church. Despite the large pretentions of the Church to a social teaching, this was limited to its starting-point, the moral behaviour of the Catholic family; and this in practice seems not very far from re-inforcing the dominant mores of society. The peculiarly Catholic pre-occupations with such things as birth control were elements within this already given framework. Apart from this concern for the family, the Church would confine itself to the separate world of the sacred.

In this it complied with the changing place of religion in English society. The Churches were required to support the establishment either directly (as in the case of the Church of England) or indirectly by con-fining themselves to a form of religion that did not interfere with the more mundane sorts of reality that were the establishment's principal concern. The Churches were the object of hostility or indifference among the working class. For the Irish, however, this did not destroy the Catholic Church's relationship to their distinctive position, even though the clergy might take up a position contrary to their interests and those of later Catholics, opposing Fenianism, having the general reputation of being Tories, distilling *Rerum Novarum* into the single prohibition against wasting an employer's time or money, and teaching that people should 'accept the position you're in and in that position get closer to God'. Because of its additional, symbolic dimension, the Catholic Church was less affected than others by the first World War which 'dealt a shattering blow to organized religion. . . Thereafter men looked elsewhere, if any-where, for their moral certainties' (Koss, 1975). Gradually the image of the Catholic Church became transposed into the inherited symbol of particular working-class communities. (Later immigrants, as those of the 1950s, were not alienated in the same way as their predecessors had been.) Catholicism was one of the means by which their identity was ex-pressed. It provided a precise and demanding framework. Its defining points were: the pope, Sunday Mass, marrying a Catholic and sending one's children to a Catholic school. The strict and inherited nature of the demands armoured Catholicism against otherwise prevailing attitudes: 'It's a bit cissy to be a Christian in this (a working-class) area, but of course Catholics are brought up in the knowledge that they are Catholics and there's nothing they can do about it — it's not something you can hide even if you want to, through school you have to defend yourself'. Or, in a more middle-class mode: 'People still think a good belief is splendid. In a funny kind of way you were quite proud of being a Catholic. Even though Catholics stood out like a sore thumb they were admired for their principles, very much so'. In the Mass, which was its centre, this framework could also hold together the different classes.

The Mass most eloquently expressed the Church's removal from the mundane concerns of its members. Eliminating both the human (the priest was a vestmented back and the congregation was to remain silent and still) and the physical (at communion, for example, the host was not to be touched or chewed), it achieved a timeless quality. Exclusively about God, a means of personal and private sanctification, the Mass was detached from everyday life. This meant in fact that the *status quo* was wholly accepted, but superficially it served to conceal class differences. Catholics had no quarrel over God and the sacred and the classes did not mix in other situations. There was nothing in the Mass that might jar with their pursuit elsewhere of conflicting class interests.

Officially, the Catholic framework was quickened by fear, instilled at school and maintained thereafter through the confessional box. The rationale may be provided by Cardinal Heenan: 'Why does the Church make us go to Mass? If Catholics go to Mass only because it is a sin to miss Mass, doesn't that show fear rather than love of God? The answer is that the Church, knowing the faithful as a mother knows her children, tells us what to do for our own good. . . If the Church did not make us go to Mass we might cease to worship God. . . . Most Catholics don't bother to go to church on great feast days like Maundy Thursday, Good Friday and All Souls. Why? Because the Church does not tell us to go and grown-ups are like children: they have to be told what to do'. Fear was the only language offered in which to express religious commitment.

But fear was not the effective force behind Catholicism, as was evident to the clergy from the figures they collected of Catholics who did not attend Mass, and from their baptismal registers, revealing as they were of subsequent losses. What the Church provided in the first place was belief in God as a way of making sense of the world. Belief does not require regular mass attendance, and non-attenders have often been recognized as 'great pray-ers'.

The middle classes acquired this meaning system through a conscious personal decision. For those who had the leisure, training and taste for extended intellectual reflection, the Church provided a well-documented tradition in which polemicists could flourish. The middle classes were more likely to make an explicitly intellectual adaptation of Catholicism: 'I made a decision to stay a Catholic but not to take some of the rules too seriously'. Having educational qualifications of their own, they were less likely to be impressed by the clergy's educational pretentions; having broader opportunities, they could stand apart from parish activities.

In working-class areas attachment to the Church was in the first place a question of family and thereafter communal solidarity. That loyalty incorporated the common working-class ethos, focused on the family and with a strong local attachment. Religion, like politics, was a private affair and not discussed (even in the family). Characteristically, it was 'the woman who looks after the spiritual side of things', even if in the case of a mixed marriage that meant a non-Catholic wife bringing up the children as Catholics. Generally, although Catholicism was obviously different, it was neither truer nor morally better than other forms of religion; other people too had the prerogative of belonging to their own kind.

Catholicism was a vehicle for the working-class conviction that there was some point in an insecure and often unfair life. It provided a sense of being allied to the spiritual forces of good and protected from those of evil, and a somewhat fatalistic acceptance of the world: 'God let it (death) happen even to his own son'. There were many formal ways of indicating the necessary attachment to the Church; the importance to Catholics of Mass attendance has, like fish on Fridays, been much exaggerated. Contributing to the outdoor collection taken from house to house in some areas, or sending children to a Catholic school, fulfilled the same function.

The strictness of Catholicism was more apparent in its ritual and only secondarily in its maintenance of orthodoxy among those not within the cognizance of the Holy Office. Ritual was under the clergy's control, and recognized to be so; people were free to come and go from the sphere of the sacred as they wished. As to orthodoxy, the clergy's definitional control was generally undisputed. The strength of Catholicism was precisely that somebody knew what it was all about and had a total conviction; the priest really was there to radiate the certainty that 'all would be well and all manner of things'.

There were various ways of relating to the fixed point of the sacred. Most recommended was the counter-reformation method of organized enthusiasm enshrined in the high Mass and benediction. The style, with the host forming an immobile piece of property detached from the congregation for their admiration, provided an image that justified the *status quo*. For men, the Mass was more usually a refreshing break from the mundane, with an inescapable echo of the dominant view that the purpose of leisure was to increase the effectiveness of work.

Life-cycles other than the ecclesiastical could also be invoked: the regular attender every Christmas at midnight Mass; 'We didn't bother much with church but we did go when it was necessary for marriages, funerals and baptizing'; or the family cycle of the children's first communions and May processions 'with the kids all dressed up'. It is a range always evident in baptism, moving as it does between the pragmatic 'that's how they get names', the notion of insurance, and the more specific entry into a religious world in which God's aid cannot be sought for a baby if 'you've never bothered to take the baby to have it baptized'.

The Church had always encompassed this variety. It was able both to maintain that there were no guarantees of salvation and to promote such practices as the devotion of the 'nine first Fridays' which appeared to promise just that. The promise of results was also implicit in practices such as novenas which worked (when they did) as an intervention of the miraculous in everyday life — a characteristic which reflected the Mass where, divorced from everyday life, the consecration worked as a miracle, regularly performed. With such resources available to its members, the Church had little to fear from rivals such as astrology or C of E. This kind of Catholicism flourished into the late 1950s when it began to be overtaken by events it could not control. The second Vatican Council, which initiated the changes in the Church, was unanticipated and its effects unforeseen. However, although the pressures for the council came from abroad, the factors contributing to change were present in England too.

The old working-class communities had been breaking up as a younger generation was moved out of the inner cities to the new housing estates. Increasing contact with other styles of life provided a challenge that was not easy to meet. Catholicism was formulated in terms of detailed practices such as the duties of Lent; when these were put in question by a change in a Catholic's circumstances or by meeting other people, Catholics found it difficult to recall quite what was the underlying content of Catholicism. For children, this process began with the end of the single, all-age parish school. The few Catholics who could remember the catechism's 370 questions and answers found its efficacy depended on being among people who shared a common assumption that these were the appropriate questions and the proper answers. Catholicism was not impervious to the dominant ethos encountered by Catholics: the pressure to think and behave in the same way as other people.

Catholics — or more particularly their children on the new housing estates — began to wonder why they were Catholics. The Church's symbolic function in the old working-class communities was declining. It could hardly be a symbol of solidarity after they had ceased to exist or for people who had left them. These communities had in any case been bound together primarily by the shared values and experiences of working-class life rather than by any specific activity of the Church, which was ceasing to have any distinctive service to offer. Even the dances and social events were available elsewhere at a price most Catholics could afford. The notion of Catholic identity was in decline; the assimilation of Catholics into English society was advancing; no further need was felt for a vehicle of such conscious difference as Catholicism.

The Catholic Church was ceasing to stand for anything with which working-class people could identify. It was just one of a number of bodies providing religious services when required. The Church, not the simple faithful, proved vulnerable. After all, they were not idiots. There was nothing of particular interest going on for them in the Catholic

Church, any more than in the Church of England. The two bodies were much the same.

At the same time a new middle class had been growing up within the Church. It had benefited from post-war educational reforms, was free from the hold of the parish, and included many of the descendants of the Irish immigrants. Some of these were infected by the taste for open debate, spontaneity, social concern and doubts about authority and institutions that were found among their contemporaries — of whatever class. Their attitude (not shared by their successors) was not to reject their religion but simply to want to understand it. The bombs of scripture, theology and history had not been wholly smothered when the Church closed in on itself; they had now gone off. The whole seamless Catholic culture — historically dubious, but at any rate the way the show was presented — was coming apart. The working class voted with its feet and left; the middle class stayed and argued. The Catholic Church in Britain had not allowed for the possibility of change. The basis of the restoration model was to do what had always been done. There was no way to communicate the rationale behind the changes to the majority of adults (who did not read the Catholic paper or more or less esoteric paperbacks), except perhaps through the Sunday sermon. But Catholics traditionally switch off at the sermon, and go into an even deeper coma when it is replaced by the reading of a written communication from the bishop.

Hitherto essential features of Catholicism disappeared overnight in a wholly inexplicable fashion. Nothing took their place. Abstaining from meat on Friday was to be replaced by some other expression of Christian commitment. There was no way of instilling whatever desired new value (it was not apparent what it was) that was to replace the former exercise in the discipline of obedience. The former things of Catholicism simply passed away. The saints apparently had abandoned their powers of finding things, curing sore throats or intervening in hopeless cases.

Oddly enough, pruned of all the impedimenta, the priest with the sacraments under his control became even more the source of grace. The changing Church became more, not less, clerical. The radical curate going round saying house masses was no more out of the peculiar world of the sanctuary or into his parishioners' world than his parish priest leading the school assembly in the rosary while the fourth form slipped away. Whatever their theology, they continued to administer the church plant and make all the parish decisions. Despite the decline in numbers, the clergy had to maintain the sacrament machine: Masses, confessions on Saturdays (at the rate of some forty an hour), marriages, funerals and baptisms, and the visiting expected by the parishioners — on whose money they lived. Expectations long instilled in older parishioners could not easily be over-ridden, nor could the arrogation of so much by the clergy be easily undone. There was no way the clergy could get it right.

Meanwhile the pilgrim people of God replaced the perfect juridical body as the official account of the Church. Effecting this change of image, however, involved the Church in contradictions. Uniformity was the basis of its self-understanding, but it began to talk of local differences, adding always that what amounted to a local difference was not to be decided locally but in Rome.

The Church, which had centralized itself, took to talking of decentralization in an apparently democratic mode. Here, too, the Roman authorities, through John Paul II, have begun to reassert their power and the universal Church is again being marshalled in the ultramontane manner against an outside threat, this time the Communism of eastern Europe. But it will be difficult to go back on the movement promised from a cohesive authority which knew best and demanded obedience to an authority whose decisions would be legitimated by reason and argument. This leads to a local contradiction: those in authority remain the same and continue to know best.

In England, at first, the changes were imposed from above abruptly and without enquiry. The bureaucracy disappeared behind a cloud of commissions, consultation documents, discussion meetings, pastoral congresses and the like, sustained by the rhetoric of illusory participation. The reality was consultative and advisory. There was to be no giving up of power. Collegiality was for bishops only.

These new bodies provided something for the established middle class. Their world is one of verbal dexterity they can manipulate for their small victories; the Church, anyway, is run in their interests. For the working class such meetings are simply a frustrating waste of time. They can see that nothing of interest to them is going to happen. They do not attend. The exercise of power in the British and Irish Churches, since it affected nobody except the clergy who could not escape it, was better regarded as a kind of parody of the exercise of power at large. Indeed the elements of parody increased. The liturgical changes were supposed to lead to a renewal of Catholic hearts and minds along communal lines. They did not, but Catholic documents continued to speak as if they had. There was a blossoming of the Roman characteristic of announcing something desirable in the present tense as if *ipso facto* it were to become so. Catholics found themselves being exhorted in general terms by church authorities. They ought to be apostolic, take a part in church affairs and so on. But they were never offered the power and authority that would make it reasonable to respond to these directions.

In the 1960s the Church suddenly started inventing liturgy — albeit by reference to a preceding golden age and a consequent shedding of accretions — speaking the while of local adaptation but curiously doing so by *fiat* from the centre. If a group followed instructions by adapting to local conditions it was almost bound to depart from the norms within which alone adaptation was permitted. It was however tacitly agreed that students and other middle class groups might experiment. Young working-class people who were not regarded as a special case, and did not attend renewal weekends or university chaplaincies, went without this opportunity.

The changes in the liturgy were what most impinged on Catholic congregations. The majority of Catholics were not greatly concerned about any logical contradictions in Catholicism; theological renewal passed them by for they were already beginning to take their views (especially on moral questions) from elsewhere; and, unlike church officials and their radical critics, they did not care either way about church structures — except that they did not want (though they often got) an arbitrary structure where the manner of the liturgy was at the whim of the local priest.

In the new liturgy Catholics who had once 'followed the Mass' were now to be 'a congregation meeting together regularly under a president'. It was presupposed that the participants would be part of an existing group already known to each other; the old Mass, when this often was the case, depended on no such assumption. The new Mass became neither one thing nor another, but an uneasy compromise. No group was gathered round what was neither a table nor an altar. No one knew whether they were talking of bread or hosts. If (say) the symbolism of the death and resurrection of Jesus — the bread (and body) broken and the wine (and blood) poured out — was to replace the symbolism of the consecration of the host as the encapsulation of the eternal God in a moment of time, it did not succeed. The meaning was merely evacuated from the old symbolism and its gestures emasculated.

Requiring co-operation as it did, the new Mass was singularly vulnerable to clerical or congregational sabotage, accidental or otherwise. The priest could still say Mass as unintelligibly as if it were in Latin, or (at the other extreme) do it as if he were a revivalist reliving his personal conversion. There was nothing to prevent the congregation from withdrawing by dotting itself around the back of a largely empty church or gazing silently at the priest when he said: 'The lord be with you'. The presence together at the same Mass of those who were hanging on gallantly despite the changes and those who wanted to try them led inevitably to what in most parishes both regarded as the dreary disaster of Sunday Mass.

However, to say that no change at all was wanted is generally a product of the somewhat patronizing notion that there is an unchanging working-class, or even Irish, culture. To acknowledge that change was wanted is not necessarily to fall into that other élitism, the official view, which is that the wisdom of the changes that have been made will filter down from the middle class, the natural leaders of the Church, to the working class who will gradually come to accept them.

Nevertheless the old Mass allowed people to engage the sacred in their own fashion, provided for a whole range of religious demands and sensibilities, and drew people into a space where there was something more to life and a fixed centre to which they could relate their changing worlds. The total unintelligibility of most of the Latin and much of the now-vanished impedimenta helped in this. They served as a reminder of the human condition. The Mass did take place 'in this vale of tears'; it was surrounded by the hosts of angels and statues and the ambiguous dark places of the church; it did know that black was the human colour for funerals and that the *Dies irae*, however pagan the words, was a genuine cry of anguish.

The new Mass has excluded much of this. From its opening invitation to 'call to mind our sins' via its demotion of the 'Lord God of Hosts' to the 'Lord God of power and might' and its plea for 'peace in our time' the English Mass has avoided the kind of language that might be genuinely popular while eschewing any attempt at 'fine writing'. It has also excluded any language or gesture that might seem excessive. At every point only one clear meaning must be conveyed verbally; it is like a lecture in which drama and silence have no place; it allows no scope for either gloom or ecstasy; *it has become trapped in a passing fashion of the 1960s*.

This open-plan Mass with its clean and functional lines, said ideally in an uncluttered church with plain (but good) wooden furniture is the epitome of middle-class taste of the 1960s. It is the English liturgical reflection of Vatican II, which was a continuation of the rational and intellectual impetus of the Counter-Reformation. The new, like the old Mass, maintains its neutrality. It speaks of sharing but does not mention food or property. It speaks of love and peace but not of justice. It makes no demands and draws no implications that might reveal the divisions in the congregation. It floats above the question of class and blesses the way things are.

The new Mass, however, was merely co-incidental with the circumstances that had been building up and that had led people to question their Catholicism. The failure of the Mass was only that it could not provide anything that might hold back this process. A new, younger generation was growing up and again finding the Mass boring, though not wishing to return to the former sort, and asserting the right to stop going at an earlier age. It no longer seemed natural to settle even nominally into one's parents' religion, nor a matter of course to initiate one's own children into it: there was no longer any question of community or loyalty involved. The Church did not maintain the line against the prevailing attitudes of society for the Church was one of their vehicles. There was no very evident reason for being a Catholic.

The working class had always tended to think that all religions were the same. The younger members of the more intellectual middle class were beginning to agree. Most had arrived at the individualistic, private and adaptive style associated with the development of liberal Protestantism. Now some may use religious groups to pursue the current middle-class obsession with self-fulfillment; others, looking for friendship, do not find that the parish structure of Catholicism can provide it; most consider they can handle such religion as they want by themselves.

If a Church is to maintain quite specific beliefs and practices and demand total allegiance, it has to be the handed-down patrimony of an appropriately specific group. The Church, however, no longer plays this part for the working class. The attempt of a few, largely middle-class Catholics to hold on to the traditional strictness of Catholicism by reinterpreting it in a politically radical fashion and attaching it to someone else's patrimony (first to the proletariat understood in Marxist terms, then to Latin American liberation movements) was short-lived. The old Catholic gentry and those whose first commitment was to the social *status quo*, observing the decline of Irish and working-class Catholicism, and the weakening of the Church of England, re-emerged to seek a rapprochement with the establishment. Perhaps, somehow, the Church could share the Church of England's rôle as the official state religion. The Duke of Norfolk slipped again into the mantle of leading Catholic layman and the Abbot of Ampleforth became a suitable choice as archbishop of Westminster.

Most often, individual experience of God was provided through the charismatic movement which abandoned the precise framework of ideas and offered a direct and self-authenticating experience of God. But the emotional and unreflective nature of the charismatic movement, and the unmediated guidance of God, make it especially open to an unquestioning acceptance of the dominant values of society. The elimination of the tensions inherent in the world and in Christianity tends to trivialize the experience ('Jesus *always* answers when I turn to him') and the internal assurance provided turns out to be the simple though divine direction to get on with what people would be doing anyway. It is the business of the middle class to absorb and propound the ruling ideology of society. (The liberal concerns for such things as the ordination of women and a married clergy do not challenge this). The charismatic movement does not attract working-class people.

Small groups based on a communitarian model and concentrating on inter-personal relationships foster the same sense of assurance and well-being. Increasingly, such 'eucharistic communities', envisaged as meeting regularly and often as comprising as few as twelve people, have been proposed as the new principle for restructuring the Church. But why should anyone (other than the clergy) make the Church his or her first community? Nor is it clear why groups of this sort should be regarded as a point of growth. Small groups are not in themselves necessarily interesting. They are often inward-looking and unattractive to any outsider, in so far as their existence comes to any outsider's notice. Working-class people, in particular, have shown no interest in these small groups. In work and in social life, they belong to wider overlapping communities, and are accustomed to finding their solidarity in larger numbers.

By and large, the Catholic Church in Britain and Ireland is set on a path that will make it just another Christian denomination, without any very outstanding characteristics of its own, primarily middle-class in composition, unable to make effective any particular demands as to belief or practice, and through its unquestioning acceptance of the rightness of the way things are arranged giving its support to the prevailing social ethos.

The moral positions on birth control, divorce and even abortion on which church officials have apparently set their hearts, are all being eroded by the stronger ethos of society. Theology has lost its purchase on society and with it all access to a popular audience where distinctions of this kind can be made. The crude and oversimplified conduct of the official campaign against abortion illustrates this difficulty, and shows how the assumption that the simple faithful cannot handle reflection has compounded the difficulty. In the light of this erosion, Cardinal Hume's insistence on prayer as the primary concern of Catholics appears not only as an attempt to hold different parties together while concealing their differences, but as an acknowledgment that all that is specific has departed from the Church.

Two features of the Church undermine prediction: its international nature and its resolve to put its house in order. Our Church cannot be immune to the decisions and demands of the Church abroad, which has initiated a series of changes. Certainly the present drift of the Church can only be reversed by a new upheaval of British and Irish society, which would either lead the Church to reflect different concerns (those of the new people in power) or force it to take a stand (not necessarily that of the people in power) on some issue regarded as significant by the whole population. The Church may yet abandon its policy of imposition and set out to discover and build on the religious needs of its members in the groups to which they actually belong. If it were to do this while it still has some working-class members its whole perspective and style could be transformed into that of a popular Church of interest to the working class.

The Church and social responsibility

TERENCE TANNER

FOR A CHRISTIAN moral responsibility cannot be separated from social responsibility any more than the love of God can be separated from the love of man. The two are one. They are bound together in our flesh. As St John wrote: 'he that does not love his brother, whom he sees, how can he love God, whom he does not see?' (I Jn 4:20). Social responsibility is as morally binding as the moral law. It is socially necessary. That is a first principle. It must be understood and acknowledged if you are to avoid trying to divide the indivisible.

It was first stated as a principle in Christian times when Paul withstood Peter to his face at Antioch. Nowadays no Christian considers that it is immoral to eat what Jews consider unclean food. Peter saw it that it was a social necessity to conform to the customs about him and to eat or not to eat unclean food, depending on the social habits of his hosts. The issue threatened to split the Church. Paul's argument was that Peter's actions had to be consistent because he was the moral leader of the Church. In the last thirty years the 'withstanding' has taken the form of theologians and laity saying to the *popes* (note, not the Pope) you must be consistent with one another; or theologians and laity saying to the bishops, you must be consistent with one another. Otherwise a schism is inevitable or, even worse, indifferentism will be rife. Moral or social indifferentism is a disease in any society and most of all in a religious society.

Ours is called a permissive society and in a book entitled *The Church Now*, it seems right to examine the links between church leadership and society's ills.

In March 1980, the Irish Hierarchy issued a Pastoral Letter in which they discussed the respect due to papal authority and to the authority of progressive theologians. Years ago (when it might have been asserted that the Irish laity were not informed), this Pastoral would have carried moral authority throughout the land and the laity would have had nothing to do with progressive thought. The Irish, however, are now as informed as the rest of the world and know that theologians at the second Vatican Council (the *periti*) were largely responsible for its conciliar decrees, but that Küng, Schillebeeck, Curren and other theologians on whom the bishops relied then are now being attacked because they are 'progressive' theologians. This version of 'Peter not being consistent with Peter' both creates the need for such Pastoral Letters and breeds social and moral indifferentism. The blame does not lie with the laity. They are only the onlookers.

Contraception is another issue, with serious social consequences, on which the bishops have not spoken with one voice. It is such a recent issue that it can be regarded both in the context of history and in the context of contemporary behaviour. No sooner was *Humanae vitae* published than it was obvious that the divisions in theological thought which had preceded it were not resolved by its publication, nor have they been since then. Sacramental discipline (or moral theology) differs widely depending on which part of the world you find yourself in. The inconsistency reaches a ridiculous point when it depends on whether you speak to the curate or the parish priest. Historically, the position is even worse. Certainly when I was ordained (1941) and for a few years afterwards it was approaching *de fide* that contraception was always and everywhere wrong and later there were those who held (and for all I know there are some who still hold) that *Humanae vitae* was an infallible document. That encylical created grave social and personal problems. Some Catholics accepted its rulings 'strong in faith'; others dropped out. Both groups can now look back in cynicism, the breeding-ground of indifferentism, but most Catholics in both groups were not themselves at fault.

The laicization of priests and religion is the latest issue. One pope permits it and another does not. That does not enhance papal authority. It destroys it.

I date my first awareness that I thought this way to the Sunday in the mid 1950s when I refused communion to Mr & Mrs X. They always came to Mass but never came to communion because they made no secret of the fact that they used contraceptives. Then Mrs X had her menopause and Mr X had no need to use them. There had been a change in her body but not in their wills. I was roundly told off by my parish priest and by my bishop. After that, I decided that if sacramental discipline did not consist in an attitude of the will but in a physical thing, there was no moral difference between a contraceptive and the menopause. That was the first manifestation of thoughts which had been developing for a long time.

An analyst told me I was a man of simple faith who had developed late and become a maverick. Looking back, I identify three issues that concerned me when I was a man of simple faith and accepted everything without question, but which became seed-beds in my late development. They are as important (perhaps more important) as taking-off points which have led to my present thinking as they are in themselves. All

three concern the sacraments and all three have moral and social con-
notations.

The first issue was masturbation and those terrible morning queues
outside the confessionals at a boys' boarding school. Most boys accepted
that masturbation was wrong (because they were told so) and had no
'wish' to do it; yet they went on masturbating because of physical and
emotional pressures. It was a case of 'the evil that I hate, that I do'
(Rom. 7:19). The Church's teaching evoked a sense of guilt and social
stigma in young boys but it was never explained to them why masturbation was wrong or, indeed, why they had the urge to masturbate. They
were simply told it was wrong; that it would lead to hell, blindness, mental illness and, worst of all, spots; and that, if they did it, they could not
go to communion. As a late developer, I taught otherwise in the confessional. As a maverick, I snapped when I refused Mr & Mrs X communion because here the Church accepted a contradictory practice. If that
is not clear, I will explain. The masturbating boys' will was in line with
the Church's teaching but their physical action, through no fault of their
own, was not; and they were refused communion. The Xs' will was not
in line with the Church's teaching but their physical action, through no
merit of their own, was; and they were admitted to communion.

The second issue was imposing on people a duty to attend Mass every
Sunday, while (in certain circumstances) at the same time imposing on
them an obligation not to present themselves for communion. For any
Catholic the Mass is a eucharistic celebration. To be compelled by one
law to be present and by another not to celebrate reduces the non-
participating observer to the rôle of an observer at a ritual dance. A
moral leadership that imposes that duty as a way of keeping in touch
with Christ is not entirely free from responsibility for moral and social
indifferentism. Recently one of our bishops was reported as saying that
'to go to mass and not go to communion is like playing football without a
football'. I agree with that entirely, but I wish he had openly drawn the
conclusion: 'Do not go to Mass unless you go to communion'. As a late
developer, I taught that. In a few words, my reasoning was that communion with Christ exists in the heart and will; if you are in communion
with him there, go to Mass and communion. You need to in order to
keep a personal relationship. If you are not in communion with Christ in
your heart and will, stay away from the eucharistic celebration because
in so doing you will respect it and yourself more.

The third issue was the Church's habit of using sacraments and
anathemas as sanctions in order to impose penal or disciplinary laws.
This worried me then. It worries me now, and it will worry me till the
Church gives up the practice. If I said it was using a sledge-hammer to
crack a nut, it might sound blasphemous. The practice itself is more
blasphemous. We have seen the evil of it in our own day. There have

been so many changes over the last few years. Not so long ago to say Mass in English would have been an act of schism; now to say Mass in Latin is. Must we believe that our eternal union with God depends on whether we obey a changing disciplinary law of the Church? Or doesn't it matter?

Issues like these (and we can all add to the list) have social consequences. Abortion is an example. Whether a child is born wanted or unwanted, deformed or not deformed, provided for or not provided for, is not only a moral question; it is also a question of social responsibility and raises many issues. The prohibition of abortion is promulgated as an edict of the moral law: abortion is the murder of the foetus; the foetus is a child; to murder a child is against the divine law. Contraception was once said to be against the natural and, therefore, the divine law. Not everyone would hold that now and the question in many people's mind is: 'Will a loop-hole be found in the Church's argument against abortion?'. The argument against abortion as stated by the Church appears so simple and incontrovertible, but outside the Church there are millions of good, holy and learned men who do not agree with it.

As I have never had to advise anyone on whether to have an abortion, the only decision I have made has been whether to sign a petition for the repeal of the abortion laws. I decided not to because of the parallel with the way masturbation was treated in my youth: as an edict without explanation or discussion. Is an acorn an oak, and if I crush it, do I crush an oak? Is a foetus a child and if I kill it, do I kill a human being? Does an IUD commit murder?

The mother-and-child controversy has been with us a long time. If giving birth to a child puts a mother's life at risk, to terminate the pregnancy is wrong, but if the mother has cancer of the womb, her womb may be removed and the foetus comes with it. Is this casuistry or morality? A theologian can distinguish between direct and indirect effects but can the layman? Yet it is the laity who must obey the law, and the women who must die.

Have the arguments for ensoulment and the possibility of independent life been fully discussed? A few years ago these questions would not have entered my head. I would have accepted the authority of the Church without question but now, who has changed more — the Church or me?

Since the Church teaches that abortion is wrong, it has a duty to provide for babies who are not wanted, or not provided-for, or deformed. It might also have to provide for their parents. It has a good track record in this (mother-and-baby homes and special schools, and so on) and the English hierarchy are to be praised for including this duty in their recent statement in favour of the unsuccessful John Corrie amendment of

English law on abortion.

The Church has paid heavily (and not only financially) for its faith in Catholic education, even though the old battle cry, 'No to Rome on the rates', is still occasionally heard. From the beginning of the housing movement, its involvement in it has been considerable although largely un-recorded. Because of the growing number of medical and therapeutic abortions, soon it will be mainly Catholic parents who have unwanted, deformed and not-provided-for children, and those children and their parents may need social support. If the decline in vocations continues, this could pose a serious problem. Will the Church fight to have these children brought up in expensive-to-run state institutions (as it does in regard to Catholic education today), or will it shoulder its own burden (as it used to in regard to education)?

This is not only a matter of finance because, as I have written, many of these babies and their parents will need social-work support and many social workers hold radical views which they frequently express. There will soon be a need for a large increase in the number of Catholic social workers. Priests, career teachers and youth leaders should be aware of the need.

These are not the only issues connected with the Church's teaching on abortion. If we may not morally prevent the birth of malformed children, to what extent are we bound to prolong their lives? Are we, for example, morally bound to put them in an oxygen tent or to keep them alive by round-the-clock attention and expensive equipment? Is this decision the parents' or the doctor's? This may seem like going back to the days when unwanted babies were exposed on the hillside to die, but with the continual advance in medicine part of the decision may soon be to turn off a life-support system. Perhaps there is a need to popularize the Church's teaching that life does not have to be prolonged by extraordinary means. At the emotional level it will take a long time for parents and the medical profession to acclimatize themselves to letting a baby die and, in the present climate of opinion, a mother who *took no action* and let her baby die would be lucky to avoid a charge of manslaughter. She would probably be acquitted on the grounds that she was distraught but I am concerned about the morality of the act and about its becoming a specifically Catholic problem.

If we are not bound to take extraordinary means to preserve a malformed baby's life, I can hear cries of protest that we will let a baby die once it is born but will not abort it and save the mother all kinds of mental suffering. I know the answer — the distinction between active and passive means — but the accusations of inhumanity and casuistry will abound. I am reminded of one of the first jokes I remember being told — the story of the old lady who lost her purse and prayed that a theologian would not find it. There is a difference between the way theologians and ordinary people think and the theologian, for all his years of study, does not always carry conviction. So how does the ordinary person act — by faith in a theologian, or by faith in his own reasoning? One of the consequences of education, of conflicting theological opinion, and of different opinions being taught at different times in history, is that more and more people are taking their own moral decisions, especially where these involve social responsibilities.

I want to write something about charity because here again moral and social responsibility are one. Mother Teresa of Calcutta was quoted recently as saying: 'Jesus said love one another. He did not say love the whole world'. I find that quotation remarkable because if there is one person alive today who most people would say loves the whole world, it is Mother Teresa. I cannot find the context in which it was said and have, therefore, to interpret it my way. I do not know much about her but the little I know has taught me a lot. Another of her quotations, 'If you meet a starving man, you do not ask questions, you give him food', has inspired my work for drug addicts. As I interpret it, it means that charity is unconditional. You do not say: 'If you will give up drugs or prostitution or drink or whatever, I will help you'. The need is there while they are still taking drugs or drink, and you help them unconditionally. It leaves you exposed to all manner of accusations like supporting their life-style or housing them in preference to others with genuine and desperate needs, but it is part of your concept of charity and one of your priorities, or it is not. To illustrate what I understand Mother Teresa to say about love, I return to childhood and an early lesson in English: 'There were three barbers in the same street. One put over his door, ''The best barber in the world''. The next followed with, ''The best barber in this town''. And the next (of course!), ''The best barber in this street''.' The more you narrow charity down, the more intense it becomes. We cannot physically, financially or mathematically love the whole world but we do have an obligation to love within our reach and within our limits. I do not accept the argument that modern means of transport have shrunk the world so that the man in the gutter in Cambodia is as much my neighbour as the man in the gutter outside my front door. It is not true and is in danger of reducing charity to an occasional prayer and a donation without personal involvement. In a sense it is like seeing the beam in the eye of the world and not seeing the mote in the eye of this city. I hate Sundays. They start with This-Week's-Good-Cause on Radio 4; then there are more appeals in church and in the papers and on television; then there are the needs you read and hear about — they are all so obviously genuine and frustration grows. Then I walk down the street where I live with its sixty drug addicts and as many alcoholics and its scattering of ex-offenders. They need help, too, but few hear about them; and fewer still help them and no one visits them. Sometimes frustration turns to anger and I wonder whether Mother Teresa meant: 'We should love the world less and our neighbour more'.

Charity begins at home... and so does social responsibility. I suppose the Catholic Church in every part of the world has its indigenous areas of social responsibility that it can be accused of neglecting. Writers producing books like *The Church Now* in those countries can identify them but I cannot even identify them in these Isles because I am sure that, if I lived in Belgravia or Chippenham, my experience would be different. I can identify them in my street and the streets about me. We are a cosmopolitan lot but mainly English, Irish, Scots and West Indians, and I used to spend a lot of time in the even more cosmopolitan area of Soho. My world recently has been drug addiction, alcoholism, compulsive gambling, prostitution and single sex clubs. Not a pretty world, but one in which the number of Catholics is out of all proportion to their percentage of the population. I am told it is still above the national percentage in prison but not so much above as previously. I know that Catholics are over-represented below the poverty line and in psychiatric hospitals.

There is no generic word to describe the people who inhabit my world. They (and many sociologists) reject words like deviants, dropouts, social inadequates, outcasts, misfits and the rest, so I will call them what they call themselves: junkies, alkies, whores, cons, queers, shits and the like.

I start with junkies. I must know 25% of those known to the police and the Home Office. A correspondent in *The Tablet* recently suggested that on the experience of one sample-testing 75% of junkies had a Catholic background. I used to say 50%, but I am now more inclined to say 40%. It is bad enough.

I know a lot of alkies but many less than junkies. Dermot Walsh and Brendan M. Walsh are the experts on alcoholism in the Republic of Ireland. If you read the *1972 Report of An Bord Taighde Pobal-Liachta* (the article is in English) or 'Alcoholism in the Republic of Ireland' (*The British Journal of Psychiatry*, Vol. 115, September 1969) or 'Validity of Indices of Alcoholism' (*British Journal of Preventive and Social Medicine*, Vol. 27, No 1, February 1973), you will discover the size of the problem. The latest figures I have show that in England (where alcoholism is growing) 5% of our national income is spent on alcohol and in Ireland it is 13%. A lot of Irish and Scots are Catholics and, in my experience, an unduly high proportion of compulsive gamblers, strippers, whores, and rent boys are. I am told by the whores and rent boys that many of their clients are as well. I have no way of proving that but they do not often lie to me.

I have frequently argued that the Church in this country has a duty to commission professional research at the highest level to try to discover whether there is a link between this phenomenon and the Catholic religion; whether it exists in other countries; and whether a diagnosis can be made of its causes. So far nothing has been done. I have also argued that, even before this research is commissioned, the Church has a duty to provide more social work support, rehabilitation centres, street agencies, shelters and the like. A little has happened but not enough and I am sure that what has been done has had nothing to do with me.

If the laity think there is any substance in my argument they should make their voices heard. It is their money and their children. They should demand to be reassured. If there is a link between these groups and the Catholic religion, I may be seeing it only at its most obvious and there may be many others who are tarred to a lesser degree with the same brush as these groups.

I do not want to end before referring to Mt. 13:12: 'For whosoever hath, to him it shall be given and he shall abound: but whosoever hath not, from him shall be taken away even what he hath'. I know and, perhaps you know, that this refers to the gift of faith. If I accept it, my faith will grow and grow and if I reject it, any little faith I might have seemed to have will disappear. Not everyone knows that, however, and have-nots and people with very low IQs think it means that the Church is on the side of the meritocracy, and what they see around them and some of the sermons they hear and the lectures they get do nothing to disillusion them. The Church presents a rich face and although it works among the poor, it rarely gets its hands really dirty. There is a large population made up of the (again I am stuck for a generic noun) lowest of the low — I do not write 'poorest of the poor' because, although they are poor, many of them need not be — people like meth-drinkers and elderly vagrants and junkies and alkies and so on. It is very rare that the Church is seen caring about them and working for them but the Church is seen at civic receptions and the like. I am not saying that it should not be, but I am saying that it ought to be in both places and more often in the lower place. Otherwise it risks creating the impression that an uninformed reading of Mt. 13:12 gives.

Some of what I have written may seem unduly critical of the Church and I want to end with two very positive conclusions.

About twenty years ago, when the Church started to relax its discipline, it was generally said by intelligent people who did not belong to it that that relaxation was a bad thing because it would lead to a weakening of discipline in other Churches, and in the nation as a whole. I do not think that this is happening. I think it has hastened individuation in Catholics. Previously many Catholics 'just did as they were told';

now more and more are making up their own minds. I trace that to less regard for the authority of the Church rather than to the Church's relaxing its discipline but, whichever it is, it must ultimately be good for the Church. It will lose its monolithic image (and let us hope it does not try to grab it back) but it will gain real men and women.

I think Christ's words in Mt. 21:28 might be stretched to include that idea: 'A certain man had two sons, and coming to the first, he said: Son, go work today in my vineyard. And he, answering, said: I will not. But, afterwards, being moved with repentance, he went. And coming to the other, he said in like manner. And he, answering, said: I go, Sir; and he went not' (I think that 'Sir' is a splendid ironical touch!). The Church is breeding a new kind of member who will not do as he is told, but I have sufficient faith in the Church to believe that in all essential things it is right, and enough faith in my fellow Catholics to believe that most of them in the end will say so. I think that is a healthier position than what we used to have: a lot of people who said they believed but didn't.

The second positive thing I see happening is that Catholics are moving away from the Church into society in regard to voluntary works and community interests. There was a time when the Church was a closed shop but it was the Catholics who closed themselves in, and many times in the past I have preached to my unfortunate parishioners that they thought that, having kept the moral law and put their money in the plate, they had fulfilled all their responsibility to society. I do not think that is as true now that Catholics are moving more and more into local government and local societies.

I am particularly impressed by the number of young Catholics I find working in street agencies. Sadly, most of them say they have left the Church, but the Church has done something for them in getting them on to the streets, and many of them, I'm sure, will be like the son who said, 'I go not' and went.

The Church and crime

TERENCE MORRIS

I RECALL two incidents during my career as an academic criminologist when I was confronted with a particular stance taken by the Church 'on crime' — or rather two incidents in which I was brought up somewhat short in my thinking. The first was when I came across a Catholic priest serving a prison sentence for smuggling who was being allowed to say Mass each day in his cell. I wondered at this, not least since the prison system, then as now, has a habit of doing its best to restrict people from doing good things in prison while usually failing miserably in its efforts to prevent them from doing wrong ones. I was more concerned that, having been convicted of crime and sentenced to what a Lord Justice of Appeal once referred to as the 'socially disgraceful penalty of imprisonment', on account of the grave scandal he must have given, the ecclesiastical bureaucracy might not have put the priest under some kind of interdict. 'No', I was told later, since his offence against the customs and excise regulations was not a sinful act in the sense of being an offence against the moral law; such rules were merely enacted for the convenience of States and, being arbitrary, had acquired no fundamental moral status. I recalled this explanation many years later when noticing that deprivation of faculty as a sanction was not even applied in the case of a priest convicted of being involved in IRA violence. Bewildered by that, all I could utter silently was *O tempora! O mores!*

The second incident, some years later, was while I was sitting in St Patrick's cathedral in New York during the 'Red Mass' for a meeting of the American Bar Association, listening to a sermon by Bishop Fulton J. Sheen. A formidable preacher, Sheen used the opportunity to 'sock it', as the saying goes, to all those wet liberal lawyers and penologists who had so clearly gone overboard in their concern for criminals and had totally neglected the needs and feelings of the victims of crime. Perhaps concern for victims has always been underemphasized, but I was left with the clear impression that our preacher was not averse to more than a little good old-fashioned retribution. With the recollection of the appalling conditions that I had been observing in some penal establishments not a million miles from St Patrick's, I felt a sense of irritation rising towards hostile dissent. I realized how Jenny Geddes had plucked up the courage to hurl her kneeler at the preacher in St Giles in Edinburgh (though perhaps for different reasons), but above all I began to realize what a way there was still to go before the Church could speak about *justice* in a way that left the hearer — whether he was a believer or not — in no doubt whatever about the manner in which human justice, reflecting the justice of God, must also reflect God's love for man, be he ever so sinful. Unkindly, I wondered what would have been said if all of us in that great congregation had been transported in a time machine to the foot of the cross just at that moment of the conversation between the two crucified thieves, and the good thief and the Lord Jesus himself.

The truth of the matter is that down the centuries the Church has taken a variety of positions about crime, and certainly about the ways in which it should be punished. It is perhaps unfair, then, to judge every voice in the pulpit by those standards which, post-Vatican II, we have come to accept as normal, but which not so long ago were regarded as wildly radical. Part of the problem no doubt stems from the fact that at an early stage the Church had to make clear distinctions between civil and canon law, between the laws of God and the laws of princes and — not least — the ways in which Christians might render to Caesar that which was his while ensuring that God's laws were obeyed. The situation was still further complicated by the fact that, the Church having modelled its bureaucratic organization on the pattern of Imperial Rome, the efficiency of that Roman arrangement endured long after the grass had grown over the broken aqueducts and the tramp of the legions had passed into history. Incompetent and illiterate medieval rulers were generally dependent upon the Church to provide their most senior public administrators including, in England, the senior member of the judiciary, the Lord Chancellor. Admittedly, many of these men were only in minor orders but the ecclesial dimension was unambiguous.

At the same time, just as the civil law reflected the precepts of the canonical code, so the attitude of the Church towards the treatment of malefactors tended to reflect the standards of the time. Punishments for crime tended to be limited to the corporal — flogging, mutilation and frequent use of capital punishment. Torture, in order to extract confessions, though officially outlawed by the Church as early as the beginning of the thirteenth century, persisted well into the seventeenth: it was as commonplace in the interrogations of the Spanish Inquisition as it was among the priest-hunters of Elizabethan England. The Church, moreover, had an oddly illogical stance where heresy was concerned in that the heretic, *even after* recantation, could still expect to die. Heresy, more often than not, was closely connected with political considerations — the burning of St Joan of Arc being a classic instance. The political dimensions of heresy and those of crimes that have political overtones are as interesting as they are complex. Henry VIII, for example, dealt with those Protestant reformers who denied the true presence in exactly the same way as those who denied his claim to be supreme head of the

Church in England: he killed them, and brutally. So too in modern times political dissent within the Soviet empire has been treated as heretical departure from the truths of Marxist dogma and its advocates as criminals offending the people. Note that there is more than a passing parallel between 'the people' and the 'Church' in the literal meaning of *ecclesia*.

Arguably it was the rupture between Church and State that brought about the public distinction between crime on the one hand and sin on the other. Before the Reformation, or more precisely, before the emergence of the new Nation State from the remnants of medieval Christendom, the ecclesiastical courts had not merely dealt with all the transgressions of the clergy — and there were many instances of serious offences including homicide and rape — but with all those deviant acts that were thought to impinge primarily on the divine law, such as sodomy. In England, by the end of the sixteenth century, the ecclesiastical courts of the new *Ecclesia Anglicana* had been reduced to dealing with little more than matters of clergy discipline whereas the civil courts had assumed responsibility for control over a whole range of acts that went far beyond the offences of violence and against property for which they had always had jurisdiction as keepers of the sovereign's peace. As the state arrogated to itself increasing control over the lives of its citizens, many rules bearing the force of law came to have less and less foundation of any discernible moral or religious character and become increasingly arbitrary and instrumental. The high point came in sight during the nineteenth century when, in order to regulate an increasingly complex urban industrial society, the law of England at last recognized that the traditional *mens rea* that had to be at the heart of every properly proved criminal offence might be dispensed with in what had become known as statutory offences — which the police were already referring to as 'quasi-crimes' in their official reports.

This distinction, between an act that is wrong in the sense of being *mala prohibita* and one which is *mala in se*, is crucially important. It explains, among other things, how the smuggling priest could be held to be giving no scandal. It also has a bearing, albeit somewhat indirect, upon the Church's traditional teaching — or at least that part which derives from St Thomas Aquinas — that the mental element in crime is not merely central, but is modified by the content and character of extraneous circumstances. Thus the doctrine of necessity may have a bearing upon the crime of theft. If a person is starving and in imminent danger of death, argues St Thomas, then he may legitimately supply his own needs out of the goods of another and indeed a man may do so in order to save someone other than himself who is in extreme need. What is contained here, albeit strictly defined, is a kind of dynamite in any society where the unequal distribution of goods results in contrasts of almost obscene dimensions between rich and starving poor. One might legitimately wonder how many of those whose lives have expired on wayside gibbets down the ages while Holy Mother Church looked on might have pleaded necessity had they but known their *Summa* or had the benefit of enlightened advocacy.

As St Thomas put it: '. . . human law cannot derogate from natural or divine law'. This was the basis upon which that other Thomas — the courageous More — argued that the Henrican supremacy was inconsistent with the Catholic faith. Christ alone could be Head of the Church, in England or anywhere else. Henry's more thoughtful daughter Elizabeth knew what she was about when she rejected the title 'head' and substituted 'governor'. Because the law requiring him to swear allegiance to the crown in this form was an affront to divine law he could not do it. Moreover it came within the ambit of the maxim *lex injusta non est lex* — an unjust law is no law. It was an attempt on the part of the Sovereign to exercise *power* under the guise of *authority*. If we are to follow St Thomas Aquinas, we must recognize that those who hold the Catholic faith must of necessity subscribe to the belief that human (that is, civil) law cannot contradict divine law or indeed natural law and survive as legitimate. So too we must recognize that all earthly authority derives from elsewhere; as Jesus had to remind Pilate: 'You would have no power at all over me unless it had been given you from above'.

But, it may be argued, this tells us more about sin than about crime since the modern State, at least in the West, does not generally ask of its citizens the sorts of things that were demanded by renaissance monarchs. Its laws, insofar as they offend against divine law, do so in the context of permissiveness rather than that of active requirement. Hence the State *permits* the sinful killing of unborn children for social convenience but does not *require* that certain children should be killed in the womb. Yet there remains a terrible nagging question which links the doctrine of necessity with the concept of the unjust law.

If the distribution of goods in a society is so blatantly unjust, do the poor, or their advocates, have a mandate to infringe the laws of property, *à la* Robin Hood? Do the laws of tyrants belong so clearly to the category of injustice that they are obviously 'no laws' and guerilla resistance is justifiable?

If that sort of question seems a million miles from contemporary Britain it is certainly not far from the north of Ireland. Long years of bombings and killings have induced a belief in the minds of most Englishmen, many of them Catholics, that the Irish are little better than a pack of homicidal numbskulls who carry bomb-making equipment about as other people carry the shopping and who are bent on keeping the whole ghastly business going indefinitely. What many do not know, or if they did, have forgotten, is that the Catholic people of the north have been subjected to discrimination of the vilest and most blatant kind for many years, and especially since partition in 1921. Worse, that the social élite of the Orange Order has encouraged discrimination by the Protestant working class whose social and economic position has been only marginally better than that of the Catholic working class. The response of the working-class Orangeman has been not unlike that of the poor white in the American South who joins the Ku Klux Klan or the unemployed urban teenager who imbibes the noxious ideology of the National Front and turns his boot on the hapless immigrant. What the English (who may comfortably regard as violent crime acts committed by those who argue that the bullet and not the ballot box is the solution to Mother Ireland's seemingly incurable issue of blood) do not recognize is that those whom they call 'criminal' see themselves as 'freedom-fighters'.

Here the Church's position is more than a little ambiguous. Generations of Catholics with an Irish ancestry, priests included, have been brought up on a semi-distorted and essentially romantic view of the long struggle for Irish independence; and in Ireland, as in Poland, the Catholic commitment of the people has been the central focus of their political and cultural identity. Hence there has almost always been a priest about to see off the coffin as it goes down under the volley of illegal rifle fire. In the more elevated places in the Church this sort of thing has caused some embarrassment, to say the least, but it took the Pope himself to lay it on the line to the gunmen. The question remains. Are these men criminals, using violence unacceptably for political ends, however desirable, or are they legitimately employing force against an alien tyranny? One is tempted to apply pragmatic tests: such as whether Long Kesh is indistinguishable from Belsen or Dachau; whether the 'Brits' are indistinguishable from the SS in wartime France; whether Bloody Sunday in Derry in 1972 and the ambush at Burntollet Bridge are analogous to the total destruction of, and massacre of the inhabitants of, Lidice and Oradour by the SS. My own view is that they are not. Nor, I would argue, is it licit to wage war against a lawful sovereign when that sovereign does not come into the category of a tyrant bent upon defiling both divine and natural law and whose overthrow might then become a legitimate act.

The original concession of the British government by which political status was granted to IRA and Loyalist paramilitary prisoners was clearly a disastrous mistake resulting in the degrading spectacle of the 'dirty' protests. Governments, however, have a habit of cutting logical corners from their thinking. Just because the Greek Cypriots who carried out terrorist acts for Eoka in the 1950s could be handled in this way (Makarios went from the Seychelles to Government House in the end), assumptions must have been made that the Irish Question would be solved in time for these men to be rehabilitated like those who survived the firing squads of 1916. It hasn't; and in colloquial terms, the British government of the UK is well and truly lumbered. The one gleam of hope seems to lie in the growing recognition among Irish patriots, both clerical and lay, that the men behind the teen-age terrorists are not like those who founded the Free State; their totalitarianism inclines not towards the theocratic focus that outlawed divorce and contraception but towards a materialist creed that must eventually conflict with Catholicism.

The rôle of the Church in the context of violent crime in Ireland illustrates another dimension of political reality. Until the Reformation the shifting alliance between prince and prelate ensured that, in spite of potential conflict, Church and State were indispensable to one another. The erastian position of the Anglican Church never quite mirrored that relationship since there was no appeal to Rome, and Canterbury, in the last analysis, was the creature of parliament. The Roman Catholic Church established itself again largely on the basis of England's and Scotland's immigrant Irish populations. Roman ecclesiastics were social outsiders. Russell drove through his Ecclesiastical Titles Bill to prevent the possibility of rival archbishops in Canterbury and in this century Dean Inge of St Paul's observed that no Roman priest could be a gentleman. Until very recently the Church has been the Church of the underdog, in England and Scotland no less than in the North of Ireland. But that situation has also featured the phenomenon of authoritarianism.

By that I do not mean the kind of thing that is sometimes confused with *magisterium*; rather I associate it with a mixture of what the American political scientist S.M. Lipset has termed 'working-class authoritarianism' and of that prudish rigidity that not infrequently characterizes the culture of peasant — in this case Irish peasant — society. A generation ago it could be said that the official Catholic Church in England was a Church almost wholly lacking any kind of intellectual dimension. Virtually all Catholic scholarly activity could be found only within the religious orders. Many seminaries offered education and mental stimulus little better than that provided by third-rate secondary schools. The intellectual focus of Catholicism was among the descendants of the recusants and those essentially upper-crust English folk who despised the Irish but were generally too well-bred to say so in public.

Unlike the Church in France, or in most other European countries for that matter, the Church in England was not connected with the universities; hence neither in the areas of law or philosophy nor in those of political and social science was the Church engaged in dialogue about morals with either the agnostic world or the world of unbelief. It was emphasized to me as a boy that my Penny Catechism — now old, dog-eared but still clearly marked 'CTS, Price One Penny' — was all that I needed to guide me through the complex problems that would beset me. Caught reading a translation of *Rerum Novarum* at Mass, I was reproved and told that it was definitely *not* devotional material. Thinking in the Church about problems of crime and punishment, like thinking about social justice, was starved of vitality: the faithful were expected to feed on a miserable diet of intellectual gruel. Among Quakers I found a strong commitment to penal questions. I discovered that an Anglican archbishop, William Temple, had actually concerned himself with prison matters. From the Roman part of Westminster there was nothing but silence.

In a sense the Church of a generation ago was anti-intellectual. The parochial clergy, like the parochial schools, seemed to distrust anyone who sought to go beyond a rote-learned basis for faith. I recall being told that I would 'argue myself out of the Church'. As little as ten years ago I heard a vigorous exhortation from the pulpit not to trust the '. . . tuppeny-ha'penny theologians in the colleges and universities. . .' but to 'read your catechism and listen to the words of our Holy Father, the Pope'. But what is the connection between all this and crime and its treatment?

If the Church was little concerned with the moral philosophy of crime and punishment it was certainly involved in its practical realities. An arrangement with the Home Office meant that all Catholic children who came before the courts and were committed to institutional care were committed directly to Catholic Approved Schools or to children's homes. This was to retain consistency with the provisions for education in Catholic schools. The Catholic schools fell into three broad categories: (i) Catholic public schools, run by the religious orders that catered for the tiniest minority, since so few Catholic families were in the right financial bracket; (ii) day schools, again often run by the religious, again catering for a minority, and taking a good many non-Catholic pupils whose parents felt that convent schools — for girls especially — would make up in gentility what might be lacking in grey matter; and, finally, (iii) parochial schools that catered for the children of the working class who made up the bulk of the Catholic population. I was unhappily plunged for a brief period, by wartime evacuation, into one of these schools 'somewhere in the west Midlands'. I remember even now my horror at the institutionalized violence used by the teachers. They had no illusions about how to deal with offences of any kind. The calling of the Monday Mass register was followed by the caning of those lads who had missed Mass; a boy who had been found in possession of a torn-out page from *Health and Efficiency* (a naive picture of a girl with bare breasts that would nowadays not cause an eyebrow to rise) was obliged to kneel in front of the assembled school, arms outstretched '. . . in the posture endured by our Blessed Saviour'. He got a thrashing too, *pour encourager les autres*.

What was commonplace in the parochial schools was equally well-established in the Catholic Approved Schools. Many Approved Schools habitually used violence against their charges, but at least some of the non-Catholic Schools were open to radical notions like that which suggested that if you went on beating children hard and long enough, and in sufficiently trivial situations, they would become insensitive to violence, and not worry unduly about using it themselves. I would argue that qualitatively the Catholic contribution to practical penology seldom rose above a depressingly low level of mechanistic control. Ironically, in religious education the emphasis was on conformity achieved through constraint; the emphases were on the *avoidance* of sin rather than on *achieving* warm communion with God, and on the negative consequences of his wrath rather than on the potential of his love. It seems small wonder, then, that today, when about a quarter of the prison population of England and Wales is nominally recorded as 'RC', many of those inmates, especially the elderly among them, retain a mechanistic, fearful commitment to what they dimly understand as the Catholic faith. It is, in many cases, a faith of rosaries, medals and other talismans of divine protection; a child-like devotion to Mary as some Great Earth Mother; and a real terror of death beyond a state of grace achieved through auricular confession or the last rites. Of course, more fortunate Catholics must ask themselves if they have not perpetuated the same phenomenon. At least the children in the grimmer parochial schools could look forward to their fourteenth birthdays when the canes, straps and rulers — why *did* so many Irish nuns take such obvious delight in wielding the wooden *ruler* across the back of the hand? — would no longer be able to reach them. Not so fortunate the children in the Approved Schools, for whom release came only at expiry of the court order, which could go on beyond the school-leaving age.

The Approved Schools were kept out of mainstream British education by a hierarchy that feared the pollution of Catholic education by Protestant and other undesirable influences; hence Catholic Approved Schools were quite outside the classification and allocation system that, for all its faults, made a rational contribution to this legacy of nineteenth-century pedagogical penology. Illogically, there were teenage Catholics in Borstals that were *not* sectarian. I never obtained a satisfactory explanation of this. Meanwhile, in prisons the Catholic priest never enjoyed the status of the Anglican chaplain, who was invariably a full-time incumbent. The Catholic priest often had to fit in the prison with the hospital and all the other calls on his ministry.

A clue to what lay behind Catholic penal practice may be found in the words of the Abbé Pétigny in an allocution to the prisoners of the newly-built cellular prison at Versailles, some time in the 1930s: 'I see your cell as no more than a frightful sepulchre where, instead of worms, remorse and despair come to gnaw at you and to turn your existence into a hell in anticipation. But . . . what is for an irreligious prisoner merely a tomb, a repulsive ossuary, becomes, for the sincerely Christian convict, the very cradle of blessed immortality'. The Church that, in pre-industrial times, had seldom if ever questioned what was done to criminals, now went along with the fashion of the times, the penitentiary system. The diffi-culty with the penitentiary system was that, for all the enthusiasms of its advocates, it degenerated into little more than a system of punitive con-tainment. Such is the legacy inherited by the prison systems, not merely of England and Wales but of France, Spain, Italy, many of the German-speaking states and a large part of the western world. Apart from the Scandinavians, who have somehow always ordered things differently, only the Dutch have tackled the problem of prisons with anything like a radical re-appraisal of their function. If corporal punishment was an in-tegral part of penal control, the Church did not question it. Perhaps on account of its anti-intellectual bias it cut itself off, so to speak, from the currents of penal debate.

I find it a matter for rejoicing that things have changed so much, that the Church I was warned I might 'talk myself out of' is a Church 'on the move'. During the debates on capital punishment in 1948, and again in 1966, there was no Catholic voice to be heard. Quakers, yes; many Anglicans, yes; Free Churchmen galore. . . Not so in Britain last year when in the free vote in the Commons Catholic MPs voted against restoration, save for a small number, and even they gave reasoned arguments for their position. True, the hierarchy was silent, but that was probably because the issue of restoring capital punishment was so closely linked to terrorism.

Currently, in Britain the bishops' Social Welfare Commission has a Penal Affairs Sub-Committee whose work looks like going beyond the confines of social welfare for prisoners. Not that the work of groups like the SVP, Catholic Social Service for Prisoners and the Dismas Society are unimportant; but their work must be understood in the context of helping those who need help during and after their encounters with the penal system. There are many questions, part of the total problem of social justice, that need to be posed and answered.

There are grounds for optimism that the days of the well-thrashed Catholic juvenile delinquent are drawing to a close — though conditions in Ireland seem less hopeful. As Catholics get less nervous about being ritually polluted by contact with the ideas of those who perceive the world somewhat differently, though are no less caring about the fate of offenders in particular and mankind in general, so the Church becomes open to fresh ideas. Fears about a dwindling Catholic population must be weighed against the notion of a lean, agile Church, fit for action and the challenges of an increasingly confused world. In general terms the Church is now free in a way in which it has not been for centuries; free from the chafing yoke of partnership with the State; free from an all-pervading sense of defensive inferiority when so many of its members were poor immigrants of Irish stock, openly despised and often the victims of hostility and discrimination.

Without accepting naively positivist criminology, we can still say that crime is one of the most serious social problems in the urban context. We can also say that most of these problems tend to inter-act with and stimulate one another. Look at the city tower blocks standing in their waste lands, the unemployment problems and general wretchedness of the inner city and you have the outlines of the picture. Look too, at alcohol abuse, not of Victorian proportions but still unacceptably commonplace, with all its implications of violence on the streets and wife-and-child battering in the home. Urban planning and the general drift of social policy are central to any agenda for social justice.

But there is much more than the social distribution of welfare to consider. For far too long, welfare policies have been couched in an ideological framework of Fabian origins that has made assumptions about needs rather than choices, and has been as much concerned for the orderly comfort of the State as for the moral identity of individuals — perhaps more so. People with social problems are seen as often the creatures of their environment, without any capacity for moral choice. 'They need help'. Indeed they do, but the problem is a great deal more complicated. Through our system, in which social opportunity is unevenly distributed, some people are never presented with all the information they need to make sensible moral choices. Ignorance of the possibilities and a general inarticulateness often give an impression of moral incapacity.

Thanks to some psychiatrists, punishment has become a dirty word, but it ought to be otherwise. What we must object to is *unjust* punishment. Most of the judiciary, including the lay magistracy, believes that it achieves a reasonable result in attempting to assess what people deserve, but in the total context of justice this may not be so. More poor people than rich come into the ambit of the penal system in one form or another; a disproportionate number of black people find themselves in trouble; and, by and large, the lower the social status of the offender, the more likely he or she is to experience the full rigour of the penal system. Many white-collar offenders manage to pull off successful plea bargains that save the State trouble and expense and result in their being charged with lesser offences. Moreover, once in prison, a high-status offender is very unlucky if he does not find himself in the comparative comfort of an open prison looking forward to an early release on parole.

These manipulations of penal experience by the executive must be challenged in the context of the Church's commitment to natural justice, which reflects divine justice. That justice makes no distinction between rich and poor, or between high and low status. The parole system in particular collides with natural justice since it is wrong not only that a man should be denied knowledge of how long he must remain in prison, or why he cannot be paroled, but that decisions to release should be related to factors over which the prisoner has no control and which cannot be related in any way to his deserts. Parole, of course, is the creature of positivist social policy and an alert Church should be able to expose its inadequacies.

Again, we have a need to consider the question of prisoners' rights. If men are incarcerated *as* and not *for* punishment, what grounds are there for many of the restrictions placed upon those who may be serving very long sentences? Why should they not be able to correspond freely, to have what books they want, typewriters in their cells, and so on? And why, above all, should they be subject to the *kadi* justice of boards of visitors for offences against prison discipline that can result in the effective extension of their sentences? The United Kingdom has not had a very creditable showing at the European Court of Human Rights.

Prisoners' rights — and the frightful riot at Hull Prison and its equally fearful aftermath highlighted the problem — are part of a more general question of human rights in the context of *quis custodiet custodes*? Deaths in police custody, the violent deaths of people like Blair Peach in which the question of any criminal prosecution is already pre-empted by the executive, likewise raise questions that will not go away. These problems must appear on the Church's agenda of questions of social justice.

Last, but by no means least, there is the question of relating statements about right and wrong to the problems, not merely of just desert, but of penitence and forgiveness. Condemnation of crime not only re-affirms the boundaries of tolerable behaviour, but confirms the offender as a being made in the divine image, above the animals and with a capacity to choose, however attenuated. In that neo-Kantian sense, every offender has a *right* to be punished and corresponding right to resist being treated as if he were a hapless sufferer from some social disease. But the punishment must be just, and justice here must be comparative as well as individual. The natural consequences of just punishment must be contrition, and then, restoration. This is the true rehabilitation. What our society seldom permits is such true restoration. It inhibits contrition and generally confuses it with the more common phenomenon of remorse. It is deeply conscious of its secular character and its moral pluralism, so that for the most part it tries to do nothing controversial: that is, nothing which blatantly departs from policies based upon positivist philosophy and utilitarian practice.

Here, it seems to me, lies the great challenge to the Church in Britain and Ireland. It must concern itself not merely with the welfare of offenders but with the processes of criminal justice and penal practice and examine them in the light of, say, that great beacon of wisdom and commonsense, the *Summa*. It must be satisfied that its concern for the treatment of prisoners is no less definitive than its concern for the unborn; and that its awareness of social discrimination in the prosecution process is no less lively than its concerns in the field of race relations. These are no restrictive, academic concerns, but issues that affect Catholic lawyers, judges and magistrates as well as policemen and social workers. Strangely, it is in the courts that one becomes most aware of the near-zero impact of the faith. The courts, sacred places whose rituals and vestments have ecclesial echoes, tend only to hear God's name in the words of the hurried, often unbelieving oath. Eccentrically, I sometimes think that, in Britain at least, instead of *Honi soit Qui Mal y Pense* under the Royal Arms I read: 'You would have no power at all over me, unless it were given you from above.'

The Church and cultural life

DAVID LODGE

THIS ESSAY does not pretend to be anything other than a very personal and impressionistic account of its subject. First, I must define the scope of that subject. 'Culture' can, of course, mean everything that is not nature, the whole reality that men construct by work and play. The specific contribution of the Catholic Church to British cultural life in this broad anthropological sense would, however, be difficult to measure, and difficult to disentangle from the contribution of the Irish as an ethnic group. I take my brief, therefore, to be high culture: the arts and sciences, education in its non-vocational aspect, intellectual life generally — what Matthew Arnold classically described as 'getting to know, on the matters which most concern us, the best which has been thought and said'. By 'Church' I mean the institutional Church, and the activities of men and women significantly motivated by their membership of that Church, even if they act as a kind of internal opposition. Finally, I shall be commenting mainly on the situation in the United Kingdom, and especially England, since such competence as I may have to speak on this subject is limited to my own country.

Within these terms of reference, it seems to me that at the present time the Catholic Church is making little or no distinctive contribution to our cultural life. It has not always been so. The institutional Church, to be sure, has never been much concerned with high culture in these islands, and has often been positively hostile to it. Catholic bishops and priests have not, as a rule, been intellectuals — until recently they were educated in planned isolation from the main centres of academic excellence (the universities) where high culture is nourished and transmitted. They saw their main function as the pastoral care of a predominantly working-class and lower-middle-class community, who needed to be protected from the potentially disturbing influence of modern ideas in the arts and sciences, and drilled in unquestioning obedience to clerical authority. That 'ghetto' Catholicism had its virtues, but openness to the benign influence of culture was not one of them. It was indeed, in Matthew Arnold's sense of the term, philistine (Arnold himself was thinking of the Protestant dissenting community in Victorian England, but as John Bossy has shown, English Catholicism is best understood, sociologically, as a form of Dissent). Its sacred art and architecture were generally in deplorable taste, its standards of liturgical performance were low, its devotional and homiletic language in the vernacular compared unfavourably with the Anglican tradition, and its interest in imaginative literature, drama and film was mainly that of censorship.

If the institutional Church has always been essentially philistine in disposition, however, it is not true to say that Catholicism has made no contribution to British cultural life. On the contrary, in nearly every generation since Catholic Emancipation, there have been Catholic artists, writers and intellectuals, who have made an impact out of all proportion to their actual numbers: the Oxford Movement converts led by John Henry Newman, of whom Gerard Manley Hopkins might be regarded as the last; the Acton-Von Hügel circle of Liberal Catholics in the late nineteenth century; the Catholic artists and writers of the Decadence — Wilde, Beardsley, Dowson, Francis Thompson and many others; the Chesterbelloc in the early decades of the twentieth century; Eric Gill's Guild of Catholic Craftsmen in the inter-war years; the 'Catholic novel' of Graham Greene and Evelyn Waugh in the Forties and Fifties. Most of these figures were converts to Catholicism, and many of them were attracted to the Church precisely by its cultural heritage. But that cultural heritage was Continental European — or, if English, medieval. Catholicism, to most of these men, meant Dante, Aquinas, Gothic cathedrals, Renaissance painting, Baroque architecture, orchestral masses, the organic, pre-industrial society. Or else it meant the splendours and miseries of the spiritual life — dramas of sin and salvation, miracles and mysticism, still amazingly going on in the midst of the drab materialism of modern society. It had relatively little to do with, say, Rosary and Benediction on a Sunday evening at the parish church of an industrial suburb, followed by a meeting of the Legion of Mary and a whist drive organized by the Union of Catholic Mothers.

What I am suggesting is that when Catholics made a distinctive contribution to cultural life in this country in the last one hundred and fifty years, they projected an image of Catholicism as something essentially exotic and/or boldly opposed to the prevailing spirit of the native cultural tradition, whether the latter was seen as liberal-Protestant (in the nineteenth century) or secular-agnostic (in the twentieth). In this respect they were often expressing what had led them to the Church in the first place — a sense of its 'difference', that continued to attract converts until quite recently. Brian Wicker, for instance, in a fascinating fragment of autobiography ('Adult Education', *The Tablet*, Education Supplement, 24 February 1979) describes how, when he was received into the Church in 1950 he felt: 'One was joining something which put a strange gulf between oneself and the world as one knew it': 'I discovered there were people round about me who lived by *vows* (of poverty, celibacy, obedience) so strange and extraordinary that in meeting them I felt I was moving into another world. Until then I had thought only remote people of moral genius, like Tolstoy and Gandhi, lived by renunciations as total as that in the *modern* world. Now I found they existed in absurd places like Birmingham or Peckham Rye. One could actually meet them. What is more, the ordinary Catholic in the street lived a hidden life by which he shared, in his own way, that amazing world. For example by being solemnly committed to attending Mass every Sunday without fail, whatever other so-called "commitments" he might have; by not eating meat on Fridays, though the heavens fall; by actually *fasting* every so often ...'

Brian Wicker himself subsequently became a leading figure in a new phase of the Church's contribution to British cultural life; the emergence in the Fifties and Sixties of what might be called a Catholic New Left. This movement brought together several different groups and interests, which eventually (as is the way of left-wing movements) quarrelled with each other and went their different ways: pacifists, nuclear disarmers, literary crtitics influenced by F.R. Leavis and Raymond Williams, democratic socialists, anti-Stalinist Marxists, and radical theologians. It had a strong base in the universities, especially in adult education. It was indeed essentially critical rather than creative in orientation, and recruited primarily from the educated middle and working classes (for with the 1944 Education Act the mass of Catholics had access to higher education for the first time and, to the dismay of some of the clergy, something like an educated Catholic laity began to form in the post-war period). The movement looked for spiritual and theological inspiration particularly to the English Dominicans, and *New Blackfriars*, under the editorship of Herbert McCabe, was its principal literary organ.

The significant thing about this movement was that for perhaps the first time English Catholics were making a determined bid to present Catholicism not as some kind of refuge from or alternative to a social and political order seen as irredeemably secular, but as a basis for transforming that order: not an escape from history but a positive intervention in it. The attempt was a brave one, but it failed, and the article by Brian Whicker cited above is in some respects a requiem for it — and for the challenging unworldliness of the Catholic Church he had himself joined. The advent of Pope John XXIII, and his call to *aggiornamento*, created a climate propitious to change, but in the event the need to fight the battle on two fronts simultaneously — within the Church and outside it — proved too much for the Catholic New Left. Perhaps, too, the theoretical basis of the movement was always too shallow, improvised and heterogeneous. Some of the leading figures in the movement have left the Church (or the priesthood); others have remained, but grown less vocal; some have become more conservative. In many ways the history of the Catholic New Left has reflected the general fate of radical utopian movements in the developed countries in the Sixties and Seventies ('Catholic Marxism' has proved a more viable development in the Third World, where it answers to more concrete and urgent socio-economic questions).

If the present situation is one in which the Catholic Church does not represent any distinctive force in the nation's cultural life, this is not because there are fewer Catholic artists and intellectuals about, but because their work is not defined, by themselves or by observers, in terms of their religious affiliation. How many know, for instance, that Michael Dummett, Wykeham Professor of Logic at Oxford, is a Catholic? Time was, such an appointment would have provoked much throwing of caps in the air by Catholics, and perhaps raising of eyebrows by non-Catholics. The Present Minister for the Arts, Norman St John Stevas, is a well-known Catholic layman, but (quite properly) his policy is not seen to be in any way conditioned by his religious affiliation, any more than the policy of the Catholic Minister of Education in the preceding Government, Shirley Williams, was by hers. As for the institutional Church, it has in Cardinal Hume a leader who is probably more genuinely cultured than any since the days of Wiseman and Manning (and considerably more amiable than either of those two prelates), and the preservation of such artistic assets as the Church in England possesses, such as Westminster Cathedral and its choir, are more secure for his presence. The training of the secular clergy nowadays usually makes some kind of gesture towards 'liberal studies', and through television, and the relaxation of the old prohibitions against attendance at theatres and cinemas, the clergy are more in touch with contemporary culture today than ever before. But culturally, as politically, the Church keeps a low profile; it does not speak with any distinctive voice on such subjects, as it does, for instance, in France or the Netherlands.

As a writer and critic myself, I am particularly struck by this absence in the field of contemporary literature. Mr Greene, of course, still goes on writing with amazing fertility of invention and undiminished interest in metaphysical questions; but from *A Burnt-out Case* onwards his novels have become progressively more sceptical, ambiguous and inconclusive in their theological import: whereas the protagonists of the novels of his middle period were saved or damned by the certainty of their religious faith, those of the later books tend to be wry, disillusioned humanists who can raise only a wistful hope in the possibility of a transcendental world of truth and justice. Muriel Spark, who begun her career as a novelist under the generous patronage of Mr Greene, looked at first as if she would develop the tradition of the 'Catholic novel' in her own way: the tone of *The Comforters* and *The Prime of Miss Jean Brodie* was lighter and more playful than that of the *Heart of the Matter* and *Brideshead Revisited*,

but there was the same stark contrast between human folly and vanity on
the one hand and the mysterious ways of God on the other. As she has
gone on writing, however, Mrs Spark's stories — technically works of
great originality — have become morally more ambiguous, 'blacker' in
their comedy, and more tolerant of egoists and opportunists who pursue
their own ends with a certain style.

Both these novelists, it is perhaps worth remarking, live abroad, as
does Anthony Burgess, who had a Catholic upbringing and, to judge
from a recent interview with Graham Greene (*Observer*, 16 March 1980)
regards himself as some kind of Catholic. None of these three writers
(who would come high on anyone's list of distinguished living English
novelists) seems to have any great enthusiasm for, or interest in, the
practical effects of Vatican II on Catholic liturgy, devotional practice
and general life-styles, both clerical and lay. Indeed, my own novel *How
Far Can You Go?* (1980) is, to my knowledge, the first novel to deal directly with that phenomenon in an English context. Brian Moore's *Catholics*
(1972) was a polemical fable set in the near future deploring the
demystification of liturgy and doctrine in modern Catholicism by
celebrating a remote Irish outpost of resistance to it. The most popular
and successful fictional works with a Catholic content in recent years
have both been broadly comic, more or less nostalgic treatments of pre-
Conciliar Catholicism: Mary O'Malley's long-running play *Once a
Catholic* and Neil Boyd's 'Bless Me Father' stories with their TV series
spin-off. It seems odd that the great British public should be tickled by
these evocations of a now obsolete Catholicism; but it is less surprising
that the post-conciliar Church has not provided the climate for a
Catholic cultural renaissance.

The fact is that contemporary Catholicism no longer constitutes the
kind of unified, sharply defined challenge to secular or Protestant values
that it once did, and thus no longer provides an organizing principle or
rallying-point for intellectual and artistic programmes. It is, I believe, a
much more decent, humane, open-minded Christian community than it
once was, but it is also rather blander, duller, and more amorphous. As
a result of the upheaval of Vatican II, we have now a pluralistic kind of
Church, which resembles Anglicanism much more than would have
seemed possible twenty or thirty years ago, in which radicals and con-
sevatives, demythologizing theologians and charismatics, can all find a
corner to do their thing with like-minded people — who may not be
Catholics at all. As I write, there is in progress an attempt by conservative forces in the Vatican to take advantage of Pope John Paul II's
forceful, personality and ecclesiastical conservatism to call the Church to
order, and exert some of the old authoritarian discipline. They may
make — they already have made — things uncomfortable for the more
progressive clergy, but in my own opinion they will not succeed in

reversing the general tendency of the Church towards pluralism and ecumenism — a tendency now well established in the Catholic periodical press (English Catholicism has something to pride itself on here, incidentally — I cannot think of any other Christian community in this country that produces a weekly review and two monthly reviews of the quality of the *Tablet*, *New Blackfriars* and *The Month*).

If I am right, the prospect of a specifically Catholic (as distinct from Christian) contribution to British cultural life and cultural debate is likely to recede still further. I cannot bring myself to feel great distress or regret at this state of affairs. I am, admittedly, biassed towards the *verbal* manifestations of High Culture. Words cannot but *mean*, and meanings are always potentially subversive and threatening to orthodoxy. The fine and practical arts — music, painting, sculpture, architecture, design — are less trammelled by semantics, and have always thrived more happily in partnership with the institutional Church. It may be that practitioners of these arts would deplore more vigorously than I the philistinism of English (and Irish) Catholicism in these fields — its failure, with a few exceptions, to act as patron for the best in contemporary art. But as writer and academic, I would rather work in a pluralist secular state than in one in which the Church played a dominant or militant cultural rôle. History suggests that the rôle of the literary intellectual in the latter situation is not an easy one.

Ecumenism

ALAN CLARK

1. Origins

EVER SINCE the Roman Catholic Church formally entered the ecumenical movement with the promulgation of the *Decree on Ecumenism (Unitatis Redintegratio)* at the second Vatican Council on 21 November, 1964, the pursuit of Christian unity has emerged in official teaching, particularly at the highest level, as one of the most important priorities of the Church's mission. Reference can be made to the considerable number of papal addresses over the past fifteen years in which this priority has been strongly emphasized; and, through a whole series of directives from the *Secretariat for the Promotion of Christian Unity*, local hierarchies have been urged to encourage such initiatives as were judged to be of particular service in the development of attitudes and reflections that would convince people everywhere of their necessary involvement in the search for the unity 'for which Christ prayed'. The Council had defined the movement in somewhat abstract terms as 'those activities and enterprises which, according to the various needs of the Church and opportune occasions, are started and organized for the fostering of unity among Christians' (*UR*, n.4). This rather meagre description has long ago yielded to the reality of a concerted effort on the part of Christians everywhere, even though the path has been strewn with failures and disappointment, and even if it seems to human eyes that the goal of unity is still hidden in the future, to persevere in constructing the road to reconciliation after centuries of enmity and division.

However, it would be quite unrealistic to suggest that the Catholic community at large has given an enthusiastic response to this summons to regard the work for Christian unity as of the highest importance. The unevenness of the response in these islands is no different from elsewhere. The lack of total commitment is as real, for example, in Britain and Ireland as in the United States or Canada. The reason, moreover, is not difficult to understand. The doctrine embodied in the *Decree* challenged a wide set of assumptions which had been, over a long period, the basis of the prevailing Catholic attitude to other Christian Churches. However close family ties and individual friendships involving members of different denominations, all the *Churches* they represented were 'separated from one another' in a definitive manner, with overtones of distrust and accusations of erroneous doctrine and

practice — inherited, let it be said, from the violent polemics of the
Reformation period and handed on, somewhat uncritically, to succeeding generations. If Christians from another Church became convinced of the truth of the uncompromising claims of Catholicism, then it
was taken for granted that, completely dissociating themselves from
their former allegiance, they would totally 'submit' to the Church they
then entered.

In an earlier period this was, of course, also true regarding movement
between other Christian Churches. But in the post-war years, the
climate radically changed. The beginnings of closer relationships between these Churches could not fail to have its repercussions on the
Catholic Church, and, in any case, a movement had already started
among Catholic theologians to investigate the 'problem of unity'. But,
as is well-known, the ecumenical movement itself originated outside the
latter. The *Faith and Order Conference* at Edinburgh in 1910 is usually
regarded as the year 'when it all began'. With the first meeting of the
newly formed *World Council of Churches* at Amsterdam in 1948, the
aspirations of the 'Protestant Churches' of the West (not to mention the
partial involvement of the Orthodox Churches of the East in the growing
movement for unity) could not fail to lead Roman Catholics to ask questions about their own position, however secure their faith. The question
never was, nor ever has been, whether Catholics belong to the one, true
Church of Christ. Nothing in the remarkable development of doctrine
consequent on the decrees of the second Vatican Council has altered that
essential faith. What is at issue in the ecumenical debate is the relationship to other Christian Churches, whose members by baptism belong to
the Body of Christ and are thereby open to the grace of salvation, and in
a real relationship with the visible Church. For no serious theologian
could subscribe to the idea, which had its vogue in the past and continues into the present, that, while Christians are united invisibly in
Christ, they are free to express this unity in whatever visible form they
consider consonant with the Gospel. In essence, that is an argument for
the *status quo* and hostile to true ecumenism. The pursuit of unity means
what it says — the visible unity of all Christian Churches and communities in full communion with one another, even though the exact
nature and form of this future unity still eludes our comprehension.

But what has become clear, in the light of Vatican II, is that the so-
called 'exclusivist' claim of the Roman Catholic Church, once *ecclesial*
status is conceded to other Christian Churches and communities, is no
longer tenable. It is sufficient for the purposes of this article to leave this
statement as it stands, for it emphasizes the profoundly doctrinal and
theological questions that Catholics had suddenly to face. Questions of
history also re-surfaced. Were new answers demanded? How far, for example, had the schism of the sixteenth century destroyed the unity of the

Church? It is little wonder that Catholics felt they had lost that security which had always been regarded as one of the most precious treasures of their faith.

But developments in and outside the Catholic Church could not be ignored, particularly when the pursuit of Christian unity was seen as intimately linked to that total renewal of the Church preached and proclaimed by the Vatican Council. It was as though the whole Christian community, however divided, read for the first time and began for the first time to understand the *Prayer of Christ*: 'that they may be one' (John 17). The words of the Lord of the Church reverberated incessantly in the ears, and reached the hearts, of those who professed their faith in Christ and in the unique significance of the salvation he brought to the whole of mankind. Towards the end of the Sixties, the first positive signs of a willingness to obey the inherent summons to unity began to emerge in public view. The work, painful and laborious though it appeared, was recognized to be the work of the Holy Spirit. Practical means were evolved to demonstrate the involvement of the Catholic community in the enterprise. But doctrinal questions regarding the nature and mission of the Church dominated the developing co-operation between the Churches — at least as it touched Catholic involvement. Not only the question 'What is the Church?' but the more unsettling question 'Where is the Church?' could not be laid aside indefinitely. At the same time, the question of Christian belief and its proclamation to a 'secular' world entered into the heart of ecumenical relationships. Considerable tensions threatened the inner unity of the Catholic Church in Britain.

But, if we consider the overall impact of the ecumenical movement on all the Christian Churches, it is worthwhile to note the enormous value of this British experience to Churches in other countries. For, though elsewhere there was the same commitment to the universal goal of unity, the same cultural and historical obstacles were not felt with the same force. If the British Churches seemed to be moving at an unjustifiably slow pace, the explanation is to be found, whatever other factors were involved, in a growing awareness of the implications of the second part of the *Prayer of Christ* 'that they may be one *in order that the world may believe*'. The importance of promoting a common witness to the Gospel was recognized from the start: the ground was prepared for the reception of Paul VI's great encyclical, *Evangelii nuntiandi*.

The question, however, that needs to be asked and answered is: how did the Roman Catholic community fare in this enterprise? Even though there was a slow start, we can honestly say: remarkably well! There is no complacency here, for much more could have been achieved with more informed local leadership, more readiness, particularly among priests, to be open to new approaches. It was not by any means only the older generation that resisted ecumenical developments. Continental

ecumenists, to whom so much is due for their depth of *theological* thinking, have not always appreciated the traumatic experience of British
Catholics and have, at times, unwarrrantably by-passed the cautious
judgments (and disciplines) of authorities here.

However, it is equally possible to exaggerate the 'deleterious' effects
of such interventions from abroad. For the ecumenical movement finds
its place in the universal life of the Church and the problems of one
country impinge on similar problems in other countries. In fact, it is
precisely the catholicity of the Roman Catholic Church that has had a
pervasive influence on the attitudes of British Catholics, and, in particular, on their attachment to the Bishop of Rome as the centre of communion. Here was a problem, but the wiser saw it as an opportunity of
offering to other Churches a vision of what could be. It says much for
our brethren in these Churches that, though they have found us uncomfortable partners in an enterprise marked by national preoccupations,
they have been willing to understand our specifically Catholic insistence
on the universal character of Christ's Church. It had, after all, enabled
Catholics to accept, albeit not without a minority conscientiously objecting, revolutionary changes in the liturgy. It had turned them away from
over-preoccupation with the inward life of the Church to the world
where violence and injustice were reaching ugly proportions. In this re-
appraisal of the Church's mission, ecumenical links were forged with the
other Christian Churches some of which, it needed to be noted, had
always shown a deep social concern that bore the hallmark of the Gospel.
From the beginning, the pursuit of unity retained a pragmatism rooted
in a profound, perhaps unconscious, understanding of the Incarnation,
in the realization that no human experience is exempt from redemptive
grace. In such areas the grace of ecumenism has been present for a long
time.

But doctrinally? This has been and remains the most difficult context
for British and Irish Catholics in their efforts at ecumenical understanding. It has been said that the doctrinal justification for ecumenism has
failed to convince the Catholic community at large. Even if this is true,
the reasons for it are not to be limited to the relatively few pages of the
Decree on Ecumenism. The total impact of the Council's teaching is involved. But, for the sake of the historical record, it needs to be remembered
that the involvement of the Catholic Church was prompt and persevering. It may well be that for a long period Catholics had honestly
recognized the goodness and the devotion of their fellow Christians to
the person of Christ and so, without being formally aware of it, had
acknowledged the momentous shift in the teaching of the second Vatican
Council — that the centre of communion is Christ rather than the
Roman Catholic Church. It remains true, of course, that Christ and his
Church are so intimately (and sacramentally) linked that a unique place

in the history of salvation must be accorded to the latter. But the shift occurred.

So, even before 1970, the Catholic Church was committed to a doctrinal dialogue with the Anglican Communion (resulting from the historic visit of Archbishop Ramsey of Canterbury to Pope Paul VI in 1966), and had established, as one of the first commissions of the Episcopal Conference of England and Wales, the *Commission for Ecumenism*. Since then a parallel dialogue has been entered into with the Methodist Church, and at the moment of writing steps are being taken to promote permanent conversations with the conservative Evangelicals whose absence from Malines effectively blocked the success of that courageous initiative. It is, perhaps, worth noting that a *local* ecumenical commission exists in every Catholic diocese in the country and is linked to the national commisssion.

From the first it was recognized that the *re*-establishment of communion (the title of the *Decree* is significant here: *Unitatis redintegratio*) between Churches separated from one another at the level of doctrine and life, required the acknowledgment that the Holy Spirit does the work of salvation not only in the invididual but in the Churches *as Churches*. In other words, the Catholic community had to take seriously the particular traditions of Churches with which it was not in communion. This defect of communion could never be total, for baptismal unity binds all Christians together in the one body of Christ. Hence the introduction into conciliar doctrine of the notion of 'imperfect or partial communion'. Where, it was asked, were the deficiencies which prevented our reconciliation? On the principle that nothing should be taken for granted by any of the participants, dialogue, at the level of faith, became the characteristic instrument of developing ecumenical fellowship. It could not be assumed, for example, that one baptism signified an identical faith. Catholics found it difficult to adjust to the idea that perhaps their fellow Christians, in their enunciation of the truths of faith, were in substantial agreement, even though their formulation was different. But again, this could not be taken for granted either way, and this delicate and patient enterprise suffered not a little from a tendency of some ecumenists to precipitate action, without waiting for anomalies and even apparent contradictions to be resolved.

The experience of the Anglican-Roman Catholic International Commisssion, set up in 1969, is typical and representative of the many dialogues undertaken throughout the Christian world. The doctrinal agenda of this commission centred on three basic controversies of the Reformation: the Eucharist, ministry and authority. The resulting documents have already become classics of their kind. Substantial agreement has been claimed for their conclusions which urge that both communions can speak with one voice on these central dogmas of Christian faith. Yet total agreement has escaped the commission, leaving open and unresolved the question as to what degree of agreement in faith is required for the way to be open to reconciliation. In any case, these 'theological' documents do not have an immediate impact on the situation at *local* level — where Christians 'find the Church'. What is needed is practical, prayerful and trusting co-operation at this level and structures to consolidate it.

2. Local and National ecumenism

Here one must acknowledge a debt of magnitude to the steady, almost unrelenting, concentration of the mainstream Churches in Britain on the discovery and implementation of local and national structures of unity. The Catholic community, though for the most part not privy to the first steps, has to a greater or lesser degree, *responded* to such initiatives. Though the Catholic Church is not yet a full member of the British Council of Churches, there has been real Catholic participation in this valuable forum of ecumenical activity, particularly at divisional level. Moreover, Catholics are to be found as full members of a large number of local councils of Churches or equivalent bodies.

But a significant step was taken when the Catholic Church became a full participant in the Churches' Unity Commission, in the aftermath of the breakdown of the Anglican-Methodist scheme of union. Even though unable to accept the central propositions which demanded, above other things, the full recognition of other Churches' ministries (involving the acceptance of 'interchangeability' of ministers at the Eucharist), the continuing participation of the Catholic Church signified it was resisting pressures to withdraw at national level. The CUC evolved into the CCC — the Churches' Council for Covenanting — in which a new approach to inter-church relationships is being explored. Although success has not yet been achieved, the central 'idea' has already inspired many local churches and congregations to enter into a partnership, particularly in the field of mission, which uses the instrument of a local covenant to seal this co-operation. Catholics are partners to some few of the three hundred or so local ecumenical projects that exist (and are full members of the central advisory body for such projects), but, for the same reason that we register hesitancy *vis-à-vis* schemes of union which leave unresolved 'faith and order' issues of major importance, so we argue for greater flexibility in the type of covenant envisaged.

3. Prayer

Structures of unity, directed to united Christian action, have a solid importance in the development of the ecumenical movement. But the heart of all ecumenism remains *prayer*. Nothing can replace the centrality of prayer. Unity is grace, the gift of the Holy Spirit, which will be given according to the will of Christ; but, as members of his body savaged by the wound of division, we have to open our hearts to receive it — at whatever cost. This *spiritual ecumenism* has, of course, found a permanent place in the life of the Christian Churches in the Week of Prayer for Christian Unity celebrated at the end of January each year. It may be a certain weariness has set in. As Trevor Beeson remarked, not without a certain acidity: 'Prayer is not designed to rouse a lethargic God to action but to change the consciences of those who pray, so that they will become more active in bringing about what they discern to be God's will. Without much clarity and commitment the January exercise in prayer will degenerate into a Week of Christian Hypocrisy' (*The Guardian*, 26.1.80). Whatever defects there are in the coming together of Christians to pray and worship *publicly* during this particular week, the facts have shown a widespread willingness to accept Pope John XXIII's basic premiss — that without such prayer there will be no grace of *metanoia*, that inner repentance for sin and that change of heart without which no one can hope either to understand or to undertake the work of ecumenism. The anomaly of Christians kneeling and worshipping together and then going their separate ways has emphasized painfully the reality of division, and underlined the evil of our disunities. But this has only reinforced the obligation to continue to devote ourselves to prayer.

Catholic insistence on this spiritual ecumenism has enabled the ecumenical movement to withstand the constant charge, both from within and from without, that nothing has been achieved, or that what has been achieved has been only at the cost of the 'watering down of faith' and the acceptance of compromise in moral principle and practice. It is within the context of prayer for unity that many Catholics have 'changed their mind' and lived with their fears about what ecumenical initiatives might involve. This fear of loss of identity is not confined to the Catholic community; it is one of the painful experiences of members of all the Christian Churches whose prayer leads them to a vision of what Christ's will entails and to a counting of the costs.

Many hoped that the charismatic renewal would give great sustenance to the ecumenical movement. In some respects, this hope has been realized; the charismatic renewal cannot fail to be ecumenical when solidly grounded in prayer. But it, too, has not been able to resolve the serious problem of relating fully to the *institutional* Church its own experience at local and individual level. At the level of common Christian action, however, a creditable success story could be written up. The social gospel has its detractors, but at long last most people realize that common action in the cause of justice and peace, in the promotion of care and common concern for the deprived, is a gospel work — one which forges bonds where other areas of ecumenism make no impact.

4. *Fears*

The whole area of ecumenical initiative and co-operation has uncovered a mass of fears and anxieties for Catholics (the same is true in other Christian Churches). The basic difficulty is ecclesiological — which is only one way of saying that ecumenical doctrine appears to challenge the fundamental identity of the Catholic Church. This accounts for a continuing resistance which, however, the actual realities of the situation have done much to weaken. It has, for example, become clear that no one can work consistently in this new and, in many respects, undefined field without a much deeper commitment to his or her own faith — to his or her own Church. The Catholic ecumenist has to be a better Catholic if he or she is to be an effective ecumenist.

5. *Intercommunion*

From time to time, not surprisingly, the ecumenical movement reaches an impasse. The classic case is the question of *intercommunion*. It is surely understandable that the greater the 'communion' between Christians, the stronger the desire to be able to communicate eucharistically together. The official Catholic position is well-known: that eucharistic communion and ecclesial communion go together. At the same time, the Council recognized that Holy Communion can sometimes be the means for promoting unity not yet achieved. The question is how and when? Some Catholics, particularly those in *inter-church marriages*, sensitive to the pain caused by the prohibition, have felt in conscience that, *as individuals*, they should be free, at times, to go beyond what the official discipline permits.

The question is too complex to be argued out in this summary of Catholic attitudes to ecumenical dilemmas and anomalies. Even though such a relaxation would not resolve the issue of *intercommunion*, involving reciprocity, many are arguing that now is the time to open up further our altars to Christians of other Churches who approach the Blessed Sacrament with right faith. At the present moment, official discipline restricts this *admission* to limited cases.

But others would argue that more will be achieved by increasing 'communion' (*koinonia*) between our respective communities: that is, by common prayer, common witness and common care. The pain of separation at the altar is part of the cross of ecumenism and needs to be accepted. This realism has, one feels, more to commend it.

6. *Results*

As we enter this next decade, Catholics, in fact all the Christian Churches, need to know where we stand now. It seems best, by way of response, to venture on a summary list of the apparent results of ten years of humble, persevering work:

(i) The Christian Churches in Britain have become one *Community of Reconciliation*; in other words, a certain unity, however fragile, has been achieved. This unity, though not the final goal of the ecumenical movement, emphasizes the fact that the pursuit of unity is the constant preoccupation of the mainstream Churches in our countries and can point to positive results (such as have been noted in the course of this article).

(ii) The possibility of a certain pluralism has been accepted. Unity — organic unity — does not imply uniformity. There is perhaps a real need for a new creed which will affirm the essentials of Christian faith held in common and *publicly* accepted by the Churches, particularly a common belief in the nature of Christ's Church.

(iii) The temptation to withdraw and opt for some form of stable practical co-operation in the face of the struggle to reach agreement on 'faith and order' has not always been resisted successfully.

(iv) Catholics still need to be convinced that the renewal of the Church entails a whole-hearted commitment to the solid, practical pursuit of unity.

(v) But, at the end of this survey, it seems clear that the path has ben 'indicated' — *reconciliation* at every level of the Church's life and a real co-operation in a new evangelization of our country and of the world.

Theology

FERGUS KERR, OP

HANS KÜNG, to judge by print orders and sales, is by far the most widely read Catholic theologian in Britain and Ireland. Those who are alarmed by the thought may take comfort from the fact that his Catholic readers are, by and large, an informed and critical group who are quite capable of making a discriminating judgment for themselves on what they read.

Theology is primarily an oral pursuit. We enjoy a relatively high level of theological argument in the various parts of these islands. The quality of theological education in the seminaries, for instance, is as fine as anywhere else in Europe. The proliferation of conference centres, parish discussion groups and suchlike institutions, while certainly involving only a minority, nevertheless confirms the existence of many theologically-minded Catholics. The number of university graduates in theological subjects, women as well as lay men, rises every year. A high standard of theological journalism is maintained by *The Tablet* and the various monthlies, precarious as their financial support mostly is. Nobody could read the back numbers of *The Furrow* or *The Clergy Review* for the past ten or twenty years without coming to respect such consistent success in making good Catholic theology accessible. A great editor like the late Canon J.G. McGarry contributes far more than any erudite scholar or controversial thinker to maintaining and spreading a critical and articulate approach to theological matters.

Looking back from 1980, however, one notes a considerable decline, since the years of the Vatican Council, in the volume and the vigour of such theological writing. In the 1960s it seemed as though a whole new generation of young theological voices had been raised, partly no doubt simply to communicate to us what was happening in the Catholic Church at large, since we had been so isolated from the wider international movements, but mainly to make our own distinctive contribution to the changes of perspective and structure that were at last perceived to be possible. Translations of Karl Rahner, Yves Congar, Hans Küng, Edward Schillebeeckx, and many others, of course dominated the relatively small Catholic theological market. But with young priests like Charles Davis, Herbert McCabe and Nicholas Lash, as well as lay writers such as Brian Wicker, Hugo Meynell and Rosemary Haughton, a distinctively 'British' approach appeared to be in the making.[1] What was distinctive could not be captured in a phrase, but the main factor was the attempt to rethink perennial theological matters with the critical and analytical tools provided by contemporary English philosophy and literary studies. Such seminal figures as Wittgenstein and Leavis stood in the background, representing intellectual concerns and approaches that were certainly quite unknown in France or Germany then.

With a tradition of theological symposia that goes back to 1952, Downside Abbey sponsored, or anyway spawned, an increasingly important series of books which should certainly be mentioned. Avenues were opened up, and, in much that was ephemeral, such theological journalism helped to create the no doubt small but nevertheless critical and reflective theological community here.

On the other hand, writing and publishing learned and controversial books is an essential element of theological activity. It is mainly through scholarly quarterlies and by publishing such works of learning and of constructive thinking that the intellectual and academic tradition of any particular region contributes to movements of thought, and to long-term changes of policy and attitude, in the wider field of the Catholic Church as a whole. Judged by this measure, Britain and Ireland are a quiet backwater, offering very little that makes any stir in currents of thought in the wider Catholic world. We must prescind from the Irish diaspora: many Irish theologians are to be found working, more or less voluntarily, in great Catholic institutions in Rome and Jerusalem as well as in various parts of the English-speaking world. At home, however, with about twice as many Catholics as there are in Holland, and with not far short of half as many as there are in West Germany, the Irish and British Catholic communities together seem, in comparison with such hot-beds of theological activity, extraordinarily and inexplicably unproductive.

B.C. Butler, then abbot-president of the English Benedictines, was the only theologian from these islands to play a significant part at Vatican II. As a matter of fact, the bishops who represented England and Ireland at Vatican I, a hundred years earlier, included several who were more scholarly, and certainly more forceful in their theological views (on both sides of the infallibility debate), than any one in either hierarchy appeared to be at Vatican II.

Vatican II was bad luck for some major scholarly projects. Weeks before his death in 1975, for example, Thomas Gilby was able to send off to the printers the last of the sixty volumes of the new English translation of the *Summa Theologiae* of St Thomas Aquinas which he initiated in 1958. His team of translators and commentators was drawn from Australia and the United States as well as from Britain and Ireland. Several of the volumes anticipate the new approach to the classical theology of Aquinas which is bound to come sooner or later; but many of them do little more than echo the sort of neo-Thomism to which Vatican II theology put and end.

Again, three of the projected four volumes of *A Catholic Dictionary of Theology* have appeared, the first in 1962 and the third in 1971. Despite noble efforts to incorporate the results of the Council the work as a whole has clearly been stranded by the unexpectedly radical and diversified shift of Catholic sensibility and consciousness. Unfailingly erudite, though increasingly fractious, this is another monument to a generation of fine scholars caught at a watershed.

The *New Catholic Commentary on Holy Scripture* appeared in 1969, but was immediately overshadowed by the American Catholic *Jerome Biblical Commentary*. The rapidly accelerating pace of Catholic biblical studies in Germany, France, the United States and in Rome makes much of it seem defensive and apologetic.

Biblical studies, however, have become irreversibly ecumenical. A glance through the current Blackwell's theology and church history catalogue soon shows that no British or Irish Catholic scholar has produced a biblical commentary that would stand comparison with Raymond Brown's on the fourth gospel or with any standard Anglican work. But perhaps this no longer matters. Bibliographies in seminaries, like book-lists at study-groups and conferences, prove that Protestant biblical scholarship is now the staple of Catholic scriptural formation here. The Protestant scholarship upon which British and Irish students are now relying is a good deal more conservative and traditional than much foreign Catholic exegesis.

The only major contributions to biblical scholarship by English students recently have been, no doubt by coincidence, impressively detailed defences of traditionally Roman Catholic positions. *The Mother of Jesus in the New Testament*, by John McHugh, makes a good case for the biblical foundation of Mariology. The revival of the Griesbach hypothesis by Bernard Orchard promises to be the most massive attempt yet to show that Matthew is the earliest gospel after all — which would shake a good deal of modern exegesis of the gospels.

Martin McNamara, on the other hand, has broken new ground altogether. As a member of Stanislas Lyonnet's circle at the Biblical Institute in Rome he was among the first to bring renewed study of the Aramaic Targums to bear on the New Testament. His most recent work, in even more uncharted territory, investigates medieval Irish biblical exegesis.

Rome and another great Jesuit scholar, I. Ortiz de Urbina, provided the original setting and stimulus for the most important recent contribution by an English Catholic to patristic studies: Robert Murray's *Symbols of Church and Kingdom* is not only a beautiful study of early Syriac Christian writers but also an approach to questions about the relationship between poetry and theology which will only become more relevant as time passes.

Studies of Liturgy, which appeared in 1978, and will remain the standard textbook for many years to come, was co-edited by Edward Yarnold. This is the most striking evidence to date that Catholics, even in a denominational minefield like liturgiology, have become fully ecumenical. Nobody would dream of producing a rival handbook by Roman Catholic scholars alone.

Turning now to the history of doctrine, and to systematic theology (moral theology is dealt with in a subsequent chapter), we reach subjects and disciplines which are much more difficult to treat ecumenically.

The absence of systematic theology in England has often been regarded as one of the virtues of Anglicanism. The lack of servility to any theological 'system' has even been presented as evidence of the undogmatic and empirical nature of the 'English mind'. The paucity of important work in systematic theology by Roman Catholics in England might afford evidence of their 'Englishness' but for the fact that neither Irish nor Scottish Catholicism has much to show in the way of constructive dogmatic theology.

In practice, no doubt, we rely on translations of Karl Rahner when we want to stimulate reflection. It is perhaps even more important that Bernard Lonergan has been the principal influence on a whole generation of seminary professors, in Ireland even more than in Britain. The finest interpretation of Vatican II ecclesiology has come from B.C. Butler. The most substantial studies of doctrinal development and related questions have come from Nicholas Lash. Both of them refer with gratitude to Lonergan's influence on them.

The impact of New Testament studies upon our understanding of Jesus has encouraged many theologians recently to rethink the classical doctrines of Catholic Christology (with more or less success). James Mackey, the expatriate Irish theologian, wrote just such an essay while he was teaching in California, which appeared about the same time last year as he became professor of divinity at Edinburgh University.

In fact, if we have any theologians in the mature forties who have actually demonstrated that they might one day make further important contributions to the renewal of systematic theology (a desideratum, I take it, for Catholics), nobody else comes to mind but Nicholas Lash and James Mackey. It is not a coincidence that, as laicized priests, they have the background as well as the personal and academic freedom to be capable of serving the Catholic Church in this way. Ironically enough, according to the present decrees of the Roman dicasteries, neither would be permitted to teach in a Catholic institution.

This survey cannot pretend to be exhaustive, but three growing edges of Catholic theological studies should be mentioned.

In the first place we must note the publication of the letters and papers of John Henry Newman. This great project will always be associated

with the name of the late Stephen Dessain. Unlike the projects mentioned earlier, it had the good fortune to overlap with Vatican II, the Council at which many of Newman's ideas came into their own, and which
thus stimulated further study of his work. On the theological side,
important books on different aspects of Newman's work have been
published by such scholars as John Coulson, Nicholas Lash, Placid
Murray and P.J. FitzPatrick (whose *Apologia pro Kingsley*, to my impious
mind, is the best of them).

Secondly, stemming from the research and teaching of Walter
Ullmann, there is what has come to be known as the 'Cambridge school'
of historians such as Brian Tierney and Antony Black (but they are not
all Catholics), particularly concerned with the papacy and the councils of
the Middle Ages. Such studies are obviously of less interest to the
average reader than Newman's work. Indeed, they are of little concern
to the average student of theology. But they raise questions about the
structure of power in the Roman Catholic Church, and history often
illuminates dogma. The doctrine of collegiality inscribed in the texts of
Vatican II, for example, is a reaffirmation of the true values in conciliarism. Certainly, as the Catholic Church draws nearer to full communion with the Orthodox such researches into medieval institutions
and canon law will become increasingly relevant.

Joseph Gill's studies of the Council of Florence should also be noted.
But anybody who follows trends in Catholic theology by reading the
leading international periodicals knows that the work of the Cambridge
School is by far the most frequently quoted theological achievement in
recent years in these islands.

The third growth area, again largely confined to England, is the very
healthy state of the philosophy of religion, or what used to be called
natural theology. This is predominantly the work of lay men and
women. With Elizabeth Anscombe in Wittgenstein's old chair at Cambridge, and now that Michael Dummett has succeeded A.J. Ayer at
Oxford, it might be thought that Catholic theology stood in a privileged
position to gain from the best of contemporary British philosophy. It
does not seem to be the case. Hugo Meynell has linked Lonergan to the
British philosophical tradition, while Peter Geach shows how the most
traditional Catholic theology, and Aquinas in particular, may be
rethought with the vigour of a mind trained on Frege. But on the whole
these first-rate philosophers stand apart from the local theologians. The
two groups even regard each other with a certain suspicion. This failure
of communication extends well beyond the Roman Catholic community, however, since there is little evidence that *any* theologians have
assimilated the most characteristic virtues of modern British philosophy.
The most that may be said is perhaps that the existence of analytical
philosophy frightens theologians from undertaking metaphysical specu-

lation. The philosophers, on their side, seem remarkably immune from the queries and disquiets about classical Catholic theology that afflict the theologians.

In short, while translations of Karl Rahner, Hans Küng, Edward Schillebeeckx, and so on, continue to appear, the distinctively English generation of theological writers of the 1960s has faded away. This cannot be unconnected with the substantial number of young priest-writers who ceased to practise the ordained ministry in the aftermath of the encyclical *Humanae vitae* and, more importantly, because of intellectual and institutional frustrations. But in Ireland, with the unprecedented affluence of the Lemass years, and an apparently far more united and contented Church, little substantial theological writing has appeared. It may well be argued that cultural life in Ireland, even more evidently than elsewhere, is a creation of the spoken word. Communicating theological learning, or testing theological arguments, by embodying them in books, or even by committing them to writing at all, has plainly not become a normal part of Catholic life in these islands.

A word should be said about more scholarly quarterlies. Learned articles by Catholic scholars find their way easily into a variety of journals of international standing, particularly in the fields of church history and patristic studies. Nowadays, also, Catholic journals are not closed to other contributors. But three quarterlies of predominantly Catholic authorship should be mentioned, each of international standing and all with years of consistent learning and reflection behind them. *The Downside Review*, the oldest and the most 'catholic' of the three, while it may even seem promiscuous to the casual reader, in fact collects and connects disparate disciplines and interests in a way that enables, in Newman's words, 'the intellectual layman to be religious and the devout ecclesiastic to be intellectual'. *The Irish Theological Quarterly*, on the other hand, published by Maynooth, is much more a seminary professor's trade journal, particularly strong on the more exploratory and constructive side of dogmatic and moral theology, and more obviously part of the international theological circuit. The youngest of the three, *The Heythrop Journal*, combines the same interaction between philosophy and theology with a much larger coverage of current books.

It would not be difficult to make a list of valuable articles that have appeared in these and other journals over the past ten or twenty years. In a more favourable theological economy, in fact, many of these articles might have been padded out into books, not always to anybody's benefit. The length of an article often suffices to concentrate an insight. But publication in article form often also reduces impact and guarantees more rapid drop into oblivion. The great German debate on papal infallibility lumbers on, for example, with a whole cartload of books by now, either refuting or defending Hans Küng, whereas those who remember some back numbers of *The Clergy Review* and *The Irish Theological Quarterly* know that the bottom was knocked out of the argument, elegantly and succinctly, in half a dozen short articles. For that matter, Patrick McGrath's demolition of Hans Küng's notion of what a proposition is seems to have gone largely unnoticed, although it appeared in *Concilium* (March, 1973), a journal with an international circulation. Perhaps it was such a simple point, or anyway such a typical piece of Anglo-American philosophical analysis, that theologians more at home in metaphysical traditions could not be expected to notice it.

At the outset I stressed that the state of Catholic theology in these islands cannot be measured solely by the quality, and even less by the quantity, of learned publications. But it is very largely through books and quarterlies that any particular theological community shares its discoveries with the international Catholic community and with theologians in other communions. The Catholic Church in Britain and Ireland makes little impact upon international movements in theology, and our Anglican and Protestant neighbours would be hard put to see what our theologians are thinking.

To be very summary indeed, we may say that we rely on Protestant scholarship for our biblical studies and turn to translations for systematic theology. The place of Newman has become established in our theological culture, although only years after he was discovered in France and Germany. We have remarkably good 'schools' of medieval church history and of philosophical theology, with men of great eminence such as Walter Ullmann and Peter Geach. But the moral of the story is perhaps that these studies have developed quite independently of any ecclesiastical institution and the leading figures are laymen.

We live a time when, for better or for worse, Catholic theology is undergoing the most radical upheaval since the early nineteenth century and perhaps even since the thirteenth century. Is it not strange that such relatively devout, resourceful, well-educated and wealthy churches as ours should be contributing so little to this theological renewal? In particular, does it not seem strange that so little should come from the English Catholic community, given that it has such great figures to look back to as Lingard, Newman, Acton and von Hügel?

That there is a flourishing intellectual and academic tradition of which Catholics are fully part, both in Britain and Ireland, needs no demonstration. The great majority of university and such-like posts are occupied by Catholics in the Republic. It is taken for granted in England, although much less so in Wales, Scotland, and Northern Ireland, that the Catholic minority in these countries will be fairly represented in the intellectual life of the whole community. Paradoxically enough, it is really only in theology that Catholics are so inconspicuous and unproductive.

Moreover, we clearly do not make a significant impact in the areas of theology in which Catholics have traditionally been strong. When did we last produce a learned or reflective book on the *theology* of Thomas Aquinas? The challenges to Christian faith in our society are obvious, and internal conflicts in the Church little less so. How much constructive or critical theological writing have we produced to illuminate such problems? For that matter, do we even have anybody at present who mediates international Catholic theological movements to us as capably as Charles Davis used to do?

With the move of Heythrop College from rural Oxfordshire to London, and with various university developments at Bristol, Durham, Canterbury and elsewhere, together with slow progress towards establishing theology in the Irish universities, it would seem that, in due course, we should have a generation of students to undertake the research and reflection that might issue in more substantial writing. In England at least, as already elsewhere, many of them are likely to remain lay. As the proportion of ordinands declines, and if the ablest of them continue to be as conservative as present trends suggest, friction between diverging theological approches may well occur. The long-term effects of Protestant biblical formation, for instance, may provoke reassessment of doctrinal matters, or more probably perhaps, bigoted reaction. Either way, theological reflection would benefit. Reasoned dissent has always been at the heart of theological vitality.

For fifty years now the Catholic Churches in these islands have been secure enough to build up traditions, and that means to create institutions, to enable a tolerable diversity of theology to develop. But the confidence to do so has ben lacking. The systematic imposition by ultramontane bishops, after 1870, of the myth of a monolithic, homogeneous and absolutist Church, lies behind the notorious anti-intellectualism that marks British and Irish Catholicism to this day. As Newman often said, the lack of theologians of stature to challenge the clerical and popular image of the Church opened the doors to increasing authoritarianism and to the rejection of intellectual inquiry. All questioning in theology is assumed to lead to scepticism. Newman's own report of what Bishop Ullathorne said to him in 1859 conveys the tone: 'The Catholics of England were a peaceable people, the Church was peace. Catholics never had doubt — it pained them to know that things could be considered doubtful, which they had ever implicitly believed' (*Letters*, Vol. XIX, p.150). By the turn of the century, attempts to meet the agenda set for Catholic theologians by scientific advance, social and political changes, biblical criticism and so on, led to the painful confrontation between ecclesiastical authority and the generation of Baron von Hügel, George Tyrrell, Wilfrid Ward, and others. As such individuals either retreated or were destroyed there were no theological institutions in England which were capable of withstanding the anti-Modernist blizzard, so as to face the same agenda in the next generation.

Thus, at the very moment when our churches were at last socially and politically secure enough to expand, the nightmare of 'Modernism' ensured that the climate would be unfavourable to intellectual inquiry. The way opened for a new generation of scholars, of whom David Knowles was the most prominent (Downside, incidentally, has done more than any other single institution to foster English Catholic theology). But their intellectual preoccupation seldom bore on central theological questions. The answers to such questions were generally regarded as already clear, and the most gifted Catholic thinkers of the day went in mostly for aggressive apologetics.

Newman wrote in the *Apologia* of 'the energy of the intellect in the Catholic Church', and he even thought that it was never so much at home as when it was in conflict with received ideas and with ecclesiastical authority. For the past fifty years and more, however, the energy of critical and constructive intellect among us has never been noticeable enough to run up against any opposition. The bit has been there but the horse was long since flogged to death.

Lack of theological anticipation meant that we were surprized by the Vatican Council. We did not have the institutions or enough theologians to communicate and consolidate the Council's work. For this generation the chance for Catholic theology has no doubt been lost. But, provided that excesses elsewhere do not draw such indiscriminate intervention by ecclesiastical authority as to snuff out our frail beginnings, there is reason to hope that the self-confidence has been gained, and the appropriate structures have been developed, for us gradually to make an independent and distinctive contribution to both ecumenical and Catholic theology.

Some more general comments should be offered in conclusion. After all, what is the state of Catholic theology in other countries besides Britain and Ireland? How much constructive or critical theological writing is taking place elsewhere?

Two points should be made at once. In the first place, the papally-endorsed and officially-enforced Thomism which defined the shape of Catholic theological studies until about 1960 has obviously collapsed irretrievably. The abandonment of the lingua franca which it provided has led to a breakdown of communication among Catholic theologians. For all the ceaseless quarrels, and the often unedifying *odium theologicum*, of the past, at least the combatants shared a common universe of discourse. The further that neo-scholastic universe recedes, and those who have taken up theology in the past ten or fifteen years have no serious acquaintance with it at all, the greater the diversity in theological

intention and practice must become. It will soon be evident, if it is not so
already, that Latin American and African theological thought and
writing will differ increasingly from the European, or North Atlantic
theological universe to which Britain and Ireland plainly belong.

In the second place, however, the famous European theologians
whom we have mentioned, including Hans Küng, the youngest of them,
in fact him especially, are deeply marked by the neo-scholastic and
ultramontane Catholicism which is no doubt still strongly represented
among the theologians of the Holy Office in Rome who sit in judgment
upon them. But *intellectually*, because culturally and socially, it may be
doubted whether any of these theologians will have successors. As the
late Coronelius Ernst noted as long ago as 1966: 'To the younger
students and their contemporaries in the Universities, in England, at
any rate, Vatican II as a whole means very little; after all, Vatican II
represents the victory of the generation of the 1940s, after what painful
struggles they only know, and those who were born in the 1940s have
very little conception of what has really been achieved'.

In France and Germany, for example, bibilical studies are now the
staple of theological education, and it would be hard to distinguish
Catholic from Protestant work. Church historians, in both countries (as
elsewhere), are revising the recent past of their respective national churches in order (as it were) to retrieve the local traditions that were repress-
ed by the ultramontane centralism of post-1870 Catholicism. Numerous
monographs, essays scattered everywhere by J. Derek Holmes and
others, together with John Bossy's recent book, indicate a similar self-
examination on the part at least of the English Catholic community. But
the primarily systematic and speculative form in which Roman Catholic
theology has identified itself, in a tradition plainly continuous with the
scholastic theology of the thirteenth century, however artifically 'reviv-
ed', has diversified, in France and Germany, into a variety of styles and
approaches. Some French theologians of the younger generation, for
example, following a wider movement away from deductive argument
in theology to story-telling and myth, are writing 'confessions', of a consciously literary and personal kind. In Germany, on the other hand, the
transcendental idealism of Heideggerian Thomism has yielded to Anglo-
American styles of philosphical analysis, and some extremely technical
exegetical work has resulted. The influence of post-Marxist sociology, of
structuralism, and of psycho-analysis, may easily be detected in much
current continental theological writing. Whether with nostalgia or a
sense of excitement, one must recogize that the contemporary babel of
Catholic theological styles puts British and Irish theologians, in their
comparative dumbness, in a less disadvantageous position than the
course of this survey may have suggested. We are not the only ones with
frail beginnings.

What we should do, if prescription rather than prediction may be permitted in concluding, is contribute much more vigorously and availably to the present recrystallization of theological studies. Much European theological writing, whether of the older or the more recent generations, has a strongly idealist, not to say Hegelian, character. The standards of argument that are taken for granted by professional philosophers in Britain and Ireland are frequently not met. Since theological work is so much a matter of saying what you must not say, as well as of trying to say what you cannot say, the critical rigour of Anglo-American philosophy has much more to contribute to Catholic theology than has so far been offered. But the effect will not be great until books appear which are either translated into other languages or connect in some other way with the wider international debate. And finally, since theology clearly is in search of its roots, and the exploration of 'myth and ritual' is the order of the day, it seems absurd that the tentative connections made in the 1960s between theology and literature should not become a major focus of interest in the 1980s, given the richness of our triple inheritance in English, Anglo-Irish, and Irish poetry and literature. But it is always easier to prescribe than to prophesy.

Notes

1. Davis, *The Study of Theology* (1962); Haughton, *The Transformation of Man* (1967); Lash, *His Presence in the World* (1974); McCabe, *The New Creation* (1964); Meynell, *Sense, Nonsense and Christianity* (1964), *The New Theology and Modern Theologians* (1967); Wicker, *Culture and Liturgy* (1963), *Culture and Theology* (1966).

Selected bibliography

Black, Antony, *Monarchy and Community: Political ideas in the later conciliar controversy, 1430-1450* (Cambridge, 1970).
Id., Council and Commune: The conciliar movement and the fifteenth-century heritage (London, 1979).
Bossy, John, *The English Catholic Community, 1570-1850* (London, 1975).
Butler, B.C. *The Theology of Vatican II* (Sarum lectures) (London, 1967).
Id., The Church and Unity (London, 1979).
Coulson, John, *Newman and the Common Tradition* (Oxford, 1970).
Dessain, C.S. (ed.), *The Letters and Diaries of John Henry Newman* 41 volumes (Edinburgh, 1961-).
Ernst, Cornelius, *Multiple Echo: Explorations in theology* (London, 1979).
FitzPatrick, P.J., *Apologia pro Charles Kingsley* (London, 1969).
Geach, P.T., *God and the Soul* (London, 1969).
Id., The Virtues (Cambridge, 1977).
Gill, Joseph, *Personalities of the Council of Florence* (Oxford, 1964).
Id., Church Union, Rome and Byzantium, 1204-1453 (London, 1979).

Lash, Nicholas, *His Presence in the World* (London, 1968).

Id., Newman on Development (London, 1965).

Id., Theology on Dover Beach (London, 1979).

Mackey, James, *Jesus the Man and the Myth* (London, 1979).

McHugh, John, *The Mother of Jesus in the New Testament* (London, 1975).

McNamara, Martin, *The New Testament and the Palestinian Targum to the Pentateuch* (Rome, 1966).

Id., Targum and Testament (Shannon, 1972).

Meynell, Hugo, *God and the World* (London, 1971).

Id., An Introduction to the Philosophy of Bernard Lonergan (London, 1976).

Murray, Placid, *Newman the Oratorian* (Dublin, 1969).

Murray, Robert, *Symbols of Church and Kingdom* (Cambridge, 1975).

Orchard, Bernard, *The Griesbach Solution to the Synoptic Problem,* 3 volumes (Manchester, 1976-).

Ullmann, Walter, *The Church and the Law in the Earlier Middle Ages* (London, 1976).

Id., The Papacy and Political Ideas in the Middle Ages (London, 1976).

Id., Scholarship and Politics in the Middle Ages (London, 1978).

Bishops and Writers, Aspects of the Evolution of Modern English Catholicism, ed. Adrian Hastings (Wheathampstead, 1977).

The Christian Priesthood (9th Downside symposium), ed. Nicholas Lash & Joseph Rhymer (London, 1970).

Church Membership and Intercommunion (10th Downside symposium) ed. John Kent & Robert Murray (London, 1973).

A Catholic Dictionary of Theology, ed. H.F. Davis, Joseph Crehan *et al.* 4 volumes (London, 1962-).

New Catholic Commentary on Holy Scripture, ed. R.C. Fuller (London, 1969).

Summa Theologiae of St Thomas Aquinas, Latin and English with notes, ed. Thomas Gilby, 60 volumes (London, 1964-75).

Moral theology

ENDA McDONAGH

1. *Teaching and learning*

IN THE COURSE of conversation some years ago an Irish bishop remarked: 'Of course I wasn't a moral theologian; I was a moral theology teacher'. The accompanying wry smile emphasized the not entirely serious self-deprecation and the not entirely jocose thrust at the self-importance and pretentiousness to which theologians are often prone. Of more significance were the implicit historical facts and attitudes about the conditions of theology, including moral theology; conditions which still prevail in Britain and Ireland. Most people with a professional commitment to theology work in seminaries and other institutions with teaching loads so heavy and resources so limited that they operate and see themselves almost exclusively as teachers. And this is how their employers and superiors, including bishops, also view them. The small if increasing number of Catholic theologians working at secular universities and not directly subject to religious superiors enjoy rather different conditions, challenges and resources, although teaching necessarily plays a significant rôle for them too. And they do not include any Catholic moral theologians, as far as I know.

The stress placed here on teaching could easily be misunderstood. Most people engaged in tertiary-level education, including universities, see teaching as a primary duty. Only at university level is it significantly qualified to the point where research (and publication) is given equal status. And that equality is often more formal and theoretical than substantive and practical. (The major organizations of university academics in Britain and Ireland have adopted 'teacher' as their self-designation in the Association of University Teachers, AUT, and the Irish Federation of University Teachers, IFUT). If the university or any parallel institution is to operate at all as a community of scholars, the initiation of new scholars through effective teaching must be vigorously undertaken. The suggestions of limitation which (moral) theology teacher and (moral) theology teaching carried in the opening paragraph should not, then, obscure the necessity, value and, indeed, intellectual excitement which the activities of teacher and teaching involve in general and in theological institutions of various kinds. The worrisome source of limitation relates more to certain dominant models of teaching theology and theology teacher.

The model of teacher rather than theologian preferred by the bishop was dominant in seminaries where Catholic priests and hence (most) theology teachers received their initial training. The teacher's task was to instruct the seminarian in the accepted moral teaching of the Church so that he, on ordination, could instruct and apply it to the faithful in pulpit and confessional. Difficulties such as answers to new questions (I recall that of the use of tampons from my student days!) were resolved by more exact applications of the received rules, by appeal to the approved authors and by authoritative decisions, almost exclusively from Rome. There were excellent teachers, of whom I knew several, who transcended the limitations of the subject-matter and of the process to convey a genuine sense of morality as richer than rule and of teaching as richer than instruction. But the basic movement was receiving the stuff from above (Rome, text-books, articles by approved authors) and handing it on below. My theology teacher was the middle-man between the authorities and the students, the primary teachers and the learners.

The element of caricature in this picture does not destroy its overall validity. And while it may be less true of seminaries today, one is frequently reminded that its passing is to be regretted and that its retention or restoration is desirable where possible.

The revolution in approach and method in moral theology already begun in the 1930s and greatly accelerated after Vatican II, which undermined the simple receiving-from and handing-on process of moral theology, is already very well-known. It might be briefly summarized as the admission of large sections of Christian and human reality, biblical, doctoral, psychological and social, into the moral-theology classroom so that the neat structures and divisions of the manuals simply collapsed. Another kind of reality principle was at work in locating the moral theology teacher in the Church's overall teaching activity. The isolation and professionalization which he enjoyed (and it was always he) gave him a responsibility and authority, for all its intermediate status which obscured where the action was really going on. Long before Vatican II's insistence on the Church as primarily *God's people* with its implications of the radical equality of faith and baptism, Christian teaching, including moral teaching, was occurring formally and informally far beyond the reach of moral theologians or their episcopal masters. Parents and lay-teachers were the primary formal educators while the informal ranged from friends and school peers to work-contacts, local political and trades-union leaders, to newspaper columnists, and the ever more informal messages of the communications media and the cultural ethos. There is abundant evidence throughout Britain and Ireland to show how the informal prevailed over the formal and the non-specialized/non-authorized over the specialized and authorized. Which bishops or theologians consciously promoted in their teaching racism or sexism,

political violence, now enjoying not only practical support but moral
justification among Christians and Catholics? On the other hand many
admirable moral movements and activities, for peace, for the care of
itinerants, prisoners, and the social, mentally and physically deprived
did not originate in the class-room or bishop's study. All this helps to
locate and relativise the moral theologian as teacher in a way that was
obscured when he was in his old rôle as intermediary between hierarchy
and ordinands (to simplify crudely), or in the more authoritative professional position which today is claimed by some theologians and
resented by some bishops. The theologian is a teacher and with, one
hopes, a mediating as well as professional and authoritative rôle but
within a community in which teacher and taught are frequently inter-
changeable. The moral theologian as teacher has to collaborate with a
whole range of formal and informal teachers from whom he may learn at
least as much as he teaches about the basic direction and particular tasks
of Christian discipleship, the stuff of Christian morality. However his
ability, training, skills, opportunities and position of leadership give him
responsibility to ensure that the various formal and informal teachers in
the Church are communicating effectively with one another and with the
historic wisdom of the Christian Church in response to the changing
problems of the day. With such an explosion of teachers, information
and challenges, the moral theology teacher can no longer look only to his
manuals, approved authors and Roman or episcopal documents. He can
no longer be content to receive from above and hand down to below.
And indeed, he is no longer simply 'he' — 'she' is also beginning to
assume her rightful responsibility and duty as moral theologian in confronting the meaning of discipleship for today's Christians. The further
impact of this development on the future of moral theology will be
enormous.

Recognition of the plurality of teachers in the Church reveals simultaneously the plurality of learners and learning processes. As mediator
between the tradition and the students the moral theologian was always
conscious of his learning tasks. But the new situation calls for a broaden-
ing and deepening of that consciousness as he engages in a collaborative
enterprise as broad as humanity itself and as deep as the mystery of God
itself. This is the Church's enterprise as it seeks to understand and live
the mystery of God's presence through the full expression of humanity
in history.

The complexity of contemporary life and the range of moral views,
practices and possibilities through which Christians must chart the
course of their discipleship emphasize the learning-rôle of the moral
theologian, his or her responsibility to provide leadership in learning to
chart that course. For theological as well as pedagogical reasons, an
effective moral teacher today must be seen to be a continuing learner.

   The kind of leadership in learning and discerning which the moral
theologian offers in face of complexity and conflict of moral views and
practices is first of all conservative. He is, after all, trying to understand
and present discipleship of Jesus Christ to a contemporary audience.
The first records of that discipleship in the New Testament provide the
starting-point for his investigations and standard of judgment for his
conclusions. The subsequent history of Christian life and reflection provides further illustration of and insight into how discipleship should and
should not be realized. Familiarity with this continuing Christian story
furnishes the moral theologian with a rich storehouse of heroes and
villains from Pope John XXIII to Pope John XII, of the ways of sanctity
and of sin, of successful experiments (monasticism) and inglorious
failures (the Inquisition), of the brilliant moral insights, analyses and
syntheses of Augustine and Aquinas and the misleading, if persuasive,
moralizing of Montanists and Jansenists, of fidelity in understanding
and living against great odds as with so many martyrs and of obstinacy
in misunderstanding for reasons of convenience, as with the teaching on
slavery.
   The richness as well as the ambiguity of the past force the genuinely
conservative theologian to be also critical. He must evaluate the past,
discern its truly Christian elements to maintain continuity in discipleship. For responsible critique and discernment he needs information,
skill, dedication and freedom — the time, energy, recognition and
resources which encourage and enable him to act as discriminating
leader in recalling to mind and so to life those truly Christian elements.
With more dedication and freedom the acceptance of slavery or the
denial of religious liberty might not have afflicted Catholic moral
teaching for so long. In face of current problems a greater awareness of
past teaching and example in peace and violence, in wealth and poverty,
or in power and service might help to break the world-wide bonds of
militarism, consumerism and exploitation, which Christians also support to their immediate profit. As an overall enterprise, in its various
systematic sections and more particular challenges, moral theology is
still seriously lacking in historical depth, leaving itself open to the temp-
tations of either a rigid defence of one unexamined version of past experience and teaching or an equally uncritical rejection of all that is past.
The conserving responsibility of the moral theologian must join fully
with his critical responsibility in more detailed archaeology of his
discipline's past.
   Retreat into the past rather than active and critical recall of it in the
present may also prove a temptation as one surveys the variety of problems and solutions which threaten to submerge all clear thinking and
right doing today. The theologian's critical faculty is no less in demand
as he attempts to order, analyze and illuminate today's problems and

solution for modern disciples. Although all Christians are called to be both teachers and learners, in charting the way of discipleship, the moral theologian has a responsibility of leadership. The exercise of this leadership in learning occurs within the community of the Church but also within the community of his theological colleagues. The theological community in the strong sense of people actively and intellectually and continuously engaged in seeking to understand the faith may include people who do not teach at theological institutes or have not even studied at such. Britain has long had outstanding contributors to theology of this kind. Rosemary Haughton and Jack Dominian come to mind as present-day examples. In the dialogue with the world at issue here, in confronting new moral problems, views and practices, the theological community is greatly enriched by people whose background and life-engagement are far removed from the seminary or even the university.

The concentrated exposure to the contemporary scene which the moral theologian may not avoid, calls for discriminating fidelity to the tradition and critical openness to the present. The search for new ways will involve risk and mistake. And it calls for that third characteristic of the good moralist and theologian, creativity. Creativity should and frequently does characterize all human communication, including teaching. A good conversation, paradigm of much adult communication and moral activity, takes for granted the rules of vocabulary, grammar and syntax, as it moves over uncharted terrain, follows the spirit of the exchange and creates a dialogue that is itself creative of or transformative of the participants. The security and trust involved in such a successful venture, the community of language and tradition on which the participants draw and the genuinely personal creative activity involved, illustrate how moral behaviour is also human, creative interchange between people with a tradition and a community. In the critical understanding and creative promotion of that moral interchange, the moral theologian speaks on the frontier between the diverse communities to which he belongs, Christian and secular, historical and contemporary. His response to frontier dilemmas or conflicts may sometimes have to transcend his conserving and critical rôles in genuinely creative work. Such creative response will inevitably involve the new. The moral theologian has the obligation to show how this novelty is not for its own sake but is demanded by his conserving and critical rôles. Sometimes this will be readily recognized by the wider church community. More often, precisely because the moral theologian has had the opportunity and experienced the need to find a way forward for disciples, it will involve time, debate, perhaps initial rejection. And sometimes the moral theologian will be wrong. How to enable the moral theologian and other theologians and Christians to engage in this creative as well as conserving and critical work while at the same time minimizing the impact of mistakes, calls for continuing effort by all church members. Where the theologian pays effective attention to the work of his colleagues, to the broader insights and needs of the Church and to its overall co-ordination and guides, the pope and the bishops, the risks of mistake are reduced. In the difficulties that may arise, perhaps the Vatican reaction to the Molinists and Banezians of telling them to stop attacking each other may be more appropriate than the silencing of John Courtney Murray in the 1950s. At any rate, in the rather deprived theological world of Britain and Ireland, theologians need a lot more encouragement if their conserving, critical and creative work is to have any hope of enabling the Church to discern and meet its needs. The mistakes of creativity, in particular, are likely to be much less damaging than the simple repetition of answers drawn from 'authorities' in other times and other lands, which were almost certainly devised for rather different questions. A moral theology teacher may never be a simple 'repertoire' if his conserving function is to involve genuinely Christian and not merely verbal and mechanical fidelity to the past. Teaching is always the other side of learning with all the risks that implies.

2. *Learning and living*

Moral theology as a theology of discipleship for disciples today relates closely to Christian living. It has sometimes appeared as if moral theology should provide a theory of Christian living which might then be translated into practice. In the Christian tradition however theory never enjoyed such a simple priority. Theology was understood to be in important senses secondary to and based on Christian practice. Reflection with its accompanying insight came after the fact. This was obviously true of those earliest 'theological' documents, the books of the New Testament. Following Jesus Christ and living out discipleship anticipated writing about it. And this has been a recurring pattern in Christian life and theology. Many of the classical developments in moral theology from just-war theory to approval of interest-taking occurred after certain critical facts: the establishment of the Church as the Church of the Empire with a belief in the responsibility of defending it, and a change in the economic system which found the old prohibition of usury increasingly ignored and eventually unreasonable.

The theory developed in turn affected events and facts. Practice was also influenced by theory or previous reflection and systematization. The New Testament writings which embody reflection on as well as recording of the primitive discipleship play a normative rôle in all Christian theology and practice. Subsequent theological writing and community decisions based on reflection contribute to the self-understanding of the Church as it teaches and lives the way of discipleship. Moral theologians may ignore individual documents or passages but their primary attention has been directed to written sources with a heavy emphasis on the reflective in the theological and philosophical mould to the neglect of historical accounts of life or the recreations of life in imaginative literature.

There has been a recent welcome recovery of history and story by theologians, including moral theologians. It has not made much impact in Britain or Ireland as yet. This will enrich moral understanding and teaching although it cannot simply replace the tradition of conceptual analysis in which moralists, philosophical and theological, must still engage. More challenging in many ways for moralists is the tendency to give priority to practice, or 'praxis' — as the jargon tends to put it. This learning through *doing* and reflecting after the fact could pose serious problems for the study-bound moral theologian and indeed for other Christian teachers.

It is fairly obvious that the moral theologian cannot do research and reflection if he is entirely engaged in activity. Apart from the very difficult question of time and energy, different skills are developed in the one and the other. Yet the moralist above all must be in close and constant contact with the life on which he is to reflect. To some extent this happens automatically if sometimes unconsciously. The moral theologian is also a member of a family, of the Church, of a particular State. His active engagement with these and other communities may vary considerably but it is seldom negligible and can, with advertence, provide some active basis for his theological inquiry. A more self-conscious engagement in particular pastoral or social activity will usually make him more alert and aware in his theology. Theologians who have worked with special groups, the handicapped or alcoholics or prisoners or divorced or homosexuals, frequently display particular insight into these problems and can enlarge theological understanding in general.

The limits of this kind of engagement derive from time, energy, opportunity and ability. No moral theologian can cover a wide range of activity. He will therefore be dependent on dialogue with people engaged in particular activities, personally or professionally. A much more profound and continuing dialogue is demanded of the moral theologian in a whole range of areas today. In the areas of medical and bio-ethics, of business ethics and of law and morality, useful collaborative work has already begun. However it is only in the medical area and in the United States for the most part that real collaboration has been sustained over an effective period by a relatively large number of collaborators to yield substantial results. In Britain and Ireland especially, a much more systematic effort will be needed by theologians, other specialists and lay-people affected if Christian discipleship is to be understood and taught and lived in response to challenges as diverse as the environment and its protection, political freedom and economic development, to take a few obvious instances.

Team-work of this kind with the moral theologian learning with and from the expertise and experience of so many others will be necessary to future moral theology. However the professional moral theologian may not be the critical figure in some of these developments. It is important to recognize the responsibility of other professionals to provide leadership in discerning the way of discipleship in their own fields, in offering leadership in moral learning and teaching for the Christian community in their particular area. The moral theologian will be a partner to the enterprise of developing Christian morality for architects and accountants, politicians and lawyers. He will not necessarily be the dominant partner. However he will remain a necessary link to the tradition and to the other areas in which Christian morality has to be exposed and lived. In this vision of a Church collaborating through its different members with their responsibilities and experience, the moral theologian will require commitment, knowledge, skill and opportunity far exceeding those suggested by phrases such as 'merely a moral theology teacher and not a moral theologian'. The demands on the moral theologian to be linked directly or indirectly with the great moral movements and issues of the day call for much greater support from the Church in its community resources and pastoral direction. Blame for the present apathy about or occasional hostility to moral theology may be variously apportioned. Its failures to meet the needs of the gospel community today will be harshly judged later.

3. British and Irish issues

What I have been saying applies to a large extent to the tasks of moral theology throughout the Church, although its particular limitations of personnel and other resources in Britain and Ireland have been briefly noticed. Britain and Ireland share many of the same tasks and issues, although sometimes with a particular quality or qualification of their own. Marriage breakdown has its own characteristics in England, somewhat different in Scotland perhaps, and more different still in Ireland. The abortion problem is, if one would excuse the crudity, developing as an export problem in Ireland while it has become an import as well as a native problem in Britain. Racism is predominantly a British issue although many Catholics of Irish origin or extraction are involved in it and had or have to suffer similar indignity. Sexism affects both islands in somewhat different degrees and fashions. Economic issues such as unemployment and the community's response to it, or the responsibilities and powers of management and unions move back and over the Irish Sea. So do the positive moral movements which have emerged to fight in some of these issues. A survey of the major current moral issues could take enormous space and time so I choose to concentrate on a few that have a peculiarly British-Irish character.

(a) *Britain and Ireland*

The first of these is undoubtedly the relationship between Britain and
Ireland and the parallel but not identical relationship between British
and Irish people. Despite their long and sometimes tragic history, their
relationships have received very little attention from theologians, moral
or other. Given the continuing tension between the countries and the
peoples, expressed most destructively in the violence in Northern
Ireland but also at work as between Irish and English in Britain (the
earliest of Britain's contemporary race problems!), and then in an insidiously destructive way within the Catholic Church in Britain, some
more attention to this question by the Catholic Church and its
theologians as well as its ordinary members is clearly called for.

I suggest three separate tasks for urgent attention:

(i) A historical-theological examination and appropriation of the
history of British-Irish relationships. This needs some further explanation. The history is so long and tangled that it could take volumes to
complete. Much of this work has already been published by reputable
British and Irish historians. What I have in mind is a joint effort by
theologians and historians on the basis of this material, to produce an accurate historical survey which would offer opportunity for theological or
Christian understanding, forgiveness and reconciliation. Some of the
work of Haddon Wilmer of Leeds on 'The Politics of Forgiveness',
despite its slightly unhappy title, would be relevant here. At any rate it
should be possible for theologians and historians with the support of the
Churches to supply a basic and accurate account of the history with such
theological reflection on its implications that it would lead to eventual
repentance and reconciliation. Such a work should be required reading
in all religious and moral courses.

(ii) The second task would involve a much more serious concentration on the rôle of religion in the Northern Irish and British-Irish conflict. History might again combine with theological analyses to help us
understand and appropriate past and present. The object would be to
enable the Churches to play a more positive rôle in the future rather than
to convict them of failure in the past, although some recognition of and
repentance from past failure are clearly demanded. In this as in other
areas, the theologian will be collaborating with other academics such as
historians and social scientists, and with more directly-involved people
like politicians, community leaders including clergymen and the suffering masses. The life-experience will be critical to the learning-process.

(iii) The tensions between English and Irish Catholics, the evasion of
these tensions and their historical and political background, have
plagued the Church at least since the Veto controversy at the beginning

of the nineteenth century. The great improvements in relationships in past decades display an unhealthy middle-class blandness while the working-class Irish feel and may be excluded and excluding. The 'Paddy' references and the Irish jokes might be taken too seriously but they sometimes reveal a nasty edge and frequently express or feed a hidden hostility. In many ways the Catholic Church in Britain has not attempted to celebrate its ethnic pluralism. Perhaps it felt threatened or overwhelmed at any earlier stage by the Irish element. Some more thoughtful examination and reflection on these tensions are now required for the health of the Church in both countries, and indeed for the health of society generally, if traditional resentment is not to be replaced by a more destructive rootlessness.

(b) *Protestant-Catholic relations*

It is impossible to discuss British-Irish relations, past or present, without facing up to Protestant-Catholic relations. The progress made in the last two decades is enormous, as compared with the starting point but looks very limited when compared with what is still to be achieved. The progress gives promise for the future but it could as easily lead to complacency in the present as the more serious and difficult problems arise. The impact of the agreed statements between Anglicans and Catholics has been limited through fear and disguised through complacency. The continuing scandal of Northern Ireland (and its genuine and universal Christian scandal may not be ignored) demands an honest and effective response from the Churches which they have so far failed to give, busy as they are with their own people, their own institutions and their own power. Only an ecumenism that involves inter-church surrender in love and forgiveness can help the Churches out of this impasse.

Meanwhile this scandal combines with a host of other religious, cultural and economic factors to undermine the traditional bonds uniting family, locality, school, common social activity and church-going. To survive as a believing Christian in the future will call for much more self-conscious allegiance by the believer and a new set of structures or communities of support. In that situation, and it is already here for many young Christians, the divisions between Churches with their restrictive regulations for joint celebrations of Eucharist, marriage or death, will look increasingly fussy and irrelevant. How to avoid simple anarchy in inter-church relations and yet prevent the current regulations from alienating a growing number of young people will be a major task for pastors, theologians and believers in the next decade. It has special urgency in our islands.

(c) *Economics and discipleship*

To ascribe all our woes to economic conditions would hardly satisfy even the Marxists among us. Yet there is an increasing recognition that economic conditions play a significant rôle in the development of a humane society and in its break-down. Church and theologians have hitherto lacked the interest and the skill to confront in any significant way the problems posed for discipleship at what the jargon calls the macro- and micro-economic levels. The present economic difficulties in Britain and Ireland, the uneasy state of the European Economic Community and the north-south or first world-third world tensions in which we are all involved, economically and politically, suggest a much more serious approach to studying the economic responsibility of discipleship. Such an approach would need the knowledge and experience of a range of Christians. In the British and Irish situation it would provide an excellent focus for international and inter-church collaboration. In that very collaboration itself new aspects of discipleship would almost certainly emerge.

4. *The cost of morality and of moral theology*

As learner as well as teacher, as learning from life as well as from books, the moral theologian is confronted with the meaning of discipleship for himself as he attempts to chart it for others. In the transparent world in which Christians now live it is very difficult to get away with simply instructing the others. My own jocose remark to a student twenty years ago, 'I teach this stuff, you don't expect me to live it as well', I would not dare risk today. The teacher and learner of moral theology must also be a disciple, and discipleship is costly. So moral theologians, by giving a lead in learning and in learning for living, have to face the further tasks of Christian living for themselves. The standard lecture on famine in the Third World after a sumptuous banquet is so crass as to be easily dismissed. The more modest but still very comfortable life-style of the moralist who is struggling to relate the pervasiveness of poverty to the meaning of justice for today's disciples is much more subtle and much less easy to cope with. But it must be coped with if Christian discipleship is to offer a way out of the present consumerist enslavement of the First World and impoverished enslavement of so much of the Third.

The insulation of university and seminary, of education and class, of prestige and worthwhile, enjoyable work all conspire to blind theologians to the real moral conditions of our world. What is the moral theologian prepared to sacrifice in order to come to grips with that real world, and in order to offer some vision of true discipleship to the Church he is called to serve?

5. *Conflict with church authority*

Recent difficulties between church authorities (pope and bishops) and theologians may have been inevitable and even healthy in the rapid transitions which the Church had to make in the 1960s and 1970s. They are regrettable, however, in so far as they reflect fear and arrogance, instead of trust and humility. They may even be more easily avoidable if the collaborative learning to which the Church is called by word and world became the dominant concern of all church members, with of course special responsibilities for theologians and final practical authority for the pastors. In the service of the Church by his deciphering of discipleship, the moral theologian has to take risks and be willing to pay the price. These are critical tests of his own discipleship and of his authority to investigate and explain it for others.

Christ in the Church

JAMES MACKEY

IT IS NEVER good policy to approach one's topic with an excuse. Yet there does seem to be some point in saying that any restriction of the discussion of this present topic to the Roman Catholic Church in Britain and Ireland might prove more difficult than it would with discussion of any of the others. For if the fragmented movement of Christian people through history can be described, in a positive and promising way, as a human attempt, still largely unsuccessful, to reach the stature of Christ, it sometimes seems just as legitimate to take a more cynical and negative attitude and to describe the same movement as a bewildering variety of models for Christian belief and practice consistent only in their common intent to evade the full challenge of the spirit of Jesus and their consequent accommodation to more manageable forms of religious existence. Somewhere in the depths of all our devious little Christian hearts we realize that any serious attempt to follow Jesus would ask far too much of us and, prudent people that we are, we trade the prospects of the cross for the relative comforts of the pew.

The Roman Catholic Church has, of course, its own peculiar variation of this common Christian disease. In the most heralded of all its documents, Vatican II declared: 'They are fully incorporated into the society of the Church who, possessing the Spirit of Christ, accept her entire system and all the means of salvation given to her, and through union with her visible structure are joined to Christ, who rules her through the Supreme Pontiff and the bishops' (*Lumen Gentium*, 14). In this definition of full memership of the Church of Christ necessary for salvation, there are two criteria which, however much we might wish them to be one, are of quite diverse character. One of these is relatively easy to describe and to detect, since it requires acceptance of public sacramental rites and allegiance to an extremely visible ecclesiastical government. The other, however, relegated to a subordinate clause in the course of that interesting sentence, the possession of the Spirit of Christ, seems less amenable to concrete and detectable detail; at the very least, and if only by default, it is made to seem so. In the course of the council document in question it is usually developed in terms of what can only be called brief and uninformative moral generalizations about love, humility and self-sacrifice. Similarly, most sermons preached in Roman Catholic churches which end in practical perorations simply

exhort the faithful to frequent the sacraments and seem happy to assume
that this will increase the Spirit of Christ so automatically that the latter
needs no further definition. And the document from the Sacred Congregation for the Doctrine of the Faith which forbade Hans Küng from
teaching as a Catholic theologian was wholly concerned with the authority and prerogatives of Church offices, and made only the briefest and
most oblique references to what the man had to say about Jesus. Almost
everywhere one looks the ritual and institutional criterion crowds out the
specifically Christological one.

So my particular   remit in this chapter is to survey . modern
Christology, to see what it has to say about Christ — the Spirit of Jesus
— in the Church. But as I reflect on this particular remit my opening excuse returns in a different form. For it seems that one has to go either
outside Britain and Ireland or outside the Roman Catholic Church in
order to find the most influential Christologies that have recently appeared. Irish Catholics have been even less prolific in theological
publication than British Catholics. In fact most Irish writers of Catholic
theology today are in exile. That fact, no doubt, invites its own comment
both upon the writers and the Irish Catholic Church, but I am too much
part of the fact to be the one to make the comment. So I shall simply
select some of those Roman Catholics who, though not of Ireland or Britain, have written Christologies which have proved quite influential in
these islands: Kasper, Küng and Schillebeeckx; and some themes from
the *Myth of God Incarnate* debate which, though it exercised mainly non-
Romans, is a very indicative straw in the wind that blows toward the
future of all our divided traditions.

It would certainly prove too flattering to this cross-section of modern
Christology to sum it up as an attempt to penetrate traditional layers of
dogma and apologetic in quest of the Spirit of the historical Jesus — and
it is certainly no part of the intention of this short piece to try to justify
theologians over hierarchs, or indeed over any member of any of the
Churches of Christ. But if the penetration is described in terms of groping efforts, the results of which largely advertise their own short-
comings, no such flattery should result, and yet serious attention could
be claimed for the direction in which such groping efforts are aimed.

1. Incarnation

Don Cupitt, one of the most radical contributors to *The Myth of God
Incarnate* debate, and the one most determined to continue that debate
(in his books *Jesus and the Gospel of God* and *The Debate about Christ*), has
singled out Incarnation as the *bête noire* of the Christological tradition.
Somewhat reminiscent of the story of the man who sneezed on a
headland on the south coast of Ireland, just as the Lusitania exploded
and sank, and got the distinct, if fleeting, impression that his sneeze had

caused the whole disaster, Cupitt blames incarnation doctrine for weakening our appreciation of Jesus' humanity; for creating a cult of the divine Christ which resulted in the true deity of the God Jesus called Father fading into the background; for replacing Jesus' challenge to choose between this loving Father and earthly power with the demand for unquestioning obedience to the earthly plenipotentiaries of the new cosmic emperor Christ; and, finally, for making God the Father into an old man, a picture of impotence, especially when placed beside the pictures of Christ the King.

Now there can be no doubt about the fact that Christians in the course of history have imagined that the intrusion of a pre-existent divine person effectively de-personalized the human Jesus, despite the fact that the word 'person ' in Trinitarian theology bears nothing more than the very remotest resemblance to the word 'person' when used of human persons. And the ensuing image of Jesus' humanity as a puppet in the hands of this pre-existent divine 'person' did certainly encourage those who thought themselves commissioned to continue Jesus' alleged offices of king, priest and prophet (i.e., teacher of orthodox doctrine) to present themselves in turn as mere conveyors through their human acts of the very will of divine persons. This in turn allowed Christian leaders from early times to claim divine authority, thus modelling themselves on the kings and emperors of the secular sphere, in spite of an express prohibition of Jesus himself forbidding them to do so (The claim is as clearly present in the document which condemned Hans Küng as it is in the ancient political theology of Boniface VIII). The rest of the faithful correspondingly could, as often as they wished, feel relieved of the personal responsibility to witness to their faith in all areas of morals, belief and worship and assume instead the much more comfortable, and sometimes cynical, rôles of passive obedience or passive resistance.

All this happened and continues to happen, but, although I would have to admit that traditional incarnation theology did not do all it might have done to prevent these aberrations, I still prefer Walter Kasper's view of the matter. Kasper insists that it was heterodox incarnation theology, specifically that associated with Apollinarius, and not the orthodox kind, which was causally connected with so many of the features of Christian history which Cupitt bemoans. For if Jesus did not have a human mind of his own (his own human 'rational soul'), then the word 'intrusion' is a valid description for the divine activity in human history; then church authorities which speak in the name of this intrusive divinity will in turn intrude upon the faithful and seek to lord it over them like demi-gods in God's name; then the faithful, deprived effectively of the witness of Jesus' own fully human life and death as the only genuine source of Christian faith will be passive before the intrusions; then, finally, the truncated humanity, represented in the very person of

the founder of Christianity, will bring on the protests of those modern
humanist movements which, in the name of a proper evaluation of
humanity, prove so persistently hostile to Christianity.

The case for penetrating beneath incarnation theology in quest of the
Spirit of Jesus would then rest on the belief that most Christians have
offered and still offer allegiance to a basically Apollinarian Jesus. There
is much to be said for that belief. Orthodox incarnation theology, on the
other hand, if it were fully understood and properly preached, would
surely say to us that the word of God is found at last in a fully human
condition, that the fully human life and death of Jesus of Nazareth is
God's definitive word in human history, a life of loving service lived in
the conviction of God's unconditioned grace to all and culminating (consistent to the last) in the death of a slave.

2. Resurrection

Some of the literature selected for this survey contains a corresponding
attempt to penetrate beneath some all too familiar resurrection theology
to the Spirit of the human, historical Jesus, though once again it must be
said that the attempt is often as laudable in its intention as it is questionable in its execution. First, it is clear that some theologies of resurrection could involve just as much divine intrusion from outside human
history (rather than spiritual creation and recreation from wihin it) as
any incarnation theology, and could in consequence just as successfully
block our view of the central importance of the life and death of Jesus for
the inspiration of our concrete Christian lives. For, to put the matter a
little too simply, if it is God's act of raising Jesus that manifests him Son
of God, and if this is thought to be an act subsequent to his earthly life
and death, then the human person of Jesus and the human existence in
which it is known can be of no more than incidental importance in
manifesting the Son of God and of revealing to us, therefore, the ways of
the one, true God with man. Second, it seems to me that in varying
degrees the Christologies of Kasper, Küng and even Schillebeeckx are
inconsistent at worst, confusing at best, on the resurrection of Jesus of
Nazareth. All want to give the resurrection of Jesus some rôle in getting
the Christian movement going (again?) after the death of Jesus. According to Kasper, though Jesus saw his death as redemptive, and it could
consequently be so understood by others, his cause was so bound to his
person that his death could just as well be considered the failure of his
mission. So the historically-evident dynamism of the new movement had
to have what he calls an 'initial ignition' after Jesus' death and this was
the resurrection of Jesus. Yet he insists that 'Easter itself is an object of
faith' (p. 131) and he describes the appearances of the risen Jesus in particular as states of being possessed by Jesus (rather than objectively
tangible events), as awakenings of faith, experiences of faith, encounters

with Christ present in Spirit. In fact, in answer to the question, if we are or are not talking of the resurrection of the person Jesus, he says: 'It is therefore not a separate event after the life and suffering of Jesus, but what is happening at the most profound level in the death of Christ' (p. 150).

Küng goes through much the same motions. 'Even the non-Christian historian', he writes 'will not now dispute the fact that it was only after Jesus' death that the movement invoking his name really started' (pp. 343-4). Here again is the insistence that his cause was identified with his person and so his death could only make it seem a failure (pp. 340ff). Once again, though, we are told: 'Jesus' cause — which his disciples had given up as lost — was decided at Easter by God himself' (p. 352). And once again, just as we wait for some evidence of this act of God that was to get the movement now known as the Christian faith going after its apparent failure, we are informed that 'the resurrection is not a miracle authenticating faith; it is itself the object of faith' (p.360).

Schillebeeckx offers us a much more elaborate exegesis of New Testament texts on resurrection in the context of alternative early credal formulae about the present and future status of Jesus, but he still sets it all in the kind of scheme with which we are now familiar. 'The death of Jesus put an end to the common life in fellowship shared by the earthly Jesus with his disciples — an end reinforced by their leaving him in the lurch. What was it then that after a time gave these same disciples reason to assert that they were once more drawn into a living, present fellowship with Jesus ... what took place between Jesus' death and the proclamation by the Church?' (p. 331). The answer which Schillebeeckx offers to this question centres on conversion experiences of particular disciples, and first of all of Peter, which, because they are already overlaid by more recently constructed resurrection kerygma in general and appearance stories in particular, are now available to us only through the rather tortuous reconstructions of a scholar like Schillebeeckx. 'The appearances stories in the gospels', he writes, 'are no longer telling us about the initial conversion to Jesus' (p. 385).

In spite of great differences in detail, then, the same pattern is found in all three Christologies when dealing with the resurrection. The origin of the Christian faith as a movement in history is attributed to something which occured after Jesus' death, but when we enquire more closely after this something it turns out that no details of it can be given which are other than those which describe exactly the thing we wanted to explain, for all we can apparently be told is that it was the first faith experience of the disciples. And since no further details of this faith experience can be found we really have no final reason for locating it after the death of Jesus rather than during his life, for instance, or even at or as a result of his death.

In fact the insistence, despite the lack of informative detail, that this something must have taken place only after his death seems unnecessarily to devalue both his life and his death; at least it demotes his life and death from the central position in accounting for the historical origin and ground as well as content of the Christian faith.

Of course, if the purpose of presenting the resurrection kerygma of the New Testament in this way is simply to supply information on the event which in fact got the first disciples to preach the faith — that and no more — then the whole thing is a harmless enough exercise in attempting to satisfy historical curiosity, and is of no further consequence for the Christian faith today.

But the suspicion must always remain that the search for this 'something unique that happened just after Jesus' death' is meant to be more than the satisfaction of historical curiosity, that, on the contrary, it is to supply us with grounds for belief and, perhaps, with what to believe today.

Once again, as in the case of incarnation theology, one can follow and applaud an effort to, at the very least, prevent resurrection theology from hiding the true source and content of our Christian faith in the Spirit of Jesus; an effort to back us away from that anxious search (forbidden also by Jesus) for such signs and wonders as would coerce assent to a divine ruler and teacher and, of course, to those whom we would like to exercise coercive authority in the name of such a one. Once again the effort partly fails, in part because the long misuse of resurrection in theology is still mistaken for its proper use, but in part also because, as in the case of even orthodox incarnation theology, there is a residue of the coercive intrusion or 'proof-miracle' element in resurrection kerygma which goes all the way back to the New Testament itself. It has at all times been difficult, but it is always necessary to insist that the essence of resurrection preaching is to say 'that God has made him both Lord and Christ, *this Jesus whom you crucified*' (Acts 2:36). Resurrection theology, too, rightly understood and properly preached, instead of diverting attention from the historical human person, Jesus, proclaims to all who will accept it that *he* is God's anointed, Lord (in incarnational terms, Word).

3. Death

The treatment of the death of Jesus recorded in that last section should advertise the fact, though it is seldom noticed, that the theology of the death of Jesus, which should be of all theologies most transparent to the lesson of his human life, can itself provide a barrier that needs to be penetrated by those who sincerely wish to recover for the Church the true Spirit of Jesus himself. No matter how many times we piously repeat the conviction of the author of the Fourth Gospel that the death of

Jesus was the consummation of his life, so much theology simply seems
to separate it from his life and so to obstruct our view of the Spirit that
breathed throughout his human life and breathed fully out into the world
at his death (John 19:30). Very obviously, those of us who are satisfied
to see in the death of Jesus nothing more than the end-result of an eternal divine decree are automatically saved from seeing that the Spirit of
the human, historical Jesus brought him into fatal conflict with civil and
ecclesiastical institutions and, more important still, we are saved from
the challenge to have that mind or Spirit in us which was in Christ Jesus
and which could unsettle us today from the comfort of our civil and
ecclesiastical positions. Eternal decrees are just as 'intrusory' as certain
theories of incarnation or resurrection, and they just as easily facilitate
the wish of the rest of the Christian community to remain undisturbed in
a position of responsibility-saving and unthreatened obedience. But
even if we were to come a little closer to the concrete details of the execution of Jesus no clearer vision of the Spirit that breathed through his life,
and breathed consummately through his death, need necessarily result.
It is difficult to know quite what to say about the faith-destroying rôle
attributed to the execution of Jesus by the writers on resurrection
surveyed in the last section. One is tempted to wonder why such
unblushingly confident historical generalizations about the state of all
Jesus' disciples are so easily admissible here when similar historical
claims about Jesus and his disciples would anywhere else run into a
scholarly barrage. It is clear enough that the failure-of-the-movement
assertion is introduced as comment on the death of Jesus, whether fac-
tually or hypothetically, simply to persuade us of the need for this unique something which happened just after the death of Jesus to account
for the origin and content of the Christian faith-movement in history. It
is much less clear how such assertion about the death of Jesus can in any
way be reconciled with the more evident Christian belief that Jesus'
death was indeed the consummation of his life, a belief which, as I tried
to stress in my own Christology (pp. 52-4) is by no means confined to the
Fourth Gospel but is at least implicit in every major expression and
embodiment of the Christian faith.

There is, in any case, no need to pursue any further this particular
puzzlement, for we have an even more effective way of evading such
exposure to the Spirit of the man Jesus as would inevitably result from
any serious acceptance of Jesus' death as the consummation of his life.
What we do is simply this: in a totally self-righteous and uncritical manner we present the death of Jesus as the murder of an innocent man.
Now a description of a death as murder of an innocent by definition
separates that death from the life which preceded it. Immediately our
attention concentrates on the (obviously) immoral qualities of the killers
and this prevents even the approach of any suggestion that something in

the dead man's life may have led inexorably to his death. So in the case of the incumbents of the highest offices of Church and State involved in Jesus' death we concentrate entirely on their malice and weakness respectively. As in the case of incarnation theology, much tradition supports this evasive action; as in the case of resurrection theology, much in Scripture supports it also.

For evasive action it is. For although, unquestionably, the most obvious by-product of this concentration on the alleged guilt of Jewish leaders and on the exaggerated weakness of the Roman Pilate has been the enormous and indelible stain left by anti-Semitism on the whole of Christian history — others, unfortunately, always suffer more than Christians for Christians' evasion of the true Spirit of Jesus — the other, connected, by-product is the evasion of the conclusion that the Spirit in which Jesus lived his life posed such a radical challenge to all ordinary conceptions of innocence and guilt and all ordinary exercise of power and authority in Church and State (now as then) that he could reasonably be convicted of a threat to such allegedly necessary authority by rulers otherwise kind and strong, in Churches and States today as easily as two thousand years ago. So the death of Jesus, instead of being transparent to his life and instead of being the consummate handing on (John's verb) of the Spirit which took historical shape in that life, lines up with resurrection and incarnation as a barrier to a keener view of that Spirit in the course of its theological presentation.

4. Conclusion

Christology, of course, cannot make Christ present in the Churches which take his name. But it has a contribution to make to that end. And those who would read the Christologies surveyed so partially here will see them united, I think, in the effort to recover the Spirit given concrete and, we believe, definitive shape in the life and death of Jesus of Nazareth. It must, of course, be admitted that this effort is prone to failure due to the barriers which Christologies old and new have themselves erected and still only partially penetrated, and that we are far from a concrete and consequently powerful picture of the man who in the name of his Father creatively ignored, despite danger to his very life, those human barriers built on nation and race, religion and law, possessions and poverty, behind which men protect themselves to this day with every weapon in their ever-increasing armouries.

At its best the contribution of academic Christology will be small. But recent events have shown that hierarchs are still more interested in alleged prerogatives of office and in models of authority of questionable relevance to Christianity. Too many theologians are foolish enough to accept, and even demand, a share in this authority conceived along lines of such un-Christian models. Not so long ago, when the encyclical on contraception appeared, both of these bodies largely reneged on their commitment to pastoral service, and engaged instead on a discussion of, once more, *authority*. The laity, meanwhile, in much larger percentages than we have until recently realized, simply went their own way with contraceptives. The growing suspicion that the Irish abortion rate is as high as the English suggests they have gone their own way here also. This can, of course, not be justified on grounds of cynicism of a Church which protects life when it costs the leaders only words but not when it costs political face (as with opposition to the insane arms race and other political malfeasance), or when it costs money for the hungry and deprived. But it does tend to suggest that the Church has nothing more to contribute to the moral crisis of the time than the impotence of repeated commands and denunciations. And it reflects as much on the laity as it does on hierarchs or writers; passive resistance to one's own leaders is a mere travesty of the true responsibility of the Christian conscience in every area of Christian (i.e., human) life.

And then the greatest Christian scandal of all: the new high priests and pharisees, clerical and lay, in all the Churches have used Christianity itself to introduce, encourage and increase divisions in the human family. The ecumenical movement continues its by now tiresome measuring of Christian tradition against Christian tradition. Few even in the Churches which stem from the Reformation are anxious to emulate the Reformers and engage in the much more devastating exercise of measuring any or all of these traditions against the stature of Christ. The imperialist claims of the Roman Catholic Church are just as clearly present in the much-heralded 'people of God' chapter from Vatican II's document on the Church as ever they were, and Rome has never given any official encouragement to any form of Christian union other than for all to join itself on its own present terms. And, as always, it is ordinary people who suffer. Christian marriage is the effective sign of the union of Christ with his Church and yet, in Ireland particularly, we witness the unedifying spectacle of a fight over the spoils, the unfortunate 'mixed' Christian children who might result from this union. What exquisite ingenuity does it take to turn one of the few real forms of union between members of different traditions into a fresh battle-ground on which ancient clerics can fight like robins for their piece of hedgerow?

Academic Christology can do little, and has done less still to bring back into the Churches the Spirit of the man who cherished all life as God's gracious gift to all, creatively ignoring the barriers men had built, and giving of this God-given bounty even to the giving of life itself; but in circumstances such as those we face at present every little, helps.

Selected Bibliography

1. John Hick (Ed.) *The Myth of God Incarnate* (London, 1977).
2. Don Cupitt, *Jesus and the Gospel of God* (London, 1979).
3. Don Cupitt, *The Debate About Christ* (London, 1979).
4. Walter Kasper, *Jesus the Christ* (London & New York, 1976).
5. Hans Küng, *On Being a Christian* (New York & London, 1976).
6. E. Schillebeeckx, *Jesus: An Experiment in Christology* (London, 1979).
7. James P. Mackey, *Jesus, the Man and the Myth* (London, 1979).

Notes on Contributors

JOHN CUMMING: Literary and educational editor of *The Tablet*. Co-editor with Lord Bullock of *Fontana Biographical Dictionary of Modern Thought*; executive editor with Karl Rahner of *Encyclopedia of Theology*; author with David Konstant of *Beginnings*. Member of editorial board of *New Blackfriars*; translator and editor of many works from German, French and Dutch.

PAUL BURNS: Chairman of Process Workshop Ltd. Formerly publishing director of Burns & Oates, Publishers to the Holy See; founder member of Pastoral Development Group and SCRIPT; translator for *Concilium* and of several works of Liberation Theology from Spanish and Portuguese.

Contributors

REV. DR ANTONY ARCHER, OP: Chaplain to University of London, Imperial College. Sociologist of religion and expert on history and nature of working-class affiliation to the Churches, on which his major study *The Two Churches: A Study in Oppression* will appear in 1981.

DR ANTONY BLACK: Lecturer in Political Science at Dundee University. Author of leading works on the history of conciliarism, papalism and politics, of which the latest is *Council and Commune: The Council of Basle and the Conciliar Movement*.

RT REV. ALAN CLARK: Bishop of East Anglia. The official Catholic spokesman on ecumenism and as such has been co-chairman of ecumenical working parties and involved in all Catholic-Anglican and Catholic-Protestant joint statements.

DR JACK DOMINIAN: Head of Department of Psychological Medicine at the Middlesex hospital. Leading expert on marriage and family problems; author of *Authority*, *Marital Breakdown* and numerous other works on psychology, psychiatry, marriage and the family. Adviser to many church boards and well-known as lecturer in Britain, Ireland and other countries.

REV. DR DAVID FORRESTER: Parish Priest at Bishop's Waltham, near Southampton. Head of diocesan commission for education and catechetics; author of several works of spirituality and biographer of Pusey.

DR MICHAEL P. HORNSBY-SMITH: Lecturer at Surrey University. The leading Catholic expert on Church statistics; Director and co-author of the recent Gallup Poll/University survey of *Roman Catholic Opinion*; author of numerous books and articles on religious sociology and statistics.

NICHOLAS KENYON: Music critic of *The New Yorker*, and formerly music correspondent for *The Guardian* and *The Observer*. Member of the Liturgical Commission and an expert on liturgy and church music.

REV. DR FERGUS KERR, OP: Prior of Blackfriars, Oxford. Expert on conciliar history, infallibility and theological history. Author of an important series of articles on 'Infallibility at Vatican I' in *New Blackfriars*.

PROF. DAVID LODGE: Professor of Modern English Literature at the University of Birmingham. Leading figure in Catholic renewal and known as lecturer in many countries. Awarded Hawthornden prize for his novel *Changing Places*; author of several other novels, of which the latest, *How far can you go?* has attracted major interest in the press, on television and radio. Expert on structuralism and author of several critical studies.

DR DAVID LUNN: Church historian specializing in the history of the religious orders. Former Benedictine monk and author of *The English Benedictines*. Grandson of Sir Arnold Lunn.

PROFESSOR JAMES MACKEY: Professor of Theology at the University of Edinburgh. Author of *Jesus the Man and the Myth* and other major studies in Christology and systematic theology.

PROF. V.A. MCCLELLAND: Professor of Education at the University of Hull. Has taught at several Irish and British universities and written many articles on various aspects of religious and secular education; author of major work on Newman, Manning and Catholic education.

PROF. ENDA MCDONAGH: Visiting Professor of Theology at the University of Notre Dame, Indiana. Formerly Professor of Moral Theology at St Patrick's College, Maynooth. Author of numerous books and articles on moral theology, always with practical reference to social and political commitment.

LOUIS MCREDMOND: An historian by training, a barrister by profession and a journalist by choice. Reported the second Vatican Council and subsequent Synods of Bishops for the *Irish Independent*. The Dublin correspondent of *The Tablet* for many years; leading writer and broadcaster on Church affairs; Director of Information in Radio Telefis Eireann.

PROF. TERENCE MORRIS: Professor of Sociology, with special reference to Criminology, at the London School of Economics and Political Science. Author of *Pentonville: Sociology of an English Prison*, *The Criminal Area*, *Deviants and Control: the secular heresy* and, with Louis Blom-Cooper, *Calendar of Murder*.

DR RASHID MUFTI: Senior Lecturer in the Sociology of Religion at Christ's College, Liverpool. Author of numerous works of sociology. Delegate to the National Pastoral Congress of England and Wales.

ROBERT NOWELL: Formerly editor of *Herder Correspondence* and one-time assistant editor of *The Tablet*. Commentator and correspondent for American, French and Dutch Catholic journals. Author of *The Ministry of Service* and a study of Hans Küng to be published shortly.

IANTHE PRATT: Deeply involved with Catholic renewal and women's emancipation movements. Author, with husband Dr Oliver Pratt, of *Liturgy is What we make it* and other works, mostly dealing with liturgy for specialist groups.

REV. ANTHONY ROSS, OP: Rector of the University of Edinburgh and former chaplain to the University. Writer and historian, magistrate and prison visitor.

REV. TERENCE TANNER: Director of ROMA, the leading drug addict reclamation centre in London. A former parish curate, he now has extensive experience of the present efforts of the Church in social problem areas in Britain.

REV. DESMOND WILSON: Formerly on the staff of St Malachy's College, Belfast, then a parish priest in Belfast. Resigned from all ecclesiastical position in 1975 and now works full-time as a community worker, on projects mainly concerned with employment and work, employed by the people of the area.